Forgetting Whose We Are

Forgetting Whose We Are

Alzheimer's Disease and the Love of God

David Keck

Abingdon Press
Nashville

FORGETTING WHOSE WE ARE:
ALZHEIMER'S DISEASE AND THE LOVE OF GOD

Library of Congress Cataloging-in-Publication Data

Keck, David, 1965–
    Forgetting whose we are: Alzheimer's disease and the love of
God / David Keck.
        p.   cm.
    Includes bibliographic references and index.
    ISBN 0-687-02088-3 (alk. paper)
    1. Alzheimer's disease—Religious aspects—Christianity.
2. Alzheimer's disease—Patients—Religious life.   3. Suffering—
Religious aspects—Christianity.   4. God—Love.   I. Title.
BT732.K351966
261.8 '32196831—dc20   96-15344
                                                              CIP

00 01 02 03 04 05 —10 9 8 7 6 5 4 3 2

MANUFACTURED IN THE UNITED STATES OF AMERICA

For

Janice Osburn Keck

who cannot read this book,
but who can still teach us all
about the love of God

Contents

Foreword

Alzheimer's disease, so this book suggests, forces Christians back to the basics of the faith more than any other contemporary plague. Yet the problems it raises are not faced by recent theologies of right or left, whether neo-Orthodox, neo-Thomist, liberationist, or feminist. These approaches have occasioned "fresh articulations of the Gospel which have provided inspiration to many, but none of them could do anything for the dead, and very little for the terminally ill." The slow, irreversible dissolution of the self in senile dementia is a sustained dying for the afflicted and a mirror of unparalleled vividness for caretakers and others in which to contemplate our very own deaths. To "love someone even as they disintegrate before your eyes" intensifies awareness as nothing else can do of what above all is the Good News that the church needs to proclaim.

Alzheimer's, as David Keck aptly says, is the "Theological Disease." Its neglect by theologians is puzzling. There is an abundant literature on the medical aspects, the practicalities of caregiving, and the philosophical, political, ethical, social, and economic dimensions of this disease, but very little on the theological questions it poses. As Keck notes, "The important emphasis on practical and ethical advice has obscured the proclamation of the even more fundamental Good News of the Gospel."

Keck's diagnosis of this failure is important. As an outsider, a historian who is theologically knowledgeable, his outlook is different from those currently prevailing in theology and religious studies. He sees truths which we who are insiders are likely to overlook, but which we cannot afford to ignore.

His prescriptions are also surprising, but even when we do not accept them, they force us to ask what we would put in their place. Keck draws on the undiluted Christian heritage of the past. He argues, for example, that the notion of the soul as more fundamental to personal identity than the conscious, agential self belongs to the basic grammar of the faith. After all, the patient in whom the conscious, agential self has dissolved is still the person—the mother, the wife—beloved by children, by spouse, and first of all, by God. Similarly, the resurrection is to be affirmed as irreducibly corporeal even if unconceptualizable. It is the restoration of the beloved, the bodily beloved, for which the Christian hopes.

The unembarrassed realism with which chapters 4 and 5 develop these ideas will make some otherwise sympathetic readers wince. They will not, however, scoff, at least not if they read carefully. There is here no recycling of tired ideas and shop-worn arguments, but a fresh and persuasive treatment of perennial problems which will endure as long as the human race. The resources of the tradition, as Keck presents them, are living waters, not formulaic parrottings. He knows the present, as well as the past, too well to think retrieval without renewal is possible. There are, he says, no theological discoveries in this book, and yet there are also no archaisms. It is both intellectually and rhetorically a thoroughly contemporary work which reminds both the theological right and the theological left of much which has been forgotten in recent centuries.

The appeal of this book, finally, does not depend entirely on its reasoning and learning, good though these are. Its rootage in experience gives it a special character which reminds this reader of parts of Augustine's *Confessions* or some of Luther's writings. The dedication is to the author's mother, Janice Osburn Keck, "who cannot read this book, but who can still teach us all about the love of God." She is the Alzheimer's victim whom he, and even more his brother and father, have cared for at home (with some daytime help, to be sure) for year after year. The theology in this book grows out of those years. It was in the struggle to find what was needed for life and death, for action, passion, and understanding, that the author found himself drawing more and more from the great tradition of the church universal, Protestant, Catholic, and Orthodox. The result is a joining of reflection and confession which has much to offer both to theologians and to non-theologians.

It is only a decade since I first came to know David Keck when he took a course from me while he was in Yale College. He was a good student, one of the best, but I did not then expect that in a few years he would write a book which may contribute greatly to the redirection of Christian theology and piety in the twenty-first century. It is Alzheimer's disease, if this book is right, which helps open our eyes to the need for redirection, but David Keck is the first to make the case with the fullness and effectiveness which it deserves. Many will be in his debt.

George Lindbeck
Pitkin Professor Emeritus of Historical Theology
The Department of Religious Studies and the Divinity School
Yale University

Introduction

Alzheimer's, the Theological Disease

Janice Osburn Keck, my mother, was diagnosed with Alzheimer's disease in 1990. For several years, we had known that things were not quite right. An ordained United Methodist minister, she showed less and less interest in the church. The woman who used to drive her family to all kinds of activities refused to drive anymore. She began to spend unbroken hours rocking in her chair. Her memory and eyesight were failing, and she needed help getting dressed in the morning. We were not prepared for the diagnosis (we were imagining all kinds of alternative causes), but the doctor's report did suddenly bring the last several years' unusual behavior into clear focus. For her own sake, she has never been told that she has the disease.

This book is the result of our family's experiences, and I have written it in the hope that it may be helpful to the many Christians who are facing this disease. While this exploration of Alzheimer's in light of the church's teachings is intended primarily for an academic audience, I hope that through theological teaching, church preaching, and the sharing of friends, it may ultimately prove useful to people in the parish, caregivers in the home, and patients in wheelchairs. The church is the institution in American society which is perhaps most capable of bridging the chasm between the university and local communities. I have concentrated on the specifically theological aspects of Alzheimer's because there has been a surprising lack of sustained theological engagement with this disease and because such sustained theological work is needed now more than ever.

I had thought that a disease involving the apparently inexorable erosion of the memory would have evoked a fair amount of theological reflection. Whether one is singing "Precious Memories" in Appalachia or reading Augustine's *On the Trinity* at a divinity school; whether one recalls a prayer or one's own experience of the divine;

whether one attends a memorial service or recites the words "Take, eat, do this in remembrance of me"; it should be clear that memory is crucial both to the life of the individual and to the life of a church. And when, having contemplated the serene faces of the martyrs in a painting, one then beholds the frightened, confused face of an Alzheimer's patient, it should be apparent that profound religious questions are at stake when memory itself dissolves.

Apart from an essay by Glenn Weaver and a book of prayers by Cecil Murphy, however, there has been relatively little discussion of this disease and its implications in theological circles.[1] Why is this? Is it because it seems to be a medical and mental health issue better left to professionals in those fields? Is it because the disease affects those who seem to have lived already a full, rewarding life? Or is it because we are simply reluctant to take on a problem which may require us to acknowledge human limitations, mortality, and our dependence on God's saving work? For whatever reasons, and there are probably many, there has not been a great deal of interest in the theological dimensions of the disease.

Books such as Nancy L. Mace and Peter V. Rabin's *The 36-Hour Day* prepare families quite well for the day-to-day challenges and the nuts and bolts of what one must do as a caregiver.[2] The local and national offices of the Alzheimer's and Related Disorders Association provides updated, detailed information on medical aspects of the disease as well as practical advice and support for caregivers. Several authors have addressed the specific philosophical and political aspects of Alzheimer's, such as questions of public funding for care, when to withhold medical treatment for the demented, the legitimacy of living wills, and euthanasia.[3] Stephen G. Post, James Lindemann Nelson, and Hilde Lindemann Nelson have explored such moral and ethical challenges of this disease.[4] More generally, gerontologists have discussed the many social and economic challenges facing the elderly as a whole (such as a diminished sense of personal worth, the lack of a sound socialization process for becoming old, and "ageism").[5] The field of religious gerontology has examined the particular religious problems of the elderly, but rarely do the particular theological questions of senile dementia come to play a major part in studies in this field.[6]

I have benefited greatly from these books (and I will not directly address the issues they discuss), but rarely have I found any detailed treatment of the theological dimensions of this disease. Important practical advice abounds, but where is the rich spiritual reflection and penetrating counseling? Clearly, our family is confronting a lethal disease which drains us of strength and my mother of her memories and identity. Clearly, this disease is raising profound challenges about who we are and how we might relate to God as well as to each other. Clearly, we are called to remember what God is "doing" in all of this. Regrettably, the important emphasis on practical and ethical advice has obscured the proclamation of the even more fundamental Good News of the Gospel. Even those discussions of the disease which appear in religious publications rarely delve very deeply into the theological questions or explore the great resources of the church's traditions. As a result of this apparent lacuna, I helped arrange a panel discussion on "The Theological Dimensions of Alzheimer's Disease" at the American Academy of Religion Annual Meeting in 1993. Papers by Stephen G. Post, David Smith, and Stanley Hauerwas and the comments of many people in the audience demonstrated that there were significant questions to be asked by a sustained theological inquiry.

In preparing for that discussion, it occurred to me that it might be possible to consider Alzheimer's as the "Theological Disease." This disease does differ from other examples of disease, anguish, and death. The unusual situation of a prolonged mental deterioration and the need for sustained caregiving over many years means that we can no longer presume the existence of the cognitive subject when we are thinking theologically. The loss of memory entails a loss of self, and we can no longer be secure in our notions of "self-fulfillment." Indeed, our entire sense of personhood and human purpose is challenged. Because we are dealing with the apparent disintegration of a human being—indeed the apparent dissolutions of many, many human beings—a thorough reconsideration of many fundamental theological questions is not entirely out of order. I will explore the questions raised by this disease more systematically in chapter 1, but let me briefly suggest here some of the reasons for calling Alzheimer's the "Theological Disease."

Alzheimer's is a particular type of a lethal disease, and because it confronts us with a sustained dying, it is an inescapable reminder that we will all die. We cannot forget this reminder of our shared mortality because we live with dying each day. Hence, a study of Alzheimer's disease, while concentrating on one particularly cruel form of death, will also be a mirror in which we can contemplate all of our deaths. The disease is a reminder also of our common weaknesses. It is easy to exaggerate the differences between patients and non-patients, but the similarities may be greater. The demented may be a mirror in which we can see ourselves all too clearly: we all have faulty memories, we all become incoherent at times, we all need caregiving. In our own way, perhaps, we all suffer from Alzheimer's. David H. Smith's presentation at the AAR emphasized that part of what seems so frightening about the disease is that we are afraid to lose self-control. None of us are autonomous subjects, and we are all, in differing degrees, needy and dependent. Perhaps Alzheimer's patients can remind us of this. Perhaps they can remind us that death and loss of control belong at the heart of our theological reflection.

Because this disease confronts us with our own radical finitude and with clear limitations of human powers, we have little choice but to turn to theology. As the title of a gospel song goes, "If We Never Needed the Lord Before (We Sure Do Need Him Now)." Alzheimer's patients who are still capable of reading this book may benefit from it and be encouraged, but they realize that their capacity for self-improvement is quite limited. This book may help people help themselves, but I suspect that it will do so most by reminding us of, as the title suggests, whose we are. Consequently, this is not a self-help book, nor could it be.

Not only because of what happens to the patient but also because of the effects on caregivers and the entire family does this disease raise theological problems. A central theme of Simone de Beauvoir's *The Coming of Age* is the belief that the true test of any society is how it treats the aged, those who are no longer productive or "useful," those who may be an unwanted reminder of our frailty and mortality.[7] The challenges of long-term dementia care magnify this test. The Law says "Honor thy father and mother." But as the burdens of full-time caregiving exceed the capacities of most, and as leaving a spouse or parent at a nursing home of uncertain quality is nearly inevitable, this disease illustrates how the Law may be unfulfillable. Hence, a theological affirmation of God's grace is needed.

Further, how can we make sense of the suffering and minister to both the patients and the caregivers? How can a patient participate in the life of a church? Because this disease isolates families, the communal work of the church will be needed in order to maintain families in their communities. Facing this disease without such a supportive community is a frightening reality for all too many. Our

16

notions of worship and religious existence now find themselves under scrutiny. How can it be possible to speak of a "personal relationship with God" when there seems to be no person left, when, in some cases, there is naught but a frenzied, incommunicable, Dionysian suffering? In the ancient world, the "sacred disease," epilepsy, was sometimes seen to be a sign that one was touched by the gods. By contrast, the isolation of the "Theological Disease" seems to threaten us with being abandoned by God. Moreover, because this disease is understood physiologically in terms of natural processes, our views of nature and the cosmos may be challenged. Has God created this ugliness? Why has God allowed it to flourish? In its face, fulfilling the call to love our God will not be easy.

We may ask if caring for an Alzheimer's patient is analogous to the worship of God. In both cases, according to some, you do it because it is right, not because you expect any reward, let alone enjoy the comfort of recognition. Both caring for a loved one who no longer knows your name and praying to God in a world full of suffering can be quite painful, even bitter. Is this, then, the fundamental religious challenges for families: to praise and love God through perhaps as much as a decade of relentless suffering? The cry, "My God, my God, why have you abandoned us?" seems justified. This disease may thus bring a certain intimacy with the Bible's narratives, particularly a constantly resurging awareness of Christ's suffering. When one beholds an Alzheimer's patient as she loses control of her body, one may see more clearly the obvious fact that when you are nailed to a cross, you can no longer control your body's motions.

Addressing this apparent erosion of memory and physical capacities requires clarifying the extent to which the theological understanding of humanity depends upon the brain, on neurochemical processes, and indeed on matter itself. This disease, it seems, poignantly raises the most fundamental questions about the *imago Dei* and about the meaning of crucial words found in the Christian creeds such as salvation, resurrection, and soul. If indeed these words refer to more than metaphors, then this disease becomes the occasion to affirm religious beliefs and to realign theological anthropology accordingly. If, on the other hand, words such as *pneuma, psyche,* and *nephesh* are merely metaphors or primitive mythological constructions, it seems then that we are in a rather difficult situation; indeed, from the pastoral perspective, a cruel one. How can we avoid despair over what seems to be a ruthless triumph of matter over mind?

There is, finally, another sense in which Alzheimer's may be called the "Theological Disease"—what it suggests about the state of contemporary theology. This disease, because it focuses our attention so sharply on many of the most fundamental questions of humanity and our relationships to God, clearly illuminates the characteristics of our theological enterprises. Are current theological agendas designed around the self's fulfillment and grounded in personal experience adequate when confronted by the apparent disintegration of the self? Similarly, how adequate are theologies based on social justice or some other criterion which is of little use to those with dementia? It appears that, like Alzheimer's patients, theology and the churches may have forgotten their heritage, may have forgotten crucial doctrines (such as the soul and the resurrection) which we need as we confront senile dementia and death.

The phenomena of this disease thus resonates with important ecclesiastical themes and evokes careful theological reflection. Although I find myself writing on the "Theological Disease," I am not a theologian. By training, I am a historian, more particularly a medieval church historian, and I approach the theological consideration of this disease out of a respect for the church's history. I hope that theologians will excuse my entry into their turf, but I hope as well that they may be prompted to further theological reflection.

While I will elaborate on my theological principles in the third chapter, a few words may be useful at the outset. This is an ecumenical study because I have wanted to reach as broad an audience as possible. This has entailed the sacrifice of depth and precision in many cases, but I hope that such a lack will encourage others who wish to pursue their own denomination's teachings in greater detail to do so. When I refer to "the church" I refer to all of the disparate churches which together form the body of Christ. I take this to include essentially Protestants, Roman Catholics, and the Eastern Orthodox. I do believe there is a fundamental unity here which we will experience perhaps only at the eschaton. When I refer to caregivers, I have in mind primarily family caregivers since their challenges are the most trying. Professional caregivers confront many of the same issues, but they, at least, can leave the patient behind and return home at the end of the day. Whereas I have used both male and female pronouns for patients and caregivers to remind us all that this disease afflicts everyone, I have retained the male pronoun for God. I do because this seems to be proper. God is three Persons, and

18

persons require personal pronouns. The male pronoun, while ultimately inadequate, does remind us that Jesus, God incarnate as a man, speaks intimately of God as the Father. This intimacy with our Creator is a gift, and I do not feel comfortable changing it.

I should note that because my family has fared better than many families, my presentation of this disease is colored by a relatively positive set of experiences. We have been spared the wandering and violent behavior which some patients exhibit, as we have avoided the acrimonious breakups which many families experience. (Recently, one son took his mother to court to obtain custody of his diseased father because the son feared that she would take his father to see Dr. Jack Kevorkian for a physician-assisted suicide.) Relatively few people attempt what has been called "granny dumping" (leaving a severely demented patient in the middle of some public space without any identification), but many families are either unwilling or unable to provide high-quality full-time care at home. The realities for many patients are worse than I can convey.

We have fared better than many families in no small part because of the church's legacies. I have come to realize that Scripture, doctrine, and tradition do make a difference. With awe and pride, I have seen my father provide loving care and service to my mother for many years, and I am certain that his many years of reading Paul have had something to do with this. To be sure, his growing up on a farm during the depression and his own parents' strong work ethic have made a difference, too. But one cannot spend so many years with someone like Paul and not be affected deeply by the apostle's understanding of suffering, service, and hope.

Alzheimer's disease focuses one's sense of gratitude, and many thanks are owed. Our family has been particularly fortunate to have found several women who have been excellent caregivers for my mother. Rita Cashin, Lisa A. Bender, Arnaldy Quismundo, Deborah Schroeder, Cindy Thomas, and Chiarina Vincent have made it possible for my father to maintain high-quality care for her in her own home. The three presenters at the AAR meeting, Stephen Post, David H. Smith, and Stanley Hauerwas, were all helpful and encouraging. I am grateful to James Lindemann Nelson who invited me to discuss my research with his colleagues at the Hastings Center. He also showed me early drafts of his own work on Alzheimer's, which I have used. Mario Francisco, S.J., Brevard Childs, Ann Gollin, and Dr. Albert Gollin, read drafts of several chapters and provided me with much advice and encouragement. The students in my philosophy of history class critiqued chapter 8 and encouraged me to develop certain themes. George Marsden allowed me to read the manuscript of his forthcoming *The Outrageous Idea of Christian Scholarship*, a work which helped me considerably. I very much appreciate the advice and assistance of George Lindbeck, whose guidance was most helpful on several important points. I am especially grateful for my wife, Karin Lindt Gollin, not only because of her careful editing but also because she understands what to do when I find myself teary-eyed at church or in my study.

Let me conclude with an optimistic thought. Could this illness, like previous watershed issues, such as infant baptism, purgatory, and the creedal issues, lead us to reevaluate the nature and purpose of our theological endeavors? Will it remind us that there are common human dilemmas transcending politics, racism, sexism, and all the other "-isms"? Is it possible that Alzheimer's and related phenomena might revitalize a serious theological consideration of *nephesh* and *psyche*, of the divine image, and of salvation and redemption? I, for one, believe that the millions of sufferers who can no longer read, no longer speak, still have a thing or two they can teach us, particularly about the love of God.

Chapter 1

Deconstruction Incarnate:
The Etiology and Teleology of
Alzheimer's Disease

Is there no balm in Gilead? Is there no physician there?
— Jeremiah 8:22

In 1907 Alois Alzheimer, a German doctor at the University of Munich, published the results of his observations of a patient's brain, which he had sliced, stained, and studied under the rapidly improving microscopes of his day. What he identified was the disease which now bears his name, a disease which is perhaps the most acute and frightening form of senile dementia, as well as being the most common. Popularly, it now becomes a way of expressing the fears many elderly have when they say, "I can't remember. . . . I hope I'm not developing Alzheimer's." Dr. Alzheimer's work marked the beginning of the story of a disease which is all about the breakdown of our personal stories, a disease ultimately about living lives with deconstructing narratives. This chapter examines the medical aspects of this disease and suggests the agenda for the theological discussion of the following chapters. If indeed memory is as central to our identities and our relationship with God as we might suspect, then this chapter's consideration of a disease which erodes the memory will leave us with a number of challenging questions.

Although Alzheimer's discovery represented the articulation of a particular form of dementia, the problems associated with this disease pertain to many other forms of dementia and cognitive impairment, such as multi-infarct dementia or brain tumors, which can be caused by over fifty different medical conditions, including strokes and AIDS. While this study of the theological aspects of Alzheimer's focuses on one disease, largely because of my own family's concerns and experiences, I believe that its considerations apply to these other forms of dementia as well. As the full name of the Alzheimer's Association suggests, it is for Alzheimer's Disease And Related Disorders. Because I am interested primarily in the theological aspects of the disease, I will keep this treatment of the medical facts of the disease brief, and I will not examine in any detail the public policy issues raised by Alzheimer's (such as matters of public funding, when to withhold treatment, the legitimacy of living wills, and euthanasia).[1]

Medical Aspects of Alzheimer's Disease

Alzheimer's disease and related syndromes currently affect up to four million Americans. (The title of the congressional Office of Technology Assessment's 1987 study of Alzheimer's, *Losing a Million Minds*, was badly understated.) Over one hundred thousand victims—husbands, mothers, colleagues, strangers—die each year, and thus, it is the fourth leading cause of death in adults, following heart disease, cancer, and strokes. Because of genetic factors, perhaps as much as 10 percent of the population may expect to develop Alzheimer's or another form of senile dementia. Risk increases dramatically with age, so that those over 85 may have as much as a 50 percent chance of becoming a patient. The disease usually strikes people as they enter their seventies or eighties, but early-onset victims have been in their fifties or sixties. My mother, having been diagnosed in her early sixties, is one such early-onset person. As the country's population as a whole continues to age, the number of affected persons will increase. According to a National Institute of Aging study, in the second quarter of the next century, we may expect to see fourteen million patients.[2] As people live longer, and as more people enter their Golden Years, the raw numbers and the prognosis, should no treatment appear, would seem to be rather bleak.

Entering the realm of diagnosing dementia itself can be a frightening process for the entire family. Not only are the biological conclusions themselves feared but also the entire series of tests can be disturbing (that is, assuming one is sufficiently insured to be able to afford the multiple brain scans and psychological and blood tests). Seeing someone taking pictures of a spouse's troubled brain; having a doctor ask a battery of embarrassing questions such as "How many nickels are in a quarter?"; trying to comfort a bewildered loved one while sitting in a waiting room—these are not easy experiences.

Once a diagnosis is reached, in many cases the doctors and family members will then have to decide whether or not to tell the patient. We decided not to tell my mother, partly because she would not have understood, and partly because even if she did, all we would have done was increase her anxieties. I am struck by the difference between receiving an Alzheimer's diagnosis and the experience of those I know suffering from certain forms of depression. The latter are often relieved to discover that their problems come from neurochemical anomalies, and medication comes as a blessing. By contrast, an Alzheimer's diagnosis, also a statement of neurochemistry, brings not relief but dread, and medication is an uncertain prospect at best.

Currently, medical diagnoses can only be about 85 percent accurate without a biopsy of brain tissue. Some hope has been generated recently by an eye-drop test, developed at the Harvard Medical School, which promises to be both simple and accurate. It may soon be possible to develop screening tests for people of any age to determine whether they will be susceptible to the disease. Such a test, however, would entail significant ethical and political problems since insurance companies and employers might be tempted to use this as a vehicle for excluding "undesirables." Oddly, this may be one case where smoking is beneficial; smokers seem less at risk than nonsmokers. While studies are inconclusive at this point, men and women seem to be affected equally, and whites seem to have a slightly greater chance of contracting the disease than blacks. This disease, in other words, is an equal-opportunity destroyer.

The causes of the disease remain somewhat mysterious, and this mystery intensifies the fears and anxieties of victims and caregivers. Many causes and contributing factors—including genetics, infections, neurochemical anomalies, and stress—have been suggested. The experience of previous head trauma, aluminum exposure, and immunological disorders, too, have seemed to be potential causes. It is not even certain if all patients suffer from the same disease, or whether what we now call Alzheimer's actually represents several distinct disorders. By the time you read this, our knowledge about the illness will have increased, but my mother's own condition will have deteriorated.

What does seem clear is this: electronic images of the head reveal that brain tissue shrinks significantly more than it does in natural

23

aging processes. Specific nerve cells degenerate, neuritic plaques and neurofibrillary tangles form within the brain, cerebral blood flow is impaired, and the amount of some neurotransmitters is reduced. Vacuoles, empty areas, appear in some cells in the hippocampus, the part of the brain responsible for memories. According to recent research at Duke University Medical Center, it may be that a genetic trait causes all this by enervating the "plumbing" that feeds the brain cells and cleans out the waste.

What all that means is that slowly, inexorably, your memory begins to atrophy; you lose the ability to walk, let alone learn new skills; you will no longer have the capacity to recognize family members or to communicate by any means (understandably, you may become paranoid, especially when strangers ask you to sign documents you cannot read); and ultimately, in end-stage dementia, you become unable to control grunting noises, screams, or seizures, let alone eat or go to the bathroom. Certainly, your family does not want to take you out in public anymore, lest your belligerence or incontinence prove to be an embarrassment. While bedridden, you can anticipate bedsores, catheterization, urinary tract infections, and eventually a vegetative state. Along the way, you may experience delusions about family members, both living and dead, and your behavior may be completely unrelated to who you once were (there will be no more continuity in your life's narrative). This process can take anywhere from three to more than twenty years, until you die. My mother has survived longer than the average patient, who survives seven to eight years with the disease, and she still seems in many respects quite healthy.

The deterioration can be gradual or rapid (doctors speak of a number of different stages), and patients exhibit a great variety of behavioral changes. Some seem to be living embodiments of the maxim, Ignorance is bliss. They can continue to enjoy music for quite a long period. Others are conscious of their plight for quite a number of years, and their feelings may well echo Job's words (3:26), "I am not at ease, nor am I quiet; I have no rest, but trouble comes." Some exhibit a mockery of the Stoic doctrine of apathy in their complete indifference to deprivations, friends, and even efforts to give them love. Those abandoned by their families may echo Frankenstein's creature when he cries, "I am solitary and abhorred."[3]

Despite this diversity exhibited by patients, I am most concerned with the more extreme cases of suffering, dementia, and caregiving because they are the most problematic theologically as well as the ones I fear the most. Caregivers learn early to expect the worst so that they may prepare for it. As Brutus said stoically of his beloved Portia's death, "With meditating that she must die once / I have the patience to endure it now."[4] But Brutus speaks of a singular event, while watching the dissolution of an Alzheimer's patient is a prolonged series of experiences, confrontations, and sorrows that tries the patience regularly. Moreover, the fear of further, inevitable deterioration is omnipresent. Hence, my descriptions of the more brutal effects of the disease, while generally accurate, are not applicable to all patients at all stages, even though they are dreaded in the minds of all caregivers.

The 36-Hour Day, perhaps the finest book available for caregivers, is aptly named. Taking care of a demented person requires enormous amounts of energy and patience, more than seem to be available in a normal day. Despite their many previous years of a mutually supportive relationship, caregivers eventually abandon hope of receiving support or love back from their patients. While caring for the victim at home, families find themselves trapped and isolated, unable to leave the house or to invite friends over after church services. As Ronald Reagan wrote in an open letter to the country after he was diagnosed with Alzheimer's, "The family often bears a heavy burden. I only wish there was some way I could spare Nancy from this painful experience." In addition to the psychic stress which all caregivers personally experience, the financial cost to families and society for day care, nursing homes, medical treatments, and the other aspects of long-term care for the demented amounts to $40–$100 billion, depending on the study. Both personally and nationally, the toll is staggering.

Women more often assume the responsibilities of providing the intense care required by persons with the disease. Here, my family's experience is atypical; my father and my brother have been the main caregivers. At the same time, we have discovered that in our area, there are a number of remarkably strong and loving women who have turned day care for the elderly into something of a cottage industry. We have been fortunate that they have been both available and able to treat a strange, sometimes aggravating, demented person as a real human being.

Caregivers need care, too. And they need the freedom to address the problem in their own ways. Some prefer support groups. Meeting strangers who face the same problems can be reassuring; you never know if that person on the bus faces the same challenges you do. My father, by contrast, is from old German farming stock, the kind where you bake your own pies and share them with friends, so he does not feel comfortable with the idea of a support group of strangers. He cherishes his friends and their aid, but because of the circumstances, people have to come to our house for pie.

"Is there no balm in Gilead? Is there no physician there?" Currently there is no cure for the disease. Treatments, such as tacrine (which can cause liver damage), sometimes help delay mental deterioration for a while. Tranquilizers increase the patient's confusion, but they sometimes provide caregivers with a brief respite from the squealing or cries. Given both the utility of tranquilizers and the dangers of overmedication, caregivers thus experience a painful forced trade-off between the quality of their day and the quality of their patients' day. We can hope and pray for a cure, but for many families of patients with end-stage dementia, because of the irrecoverability of lost memories, a treatment prolonging the status quo would be dreadful. As the title of Ronald Dworkin's discussion of Alzheimer's has it, this disease seems to be a "Life Past Reason."[5]

And, regardless of whether a treatment or cure is discovered, the problems of suffering and the complete erosion of memory will remain. Because religions often make it their business to remember the suffering of the past—be it in Egypt, on Calvary, or anywhere else—it would appear that many of the dilemmas raised by the disease may well be with us for quite a while, unless, of course, we choose to forget them.

Imagining Alzheimer's: Narrative, Prayer, and Disease

I have wondered if it is necessary to provide a description of how this disease affects families since there are so many people today who have friends or family suffering from dementia. Most people have some idea of what goes on inside an Alzheimer's home. I have learned, however, that I could not have formed an adequate picture of what caregiving is like prior to experiencing it myself. I do not have the sustained powers of imagination to do justice to a steadily enervating process of caregiving which extends over half a decade or more. Caregiving impinges uncontrollably on all aspects of life, evoking constant vigilance and making you perpetually drowsy and exhausted. The effects of this experience are not things we imagine readily.

Another way to describe the problem of communicating the effects of the disease on families is by comparing it to the sensations of being operated on while under local anesthesia. Recently, I had a toenail removed so that an injury could heal properly. The doctor injected an anesthetic into the toe, and I was completely unable to feel any pain there. At the same time, I could watch the doctor cut and pull away at my body and clean out the open wound vigorously with a cotton swab. Because I could see what was happening, I knew that everything she was doing should cause considerable discomfort, yet I remained unmoved. So, too, do I often remain unmoved by other stories of suffering. Cognitively and morally, I know I should hurt, but I recognize that in reality I do not feel so much pain. This imaginative block occurs in many of us; otherwise we could not read a newspaper, or watch the nightly news on television, for very long.

I suspect that few of us have the courage to explore in any depth what it might be like to be a patient with this disease. As Joseph M. Foley notes, there are very few studies of this question of the patient's own perspectives and experiences. He suspects that this is due to a fundamental problem of addressing data which do not seem readily susceptible to quantification. It may be that David H. Smith's observation is accurate as well; he notes that we deny personhood to, and hence close sympathetic experience with, those who suffer precisely because we want to avoid suffering ourselves.[6] Similarly, there may be an inclination for some caregivers and health professionals to "write off" patients as "out of it" even though the patients themselves are still very much engaged with the world. Hence, it does seem to me necessary to try to convey in some highly inadequate ways what this disease is like for those families who suffer from it. Perhaps by approaching the problem from a number of angles—by considering personal experiences, examining the question of Alzheimer's and narrative, studying prayers, and comparing it with other afflictions—the realities of this disease can be suggested more adequately.

I admit from the outset that I have no idea of the experiences, fears, and turmoils which patients have in their latter stages. Their minds are inaccessible to me, and I detect mere clues from their calls, bodily jerks, or other behaviors. Some movements are attempts to communicate distress or needs; others are not. How can I tell the difference? In order to imagine what might be going on, I recall an experience I had in a hospital ward several years ago. Upon groggily waking up after a surgery, I heard primal screams from several beds away. To describe them as pain or agony would be an injustice since they seemed to be so much more of a raw, fundamental terror. A nurse told me that they were from a mentally handicapped boy who had just woken up from anesthesia. He was disoriented and was not capable of understanding what had happened to him. He seemed caught in a pre-linguistic terror. End-stage Alzheimer's may be a kind of post-linguistic terror. Or it may be like being reborn every minute—being perpetually thrown into a unfamiliar world with no memories and no capacity to organize the bewildering array of strange sensory data that confronts you.

Another experience which suggests itself, and which may or may not be more familiar to the reader, is extreme drunkenness. The memory loss, incapacitation of judgment, urinary and gastrointestinal incontinence, slurring of speech—these effects of alcohol do resemble Alzheimer's disease. Drunken Dionysian excess, like Alzheimer's, can be anything from a stupor to a frenzied, violent, incommunicable suffering, a frenzy which mocks our attempts to establish Apollonian order (as well we may see in Euripides' tragedy, *The Bacchae*). We would have to imagine what it would be like to be perpetually drunken, at times blissfully impervious to the outside world, at times helplessly stumbling or falling towards the bathroom, never to return to full consciousness, never to sober up.

Another way of seeing how difficult it is to communicate to others what Alzheimer's disease is all about is to examine its narrative potential. Humans seem to be story-telling creatures, and hence when we encounter a problem with a story, we probably have come across something significant. Certainly, narratives which tell us about caregiving are possible. Since caregivers themselves are often in the position of having to try to communicate their experiences to their friends or support groups, we can learn a great deal from their attempts. Metaphors for the disease, too, can be suggestive. Jenijoy La Belle describes Alzheimer's as "a thief who grows bolder as the months pass."[7] But if we can imagine the disease from a patient's perspective, Alzheimer's, especially the teleology of the disease or end-stage Alzheimer's, seems to be all about the breakdown of narrative. Patients who survive long enough enter into a mode of being which defies our notions of time, consciousness, relationships, and self.

There are a few familiar stories which may provide some idea of what experiencing Alzheimer's disease is like. A first-person narrative is the most effective means of communicating the effects of dementia. Daniel Keyes' *Flowers for Algernon*, the story of a mentally-handicapped boy who for a brief while becomes a genius, is written in the first person, and it does convey some of the sense of bewilderment, ignorance, and confusion which many Alzheimer's patients experience. The most painful moments of the story are those when the narrator is aware of his irrevocable loss of mental faculties, and the greatest relief for the reader occurs when the narrator has become so impaired so that he is no longer capable of noticing his mental decline. In contrast to end-stage dementia, at the end of the tale the narrator is able to continue his life as before, ignorant of what has happened, but not much worse off.

Some Alzheimer's narratives do exist, and the most effective are generally autobiographical. Case studies which allow the patients to speak in their own words (often in an interview) or books such as Diana Friel McGowin's *Living in the Labyrinth: A Personal Journey through the Maze of Alzheimer's* do bring us into the world, or maze, that is Alzheimer's. Fictional first-person narratives, such as J. Bernlef's *Out of Mind*, can also convey some sense of how a patient might be affected by the disease.[8] More widespread dissemination of what Alzheimer's is like comes from works which have a patient as a minor or supporting character, such as the television show *Picket Fences* or the film *Summer Snow* by Hong Kong director Ann Hui. We are, it seems, uncomfortable with Alzheimer's at the center of our narratives.

The fact that these case studies, personal accounts, and fictional narratives are about people who are not yet in end-stage dementia is revealing. Middle-stage dementia can evoke the pity and fear which Aristotle saw as the mark of tragedy. Similarly, given the many wandering traditions embodied variously in the *Odyssey*, the idea of *homo viator*, or the legend of the wandering Jew, the wandering which is characteristic of many patients of this stage and earlier has rich potential for epic. Or, as the hit movie *Rain Man* showed, people with mental handicaps can be hilarious if circumstances permit. For example, when one of the author's names was called at the presentation of my father's *festschrift*, entitled *The Future of Christology*, at Yale Divinity School, my mother blurted out for all the assembled guests to hear, "He has goats!" True enough, J. Louis Martyn, one of our family's dearest friends, does keep a variety of animals. Similarly, when my mother was watching television and saw an old clip of Nixon claiming that "I am not a crook," she suddenly cried out, "Yes, you are! Yes, you are!" These situations can be very funny, and we do need to be able to laugh.

But there is very little that is funny in end-stage dementia, and here we see narratives break down. A first-person narrative about the effects of the disease would have to become literally unreadable as the person passed into severe dementia. A third-person narrative could still be grammatically readable, but to do justice to the disease, it would have to be so confused and disorienting as to be practically unreadable. Certainly, it should bring us very little pleasure to wander through its maze of words.

We should not be surprised that we would have narrative troubles with Alzheimer's disease. Long ago, Aristotle recognized that audience members such as you and I would not long tolerate the spectacle of a good person suffering for no reason whatsoever. In chapter 13 of his *Poetics*, he observed that good tragedy had to be about a good person who suffers because of an error or choice on his part. By contrast, he noted that watching a good person pass from happiness to misery through no fault of his own simply disgusts us (something which Alzheimer's may well do). I have always been struck by this remarkable chapter, because the historical foundation of Christianity is a narrative which should repel us and not make for a very good tale. The story of Jesus, Aristotle would seem to suggest, just does not "work." Similarly, the story of Job does not "work." In both cases Jesus and Job are blameless; readers may not be very comfortable with what God has to say in Job 40 and 41, and chapter 42 seems to be a very bad case of what is often deplored as *deus ex machina* (some might say the same of Jesus' resurrection).

Do Biblical stories provide us with some narrative insight into end-stage Alzheimer's disease? Passages from Job are often cited in literature on medical ethics, but Job seems to have retained his mental faculties even as he lost all else. In the case of Alzheimer's, by contrast, with careful estate planning, it is possible to keep many possessions while losing one's mind. Moreover, we are told that Job lived one hundred and forty years, was able to see, and presumably recognize, many descendants, and died "full of days" (Job 42:17). Old age for him, the man of woes, was indeed a blessing as it was for Abraham, Isaac, and Joseph. There seems to have been no senility in the patriarchs. Like many demented people, David "let his spittle run down his beard," but his was a clever feigned madness in the court of Achish of Gath (1 Sam. 21:13). The only biblical narratives which seem to suggest themselves directly for end-stage Alzheimer's disease are of Jesus and demons who make people mad. If anything, perhaps, Alzheimer's inverts Biblical narratives. Glenn Weaver observes that the dissolution caused by Alzheimer's seems to be "a reversal of the ordering process of creation and a return to the chaos of the deep."[9] Although there seems to be no single Biblical narrative which applies to this disease directly, we shall see that there are many Biblical passages concerning certain aspects of the disease (such as solitude) which are great resources.

Another aspect of the problem of Alzheimer's and narrative is that the relationships which describe who we are in our life's story break down. For example, the validation approach, one of the current methods of caregiving, emphasizes treating patients on a day to day basis. The person's past life and memories are de-emphasized, and the person is treated as if they exist in a perpetual present. Caregivers go along with whatever the patient says, even if the patient is wrong about his or her assumptions. The caregiver no longer says, "Your father is dead," but rather "Your father will be here in a little while, now why don't you eat this food for him." The caregiver is asked to forget what the patient forgets, perhaps even that she herself is the patient's own daughter. While this sometimes avoids undue expectations on the part of the caregiver and eases certain tensions, it also means that the patient's story has been shelved as we would shelve a book we tire of and do not finish. The relationship between author, characters, and reader has been suspended just as the relationships between spouses, parents, and children become suspended.

The difficulties with an end-stage Alzheimer's narrative, then, are three-fold. First, as cognitively functioning people, we have personal experiences which shed only partial light on what this kind of dementia might be like. Second, the very idea of a person going through such an experience is an idea we shun like the person itself. King Lear's speech, "Pray, do not mock me / I am a very foolish fond old man," while an example of someone suffering mental derangement, still retains power, dignity, and beauty. We can be drawn to the king in ways we are unlikely to be drawn to an Alzheimer's patient. And third, the complete linguistic breakdown which is end-stage dementia means the end of all possibilities of meaning and continu-

31

ity. An incoherent babbling narrator whose words seem to come out randomly is not a narrator, and many may well wonder if this person is still a person at all.

Hence, it becomes possible to say that Alzheimer's disease represents deconstruction incarnate. The instability of meaning and free play of signifiers which deconstructionists enjoy talking about become manifest most clearly in an Alzheimer's patient. Particularly in latter stages, the slipperiness of a patient's language becomes apparent. Talking about "shoes" can suddenly produce blurting out "ships" and then to a scatological outcry. (My mother has cursed more times in a month than I had heard her curse in an entire lifetime—is this the same person I once knew, the same person who was always very careful to control her anger?) This shifting of sounds, words, and meanings can be beautiful if it comes from a poet who enters into a creative relationship with the reader (as when Derek Walcott moves from "seashells" to "Seychelles" or plays off the multiple ways in which his title *Omeros* resonates historically or phonetically). But this unpredictable and unfixable speaking can be quite an ugly thing when the author is an Alzheimer's patient and when the caregiver has no choice but to enter into a linguistic relationship without meaning. Even straightforward sentences seem suspect. There becomes little way of knowing whether she actually liked the dinner you cooked and fed her or whether she is simply telling you that because she thinks that is what she is supposed to say.

To put it another way, Alzheimer's is deconstruction incarnate because it subverts our narratives. Previously, I suggested that early- or middle-stage Alzheimer's patients who wander have narrative potential. But in end-stage dementia our many narratives of wandering are subverted by people who are not able to live in their own homes, communicate with their families, or even offer their own prayers. This disease challenges and relativizes all of our assumptions about language, meaning, and humanity itself. A true first-person, end-stage Alzheimer's narrative—if it were physically possible from someone who cannot speak, type, or hold a pencil—would be the ideal deconstructionist text.

Making this argument may tell us something about the nature of the disease, but it does not really tell us much more about what it is like to be a patient with the disease. To learn more about that, I suggest we learn from Augustine's *On the Trinity* and his *Confessions*. In these texts, he explored the mysteries of the Triune nature of the

Godhead and his own sinfulness and reconciliation with God through the forms of meditation and prayer. Similarly, by studying a book of prayers for Alzheimer's caregivers we can begin to fathom the mysteries of this disease. If we listen carefully to the prayers in Cecil Murphy's *Day to Day: Spiritual Help When Someone You Love Has Alzheimer's*, we can sense how we can begin this process of understanding.

These prayers reveal many problems facing caregivers—failures of patience, lingering guilt, obsession with doubts and nagging questions, the loss of physical as well as mental intimacy—problems faced by anyone who has lost a loved one. But in this case, the loved one is still alive, and there remains the tantalizing illusion of forgiveness for wrongs and ultimate rectification. More importantly, the very form of the prayer allows us to enter into a world where we are the ones who need the caregiving. When we pray, we ask God to care for us, and we become the patient. Hence, if we wish to know what it is like to be a person with Alzheimer's, we must first pray.

When we read these prayers, we begin to see ourselves as people who resemble Alzheimer's patients. We recognize that our words and actions often make little sense to God. The inadequacy of our words becomes plain, and we see our stammering—and perhaps even our suffering—in a new light. The prayers and spiritual advice which Murphy offers do not tell us precisely what Alzheimer's disease is like in end-stage dementia, but they do indicate to us how we should go about empathizing with the plight of the patients. And this empathy is the first step in understanding. Stephen Sapp has suggested that caring for or knowing an Alzheimer's patient can help us to recognize that we, too, are creatures dependent on others and on God; I believe that we come to see this shared human dependency even more clearly when we are at prayer.[10]

Through prayer, not only may we begin to see ourselves as Alzheimer's patients, we may also begin to see God in these people, too. Jesus has declared that caregiving for another person is caregiving for him. His "I was sick and you visited me" could not be more powerful for Alzheimer's families, their friends, and their churches (Matt. 25:36). Moreover, as we meditate on the different faces of various crucifixion scenes, we begin to see that the gazes there are not at all far from the painful stares of many patients. We may suspect that there is a rather powerful identity between the two, the suffering Logos and a suffering *imago Dei*.

In addition to learning from prayer, our understanding and confronting this disease require that we compare it briefly with the medical and moral issues of other diseases. There seems to be a temptation in our society to vie for the title of Those Who Suffer Most or World's Greatest Victim status, and I would like to avoid such solipsistic comparisons. (I suspect that comparative oppression studies will ultimately reveal what the Cross reveals, namely, that we understand who we are better if we begin our reflections with the reality of suffering and the communion we will find there.) Still, it will be useful to make comparisons for the sake of clarity.

One way of locating Alzheimer's in relationship to other illnesses is to return to the category of narrative. Susan Sontag in her *Illness as Metaphor* suggested that cancer, in contrast to tuberculosis, did not lend itself to poetry or aestheticization. For many in the last several centuries, particularly those of a romantic bent, TB could be a "decorative, often lyrical death."[11] A disease which consumed the lungs was seen to free the soul from the body, and lead to greater creative powers or a heightened consciousness. It could even be something of an aphrodisiac, and as Thomas Mann's *Magic Mountain* and many other works suggest, TB certainly made for good stories.

Writing in 1978, cancer seemed to Sontag to be a particularly problematic disease, one that, like Alzheimer's, challenged our assumptions about health, the body, and medicine. The fact that most cancers do not have external signs of their presence (in contrast to the dramatic coughed-up blood and x-rays of TB patients) means that they do not manifest themselves until much harm has already been done. They remain hidden, mysterious, something alien inside the body, something to be feared. While we now look at cancer differently—we no longer see it as a sign of repression and resignation—we still see it differently from Alzheimer's.

There are a number of cancer narratives (such as Erich Segal's *Love Story*), and they generally center on the patient's and loved ones' struggle for dignity as the body dies. Many people around the world found the story of Francois Mitterand's sustained and public confrontation with cancer to be courageous and inspiring. By contrast, while Ronald Reagan can still communicate in his current stage of Alzheimer's, we know that eventually his body will outlive his mind, and that there will no longer seem to be any more Ronald Reagan, even though his autonomic functions may still "do it for the Gipper" for some time. According to the *People* magazine cover story on

Alzheimer's (February 27, 1995), the Great Communicator is sadly forgetting how to tell stories.

Cancers develop because of a number of reasons and factors—both genetics and behavior play a large part in the disease. As such, cancer patients may or may not bear a burden of responsibility for their illness. By contrast, AIDS is contracted largely, though not exclusively, through specific behavioral practices, and AIDS patients often bear a direct burden of social stigmatization as well. Still, as the successful *Angels in America* and *Philadelphia* reveal, AIDS narratives can succeed and become phenomenally popular. Unless the disease leads to AIDS-related dementia, AIDS patients can still be remarkably dignified and courageous even until the final days of life. We can like their stories because they can teach us how to die better.

But Alzheimer's does not provide us with any *ars moriendi*, any art of dying, for it defies any hope of dying well. When we think about death, we often are comforted by illusions, but this disease offers no illusions about self-composure, intentionality, forgiveness, or courage. Death has no sting because stings are quick, and this death is a slow, inexorable, leeching demise. Parkinson's disease, too, takes its own sweet time, and because the patient is fully aware of the breakdown of his own motor functions and communicative abilities, it can seem more cruel than Alzheimer's. But it does offer the patient a chance to give a great deal to his family. My father-in-law, Dr. Albert Gollin, has Parkinson's disease, and those who love him are drawing from his courage and character even as the disease makes it increasingly difficult for him to continue the life to which he was accustomed.

Alzheimer's thus seems to be unlike these other diseases in significant respects. It is disintegrative, non-redemptive, of uncertain etiology, non-contagious, amoral, and, at least at this point, inexorably lethal—and this combination helps us to see why it is so challenging theologically. Unlike TB, it would be hard to consider Alzheimer's to be enhancing the powers of the mind or soul. And even though sexuality does not cease with the onset of the disease, it would be hard to see Alzheimer's as an aphrodisiac. Indeed, it seems impossible to see anything worthwhile in this disease at all. Like some forms of cancer, Alzheimer's very mysteriousness increases our fear of the disease. And our lack of medical data on its causes precludes the type of cancer-fighting tips now common on television news and talk shows. With both diseases, the genetic link makes some relieved and others more worried about their own futures. Thinking about ourselves genetically can unfortunately lead us to think about ourselves as waiting persons, people worriedly anticipating the predetermined genetic fates that await us.

Alzheimer's appears to be a ruthlessly amoral disease in that we seem to be able to link it with no form of behavior. For many people, AIDS can be bracketed as a disease "those people" get, and to some there seems to be a moralizing sense of just "rewards" which can be attached to such deaths. Alzheimer's is not susceptible to such compartmentalization. True, except in early-onset cases, it strikes only the elderly. But as aging is something we all share, we may be able to sense that this disease waits for all of us, too (it is a rather ecumenical disease). We cannot address it with a moral notion of disease or with any simple assumptions of justice. These categories would seem totally inadequate. The depersonalizing which the disease brings to the patient seems mirrored in the very cosmos itself. Suddenly it seems that the universe is devoid of a personal, providential God. There seems to be no sense of justice "out there" which might correspond to something written inside on the human heart. With Alzheimer's, dissolution just happens. "Purpose" and "reason" seem to be no more a part of the eternal natural order of things than a patient's ephemeral memories.

Its non-contagious nature, as comforting as it may be, is somewhat illusory. Families sometimes go into a voluntary exile or self-ostracism because of physical difficulties or potential embarrassments with patients. Just as contagious diseases drive people away from patients and their families, so too does Alzheimer's keep friends and even family away. One minister has compared the disease to leprosy.[12] The fear is not contagion but the confrontation with deconstruction itself. It is not easy to see a stranger suffer from dementia—how much more difficult it is to see someone you know, or once knew, sitting there before you blankly staring into space or babbling. While I am grateful for the many friends who have come to our house, I do not begrudge those who have distanced themselves politely. Many simply do not know what is appropriate; it is a baffling, fickle disease. We are often asked, "Is it OK to go upstairs and see Jan?" In fact, as with many patients, she loves company. She often "rises to the occasion" and appears much more coherent than normal.

The theological and existential problems raised by Alzheimer's are probably closest to autism and acephalitis, conditions we normally associate with children. In these conditions, the problem is not of disintegration but the inability to develop "normally" in the first place. These are dreadful conditions and I would hope that some of the results of this study would be applicable to theological considerations of these as well. Similar issues of the soul and the metaphysical basis of personhood also appear in considerations of these afflictions. Often we ask, Who are we? But with these conditions, we are forced to ask, What are we? (With dementia, we may also wonder, What will we become?) As the title of this work suggests, however, the most fundamental question we will need to ask ourselves is, Whose are we?

Theological Questions Raised by Alzheimer's Disease: An Agenda

The prospect of maintaining good health for fifty years only to live for more than a decade in a demented state certainly ought to make us think twice about our ideas about health, the medical profession, and life itself. Is the teleology of health dementia? The recent work by Sherwin B. Nuland, *How We Die: Reflections on Life's Final Chapter*, critiques modern society's difficulty with the very idea of death.[13] This is by no means a new criticism (Susan Sontag also sought to illuminate this lacuna in the text of the modern world), but it is fresh in that it is from a member of the healing profession. As a physician teaching at a medical school, he became particularly sensitive of the need to prepare future doctors for their roles in helping people to die. He challenges our attempts to sanitize death or to remove it from public view, such as in a hospital or a nursing home. (A recent study of dying in hospitals provides statistical evidence of how poorly prepared the medical profession is for helping patients to die well.)[14] Given the great medical achievements of this century, we may have come unduly to emphasize curing over caring, and as we come to expect doctors to heal us, we become unprepared for a disease and an experience which they cannot treat.

One of the strangest aspects of Rousseau's *Emile* for modern readers will be the refusal to have young Emile vaccinated because, in the words of Allan Bloom "vaccination presupposes the existence of a scientific community that is possible only in large, luxurious, and corrupt nations, and because the world in which doctors are prominent is one where living becomes more important than living well."[15] In contrast to Rousseau's brave notion for Emile, the United States seems to be the most highly medicated society the world has yet produced. We seem to be indeed a "therapeutic culture," one given to healings and remedies of all sorts.[16] (We may want to follow Rousseau's critique, and ask if we have forgotten the problem of living well as we have pursued simply being alive.)

In our medical optimism, have we rendered ourselves unprepared for the challenges of a lethal disease? One can read many books on theology and never be reminded of the fact that one day both reader and author will die. We seem to be preoccupied with other matters, and we forget all too easily that thanatology is an inseparable part of theology. Moreover, we may ask if we are unprepared for mental deterioration as well. E. Brooks Holifield subtitled his *A History of Pastoral Care in America* rather starkly: *From Salvation to Self-Realization*. We invest a great deal of time and money in realizing, actualizing, empowering, and developing our selves. But self-realization is an idea which Alzheimer's renders suspect. When there is no self, there can be very little self-realization. When your primary concern is caregiving, you have little time for self. Does Alzheimer's then suggest that we need to return to the traditional pastoral categories of salvation, sin, death, and resurrection?

The theological and ecclesiological problems raised by the "Theological Disease" are of enormous significance for all of us since they strike at the heart of who we are and what we may become. Although there has been some discussion of the problems raised by dementia in some specialized circles, I would hope that this study would help to bring these problems to the forefront of contemporary theological discourse and ecclesiastical self-understanding. As shall be seen, the topics this study brings to a consideration of Alzheimer's are some of the most traditional and fundamental topics in the history of Christian thought. In turn, this disease, its patients, and their caregivers may tell us a great deal about the truth and the relevance of these basic teachings. As I write, the Philippines, where I now live, is recovering from a powerful typhoon which has killed many and driven many more into homelessness and deeper poverty. The lessons we learn from this disease about God's love, forgiveness, and suffering apply to these people, just as they apply to my mother and to us all.

In the theological consideration of this disease, two major types of problems present themselves—the ontological and the spiritual (or devotional). Although there is significant overlap, these categories correspond primarily to the consideration of the phenomenon from the perspectives of the patient and of the caregiver. Chapters 4 and 5 will concentrate on the particular ontological problems concerning patients, and chapters 6 through 8 will concentrate on caregivers' spiritual dilemmas.

Addressing these topics requires first some background. Hence, chapter 2 examines memory from a number of philosophical, theological, and ecclesiological perspectives, in order to see how memory lies at the heart of our existence and our relationship with God. This chapter establishes the framework for linking the problems of memory and memory loss to each of the subsequent chapters. Chapter 3 initiates the theological consideration of Alzheimer's disease with a discussion of my fundamental beliefs and theological methods. As we shall see, the central doctrines of the Trinity and the Incarnation will never be far from our consideration. Moreover, I want to stress the importance of orthodoxy for this study. Alzheimer's breaks continuity with the past; orthodoxy preserves it. We are not destitute of resources, and we are not alone, particularly when we suffer and when we love. Chapters 2 and 3, then, prepare us for the formal theological considerations of chapters 4 through 8.

Ontologically, what happens in Alzheimer's? What becomes of a person and her memories? Is there a metaphysical basis for the human person which this disease does not destroy? The human subject in many ways lies at the center of contemporary theological reflection; we are presumed to be rational, self-actualizing, and intentional. But can we be confident about theologies predicated on a self-conscious, decision-making subject when a person may live for over ten years without any such subjecthood? We cannot avoid the question, To what extent does the theological understanding of humanity depend upon the brain, neurochemical processes, and matter itself? Hence, chapter 4 considers from the outset the church's traditions regarding the soul. As we shall see, the teaching about the body-soul unity of our existence is that our enduring personhood is not limited to matter's fickleness. We need to ask, too, about the relationship between God and the patient. How is it possible to speak of a personal relationship with God, when there seems to be no person left? Does the Holy Spirit depend on a conscious subject in order to be present or provide comfort to a person? We will be reminded of how the soul is the locus of God's work and presence in us.

When we examine what happens to patients with this disease, we also need to ask what will happen to them as they die. Will the dead's personal existence end when blood flow stops altogether and brain functions cease? If we have forgotten the answer to this question, or if we have persistently overlooked this answer, then we will need to remind ourselves in chapter 5 about the doctrine of the resurrection. This doctrine, like caregiving, asserts the importance of the body. How, then, do the doctrine of the resurrection and the practice of caregiving mutually inform each other? Moreover, we may well wonder what happens to the relationship between the person and God not only during the stages of senile dementia but also at death and at the resurrection. Hence, we will need to explore imaginatively the traditions of the beatific vision in order to consider how these mysteries can illuminate our understanding of what happens to Alzheimer's patients. Can devotional meditations on the beatific vision be helpful for caregivers as well? Certainly they need all the help they can get.

Spiritually, the problems raised by Alzheimer's disease are perhaps most difficult for the caregivers, for they must confront a prolonged deterioration of someone they love. The doubts, anguish, loneliness, fear, and inadequacies which they feel increasingly (and which mercifully the patient seems to feel decreasingly) suggest that a person's relationship with God almost inevitably will be thrown into confusion and question. How is it possible to affirm the love and goodness of God amid the agony of the disease? Anger and hatred seem more understandable. Quite easily indeed they can develop an apocalyptic attitude, a nihilistic expectation of inevitable destruction. Can a discussion of the church's traditions concerning sin and the Apocalypse be useful here? Chapter 6 begins our consideration of the caregiver's plight by returning to the heart of our basic existential situation, the dynamic of human sin and divine forgiveness. The love shed on the Cross can indeed make sense out of caregivers' feelings of guilt and anger and their need for forgiveness.

As comfortable ideas about God and human nature are challenged by Alzheimer's, so too does the entire creation come into question. The physicist's notion of galactic entropy seems to be a macrocosm of the patient; the cosmos is in dissolution and decay. It is quite ugly. Can there be any sense of beauty in the world when this disease is present? Can the goodness and beauty of God's creation and his glory be affirmed? Chapter 7 rephrases the question, and asks, How can an affirmation of the beauty of the creation provide a support for caregiving? How can the beauty of the church's hymns, art, and liturgy be as a cool, refreshing stream in a humid, stifling jungle?

Finally, as this disease is about memory, it is also about history, and hence about God's providence. Can this traditional teaching be affirmed when there seems to be very little that is providential about Alzheimer's disease? How can the study of history provide a bulwark against the onslaught of this disease? As we shall see in chapter 8, Alzheimer's families have no other choice but to become historians of a sort, for they must assume the responsibility of bearing another person's own history. In turn, they may teach us how to be better historians.

The difficult challenge of worship and praise is raised by this disease, too. How can a pastor and a community of faith minister to demented patients and caregivers alike? How can a congregation sustain the presence of someone who is losing the ability to speak and eat for themselves? Although there is an increasingly useful body of research and literature on ministering to demented patients (as seen, for example, in the conference on Alzheimer's at Memphis Theological Seminary in October, 1994), the field of pastoral care as a whole has not explored these issues. Pastoral work generally pre-supposes working with a cognitive subject who is able to approach matters of faith intellectually.[17]

Although the ontological and spiritual problems each receive treatment in separate chapters, the pastoral, or ecclesiological problems permeate this entire text. In a Christian consideration of the phenomena of a disease, it is a mistake to separate the individual victim or caregiver from the ecclesiastical community in which she lives. Such an approach may respect the pseudo-autonomy of an individual, but it does not ground that person in a community which provides the collective memories and purpose which help imbue the person with meaning.

Ultimately, we will be able to summarize how the church's work as manifested in her teachings, sacraments, and community may answer our questions about this disease and tell us how to respond to its challenges. Once we listen to what the church has to teach us—

41

and once we listen to what Alzheimer's families have to tell us—we may be better prepared to answer the questions in the prefatory quotation of this chapter: "Is there no balm in Gilead? Is there no physician there?"

Chapter 2

Memory and Canonicity

And he said,
"Jesus, remember me when you come into your kingdom."
— Luke 23:42

It is impossible for us to distinguish between ourselves and our memories. Even the act of reading this sentence (let alone this paragraph) presupposes a memory of what the first words of the sentence are. We are our memories, and without them we have but a physical resemblance to that person we each suppose ourselves to be. Memories function canonically, telling us authoritatively who we are, giving us resources for who we will become. It should be obvious, then, that the apparent dissolution of the mnemonic capacities experienced by Alzheimer's disease patients raises most serious and profound questions about human existence.

But we are not simply what we remember. We are also what others remember of us, especially what God remembers. The Old Testament witness clearly identifies human existence with being remembered. In his *Memory and Tradition in Israel*, Brevard Childs observes that idiomatically "not to be remembered" is "not to exist."[1] God's very presence, grace, and mercy are expressed through the divine memory. The blinded Samson's strength is reborn when God answers his prayer to be remembered (Judg. 17:28), and Rachel is able to conceive because "God remembered Rachel" (Gen. 30:22). By contrast, in Psalm 88, the person whom God has forgotten, has no strength, is already in the grave, already in "the regions dark and deep." Although God's remembering of a person is crucial, the role of human memory is also underscored, especially in the case of the unrighteous. In Job 24:20, the names of the wicked are forgotten in the towns, and so "wickedness is broken like a tree."

The task of this chapter is to arrive at a theological appreciation of memory, an appreciation that is faithful to the Christian tradition and takes account of the modern world's contributions and contexts. This description of memory helps delineate the most important ways in which memory shapes who we are, how we should live our lives, and even whose we are. My concern will be, above all, to examine the witnesses of the two Testaments and the Christian tradition concerning the role of memory in the lives of persons and the church. How have prophets, psalmists, apostles, theologians, and others understood memory? Is it a purely cognitive element of human life? What does it mean when a narrative begins, "He forgot the lord God and. . . ."? How can it be said, in the case of an Alzheimer's patient, that family and friends (and ultimately God) remember *for* someone? As we shall see, there are important affinities between human memory and the church's canonical witnesses. Each is constitutive for self-understanding; each serves as a *kanon*, a "rule" or "measuring rod" for life. What will emerge from this examination of our heritage is a clear sense that the problem of Alzheimer's, the problem of memory loss, is no stranger to the Biblical and Christian traditions.

Because everything pertaining to human existence passes through the memory, this chapter risks employing "memory" equivocally. Just as horses yoked together to a chariot always run side by side, a consideration of memory brings along with it the topics of imagination (which draws on memories for all its work) and historical criticism and narrative (which, like memory, appreciate the fundamentally temporal nature of human existence). And as a perusal of Plato, Aquinas, Freud, and countless others would demonstrate, terms such as memory, habit, imagination, reason, consciousness, and repression are employed in quite different senses in different epistemologies. One person's "memory" may be another's "habit" or "imagination." Hence, we will need to distinguish carefully between memory itself and each of these topics.

The first sections of this chapter examine Christian beliefs concerning God's memory, human memory, and the relationship between faith and memory. Building on Brevard Child's analysis of the Hebrew root for memory, *zkr*, we unfold the many rich meanings and uses of memory in the lives of Israel, individual persons, and the church. The next section examines the phenomena of forgetting both as a perennial problem and as a condition peculiarly affecting the modern world. The final section discusses the impact of the twentieth-century revolution concerning the study of memory and highlights the Bergsonian concept of *durée* as an important element for this study. This chapter concludes with a theological appreciation of memory. In particular, it contrasts imagination with memory and draws together the many links between canonicity and memory evoked by previous sections.

God's Memory, the Foundation of Our Hope

God remembers. Despite humanity's regrettable habit of forgetting God, and despite the dissolution of human memories, the encouraging witness of both Testaments is that God does remember. When confronted by the phenomena of Alzheimer's (or when we remember all those millions who died suffering), it is ultimately God's memory, not ours, which must be, in the language of 1 Peter 3:15, the reason for the hope that is within us. Truly, our cry is the cry of the thief in Luke 23:42, "Jesus, remember me when you come into your kingdom."

Although speaking of God's "memory" may seem to be an anthropomorphism, the prophets, apostles, psalmists, and even Jesus himself all invoke God's memory, for to speak of this is to speak of God's fidelity. In this sense, it is a "parabolic" expression of the workings of the divine mind, rendered in such a fashion as to make such a mystery comprehensible.[2] Augustine in his *On the Trinity* located in memory, understanding, and will a Trinitarian image of God in humanity. Memory, he argued, was particularly to be associated with the Father, and memory and omniscience become inseparable. Moreover, we cannot forget that when the Logos became man, he possessed human knowledge, and hence human memory. When we speak of God's memory, we may be speaking of one of several aspects of God's faithfulness, creative knowledge, and redemptive work.

The first four chapters of Deuteronomy encapsulate many of the themes suggesting that God's memory is the key to our memory. The great emphasis on memory and remembering has led commentators to observe that Deuteronomy offers a "theology of remembering."[3] After the great work of liberation wrought by God in the Exodus, itself a manifestation of God's faithful memory, it is Israel's duty to remember these deeds and to employ this communal memory as a spur to the fulfillment of the law. Hence, it is not with Job or Lamentations that a study of the theological dimensions of Alzheimer's

45

begins. Rather, it commences with Deuteronomy—with the earliest cultic formation of Israel. For the community, its worship and God's own memory all precede and shape the experience of individual suffering, not vice versa.

These chapters comprise the beginning of Moses' final address to the people he has led out of Egypt and through the wilderness for four decades. He first recapitulates the history of the tribes' wanderings, a history of God's faithful memory and Israel's recurrent rebellion, and then enjoins the people of Israel to be faithful to God and God's work and law. What is suggested by Moses' address in Deuteronomy 4:1-10 is that that which is to be learned is prior to the community and the communal narrative itself. In other words, divine pedagogy precedes human epistemology. We do not discover God in order to remember, rather we remember what has been done in order that we may discover God.

Moses—and as far as Israel and the early church were concerned the author is Moses—well aware of the fragile nature of human memory, prophesies that the people of Israel, despite all they have received, will continue to grow forgetful of God's works. The particular form of forgetfulness which Moses identifies is idolatry, choosing to worship creatures such as fishes, stars, beasts, and even humans. "Take heed to yourselves, lest you forget the covenant of the LORD your God, which he made with you, and make a graven image in the form of anything which the LORD has forbidden you" (Deut. 4:23). Idolatry, in its ancient or modern guises, is a form of forgetfulness to which every generation seems to be susceptible.

Deuteronomy 4:30-31 serves as a coda to Moses' prophecies, a coda which transforms a warning of human wretchedness and misery into a proclamation of God's greatness:

> When you are in tribulation, and all these things come upon you in the latter days, you will return to the LORD your God and obey his voice, for the LORD your God is a merciful God; he will not fail you or destroy you or forget the covenant with your fathers which he swore to them.

God's mercies and God's memory are inseparable. The theme of the covenant which Moses stresses underscores the importance of the prevenience of God's memory. It serves as the basis for many invocations of God in many diverse situations in the history of Israel, and prophets or psalmists frequently invoke the covenant in the context of a confession of infidelity and forgetfulness.[4] As with the phenomena of Alzheimer's disease, because of its forgetfulness, Israel seems constantly to be in danger of complete dissolution, and only God's memory prevents total destruction.

God's remembering is not a purely mental operation; it also implies providential, salvific activity. In the Old Testament, the use of the root word for memory, zkr, with God as the subject, frequently employed the directional preposition le. Lexicographically, when God remembers, God brings something into the divine mind simultaneously with an implied divine motion towards the object. For God, remembering is thus never the same as acting, but at the same time, it is never separated from action either.[5] To confess that God remembers is to affirm that God is faithful to the covenant he established with Abraham. To confess God's fidelity is to confess his sustaining love.

In the context of Alzheimer's, families, especially those families who have entrusted one of their own to anonymous professionals, frequently beseech God to remember those who no longer seem capable of remembering. The proclamation of God's memory of those in distress occurs several times in the Old Testament (cf. the barren Rachel in Gen. 30:22 or the blind Samson in Judg. 16:28). As Jeremiah 15:15 underscores, not only is God's memory invoked, but also his divine presence: "O LORD, thou knowest; remember me and visit me." As anyone in a nursing home will tell us, not only is it important to be remembered, it is also crucial to be visited.

But God's memory, especially God's faithful visitation with the suffering, as witnessed in the Old Testament, assumes a rather different meaning in light of the New Testament, in light of Christ and Christ's suffering. God's memory of the covenant was frequently seen as vicarious. God extends mercy to the faithless for the sake of the patriarchs (cf. Exod. 32:11-14 and Lev. 26:45). Now we recognize that God remembers not only Abraham but also himself. Luke explicitly links the Incarnation to God's memory of the covenant. Mary declares, "He has helped his servant Israel, in remembrance of his mercy," and Zechariah, "filled with the Holy Spirit," proclaims that God will "remember his holy covenant" (Luke 1: 54 and 72). In some sense, the Incarnation, death, and resurrection can be seen as God's great act of memory. Because of Christ, the new covenant, God forgives, and forgiveness is phrased as the forgetting of sins. Hebrews 8:12, reinterpreting—re-remembering or re-canonizing—Jeremiah

47

31:34 in light of the Gospel, presents God's declaration: "For I will be merciful toward their iniquities, and I will remember their sins no more." God's forgetting is a sign of love and power; our forgetfulness is a reminder of our solipsism and weakness.

In Isaiah 44:21, divine and human memory become interwoven, but in the union of the two natures, God's divine memory and Jesus' human memory become one. Human nature, made in the image of God, partakes of the depths of divine memory (omniscience), and the divine memory assumes into itself the weakness of the human. More specifically, God divinizes human memory. Jesus' cry, "My God, my God, why have you forsaken me?" is the lament of a man who possesses the fullness of divine memory—yet who himself simultaneously experiences being forgotten. His soul at once encompasses all of history and more, yet he himself is cast outside of it completely. This seems to be a horrible mental counterpart to the physical pains of the nails and thorns. When God remembers us, then, he also remembers being forgotten himself, a terrifying abandonment for which we sinners all share responsibility. We may wonder, perhaps, if his own experience on the Cross facilitates his remembering of Alzheimer's patients in nursing homes.

Human Memory, Faith, and Apostolicity in Israel and the Church

"This is my body which is given for you. Do this in remembrance of me" (Luke 22:19). The central act of the Christian community is an act of remembering God's saving work. The acceptance of the canon, Christ's Supper, and his Lordship by a person is the acceptance of an authoritative shared memory and the basis of the church's apostolic communion.[6] As we shall see in this section's exploration of the many roles of memory in Israel and the church, this shared memory stands at the heart of Christian faith and is the basis of our relationship with God. Consequently, memory plays a crucial role in the dynamics of morality, sin, and forgiveness.

To remember God seems at times synonymous with belief; that a person remembers God and behaves accordingly resembles an experience of faith. It would seem contradictory to say that an agnostic or atheist can remember God—for such a memory implies a commitment to the reality of that which is remembered. And Christians often call this commitment faith. Remembering the divine is not a neutral, dispassionate epistemological process—indeed, we should expect nothing less when we uses phrases such as "Do this in remembrance of me." Whether faith is understood primarily as a series of truth-claims, a fundamental disposition in a person, or a sense of trust, whether it is viewed in terms of Barth's "truth as self-involving" or seen in scholastic terms of faith formed by love, Christian faith and memory combine both cognitive and affective elements. Remembering theologically entails not only recalling certain facts or propositions about God and humanity but also presumes a soteriological, ethical, and existential disposition in the rememberer.

Lexicographically, *zkr*, memory, and faith became related during the unfolding of Israel's history. As Brevard Childs has demonstrated, the identification of the Hebrew root for memory with not only cognitive processes but also existential claims was the result of three distinct historical crises in the cultic life of Israel.[7] The "theology of memory" produced by the Deuteronomist was in response to the need to make the Exodus experience a reality for those generations who had not been in Israel. Responding to another gulf between the experiences of the exiles and the professed history of the covenant and Exodus, Deutero-Isaiah uses the Israelite's remembering of God as a bridge spanning present experience and the history of God's salvific activity. Similarly, Ezekiel's use of memory provides a way for those of subsequent generations to identify themselves directly with the covenant.

In each case, Israel's remembering of God and God's work provides existential "memories" for those who could neither have experienced the events nor even seen the land which had been promised. Childs employs the term "actualization" to describe this process for the Israelites. The rememberer "entered the same redemptive reality of the Exodus generation." The event transmitted to another's memory becomes as real as the original experience.[8] Thus, at Passover, Jews eat bitter herbs to remind themselves, to actualize for themselves, what Jews have experienced before. Memory is thus efficacious. Childs stresses that this use of *zkr* exhibits a distinct appreciation for the dynamic, existential qualities of salvation history and human memory. For the Israelites in the exile, memory was not mythical but historical. Memories did not recreate or manifest a mythical understanding of origins, rather they linked the rememberers to God as God works in history.

49

For several reasons, the historical contexts for the New Testament understanding of memory and its relationship to faith are in important respects quite different from those of Israel. First, the Gospel narratives' concerns for the past are overwhelmed by the present reality of God in the person of Jesus Christ. Hence the Gospels speak little *per se* of memory (though the Lukan Magnificat and Benedictus, Luke 1:46-55 and 67-79, link the conceiving of Jesus and the birth of John to God's remembering of the covenant). Prophecies may be remembered, but they are remembered insofar as they point to the present manifestation of God. There is no doubt that the Pharisees remember the Exodus; the issue is whether they believe that the man before them is the Messiah. Nevertheless, Christ's words of institution for the Eucharist remind us in the central act of the church of the importance of remembering him.

Second, whereas the Hebrew term for memory was undifferentiated from responsibilities, affections, and ultimately action, the Greek understanding of memory by the time of Christ had experienced the rigorous epistemological analyses of Plato and Aristotle.[9] In the hand of philosophers, terms for mental processes became distinguished and separated. Whereas many Homeric Greek's mnemonic terms semantically resemble the Hebrew *zkr*, Greek terms after Plato and Aristotle exhibit differentiated memories such that remembering can be understood as a purely epistemological, completely neutral action in the mind. These memories do not entail any particular responsibilities, duties, attitudes, or personal struggles. Aristotle's *On Memory and Reminiscence* appears to be a treatise on data processing.

Third, and reinforcing this distinction between cognitive recalling and acts of the entire person, the New Testament emphasis on belief and conversion suggests that the process of "entering sacred reality" cannot be expressed adequately by memory. Rather, the self-conscious will becomes more important. Whereas Israelites are born into a genetic community with specific historical memories which define its existence, gentiles may choose to join a community which professes certain truths. Thus, confessions and creeds begin with "I believe" not "I remember."

Finally, the understanding of the Holy Spirit's role as Paraclete also changed the theological understanding of memory. The Spirit remains present in each generation, even though the narrative of Jesus is received through the memories and witnesses of others. As

Paraclete, the Spirit comforts directly; Christians have more than memories of the covenant in times of duress. Consequently, instead of enjoining Timothy to remember the truths of Christ, pseudo-Paul states, "Guard the truth that has been entrusted to you by the Holy Spirit who dwells within us" (2 Tim.1:14). Nevertheless, despite these historical changes in the manifest reality of God, important links between memory and faith remain; Hebrews 11:22 makes it explicit—by faith Joseph remembered the Exodus. And through our faith, we remember Joseph and the author of this epistle.

It should not be surprising that memory becomes more important in the pastoral epistles, letters written for readers several generations after the Resurrection. First, as with Deuteronomy, the author must bring those who have heard into the realm of those who were present. The same problem of "actualization" remains. Second, both Deuteronomy and the Pastorals seem to expect that sin will cause people to forget who God is and what God has done (cf. 2 Tim. 3:1ff). But because false Christs were being preached at this time, the issue became not only *whether* Christ is remembered but *how* Christ is remembered. Consequently, in these epistles which testify to the development of the church, authoritative teaching assumes a position of paramount importance (cf. 1 Tim. 4:13 and 2 Tim. 4:2). Timothy is not only to remember Christ but to remember Christ "as preached in my [Paul's] gospel" (2 Tim. 2:8). Memory is inseparable from the crucial ideas of apostolicity and canonicity.

The great emphasis on apostolicity in the writings of the Fathers emerges from this context of preserving the accurate, faithful memory of who Jesus was and why he became man. As much as we might like to, we should not choose to remember any Jesus we please. Nineteenth- and twentieth-century liberal, often Marcionite, attempts to separate Jesus from his Jewishness are, to put it most charitably, a failure of memory. Significantly, it was in part through the challenge of Marcion that the early church had to establish formally what constituted the canon of Scripture. Both in the life of a person and the life of a church, challenges to faithful memory produce a need for canonicity, a need for authoritative self-description.

Finally, the Christian experience of conversion and the willful assumption of the church's memories into one's own memories—the process of growing strong in faith—may also entail a very important transformation of memories. The Resurrection, for example, changed the memories of the disciples (John 2:22 and 12:16). The fresh insights

51

brought by Augustine's new faith as he presented them in his *Confessions* provide a clear example of how conversion completely alters old memories. He is able to recall his former life in the context of his new realization of God's work in his own life. The "once . . . but now" of the hymn *Amazing Grace* similarly expresses this important transformation of memory by faith. We look back on our lives with the fresh knowledge of God's love and work for us—our experiences are transformed and we are filled with hope for the future. For the convert as for the Israelite, faith actualizes and transubstantiates human memories. A conversion experience resembles receiving a diagnosis of Alzheimer's disease because this medical revelation compels us to re-remember the previous months of strange behavior and forgetfulness. Unfortunately, this re-remembering entails a new sense of dread, not a sense of hope.

The link between faith and memory underscore the importance of the narrative context in which we remember.[10] The discussion of Psalm 25:6-7 in the first section highlighted the importance of how God remembers. God remembers according to his "steadfast love." Similarly, human memory does not occur in a vacuum. Rather, memories interact dialectically with our own sense of who we are and how we are to live. This sense expresses itself as our life's story or narrative, and in consciously or unconsciously remembering, we bring the past into the present moments of this ongoing narrative. Similarly, past memories assert themselves by shaping this narrative in ways which we may not perceive. Accurately or not, we see ourselves as a certain type of character or characters (say, a certain type of spouse, parent, or professional) and we remember our pasts accordingly, sometimes with regret, sometimes with satisfaction. The questions become, then, What are the canonical events, principles, and habits for our remembering? Do we remember as Christians according to faith, hope, and love? With pride, despair, or anger in our hearts? Have our lives been sufficiently shaped by the church's traditions that our remembering may be guided by service to Christ's lordship?

Because of this strong identity between faith and memory, memory becomes interwoven with all aspects of our relationship with God. One of the central elements of this relationship is praise; as my father's *The Church Confident* reminds us, the act of praise ought to be the defining characteristic of the church and its worship.[11] As many passages suggest, to remember the covenant with Abraham or the liberation of Israel—to remember God's work—is also to be compelled to praise. The link between memory and praise is, in part, a feature of Hebrew. Especially in some later passages of the Old Testament, the hiphil of *zkr* can also be translated as "extol," "proclaim," "praise," or "confess."[12] Psalm 105, a great psalm of praise and memory, links praise of God with the recalling of God's works. Similarly, the rememberings in 2 Timothy 1–2 evoke praise from the author. Theologically speaking, memory is doxological, and the culture of the church is a culture of praise.

At the same time, memories can also be painful, and perhaps the most disturbing memories are the memories of sin. Ezekiel prophecies Israel's future remembering of her sins—this remembering, quite naturally, will produce lamentations and shame (Ezek. 16:61; 20:43; 36:31).[13] Yet in some elements of the tradition, there is also a clear sense that painful memories, purgation, and reconciliation are linked. In Ezekiel, the future remembering of sins appears to be part of the process of the recovery of Israel, a recovery possible only because God does not forget (16:59-63). In the medieval drama *Everyman*, the eponymous hero's recollection of the scourging of Christ is "penance strong that [he] must endure."[14] In his *Lament for a Son*, Nicholas Wolterstorff intimates that we need an afterlife to confess our sins to our loved ones, to purge our memories of all of the shortcomings, failures, and iniquities which we know all too well.[15] His son's unexpected death, as with the loss of cognitive presence in Alzheimer's, deprived him of the chance to apologize, to rectify, and to forgive and be forgiven. As we shall see in chapter 6, the burdens of sin in the memory lead us to consider the importance of eschatology.

A comparison with Greek traditions underscores the strangeness of the Jewish and Christian understandings of human memories, especially painful ones. Mnemosthene, Memory, was mother of the Muses because Memory is the source of the arts. But, according to Hesiod, the nature of these daughters "is forgetfulness of evil and rest from cares. . . . The gifts of these goddesses instantly divert the mind."[16] In Aristophanes' account of Eros in Plato's *Symposium*, sexual pleasure becomes a vehicle for forgetting the wretched state of a deeply wounded humanity. And in the underworld, the departed soul is to receive the gift of a sip of the waters of Lethe, of forgetfulness. In the *Odyssey*, the souls of the dead must drink blood for vitality and memory. Ultimately, in the Greek world—at bottom a world circumscribed by tragedy—human memories are to be forgotten.

By contrast, Zophar, one of Job's interlocutors, seeks to comfort the afflicted man by telling him that one day he will forget his miseries (11:16). Job soundly rejects this idea, for to do so would be to deny both himself and God. Liturgically, we express the importance of grievous memories when we confess, "The burden of our sins is intolerable." Christians are to remember even their sins. As patristic scholars have shown, Job's notion of his own personhood would have been impossible for the ancient Greeks. Indeed, for the Greeks, "person" could mean but a mask, a mask devoid of distinct, ontological content.[17] The unique human person as a being with a special set of historical memories, however painful or joyous, was not an idea available to most Greeks, whose doctrines of reincarnation or of Lethean forgetfulness precluded such personhood.

Dante's Christianization of Lethe suggests the special dimensions of the Christian constructions of memory. In canto XXXI of the *Purgatorio*, the poet's own cleansing in this river is a purging only of his self-confessed, woeful memories which impede his progress into heaven. After he emerges from the water he partakes symbolically of the Eucharist. He drinks a blood which is quite different from the blood which the shade of Achilles drank in the *Odyssey*. Through Christ, the poet retains his memories, his personhood, and is prepared for beholding the divine. Not all experiences of sorrow can so smoothly lead, as they do in Psalm 77, to memories of God and God's work and the concomitant evocation of praise and joy. But in the Christian world, the sufferer can hear God say "But remember, I made all this, and raised my Son from the dead, so. . . ."[18]

It is precisely this dimension of grace, this dimension of God's activity, and our ability to cooperate with it, which marks the peculiar dimensions of memory in the Jewish and Christian worldviews. Because God created humans in his own image, for example, it is possible for Augustine to argue that by remembering with the aid of the Spirit, the *imago Dei* in humans becomes more like the divine.[19] By contrast, for Polybius, ultimately, human memories of the past are embedded in a rather bleak present. He states that he feels compelled to write history because "the only method of learning how to bear with dignity the vicissitudes of Fortune is to be reminded of the disasters of others."[20]

As Polybius suggests, memory is not only crucial for our emotional and spiritual experiences but also for our behavior. At the most basic level, ethical reflection and moral growth seem impossible without memory, for without knowledge of past events there is no ability to learn for the future. Thus, Polybius declares that "certainly mankind possesses no better guide to conduct than the knowledge of the past."[21] But whereas the Greek historians provided useful lessons and character studies, Moses also revealed binding commandments. And Moses sought to strengthen Israel's ability to fulfill the law by strengthening its memory of God. In Deuteronomy, the instruction in the law is inseparable from the Israelites' memory of the Exodus. Without the latter, the former is ineffectual and meaningless.[22]

Further, the actualizing of other peoples' suffering is to strengthen the person in her faithfulness to the community: "You shall remember that you were a slave in Egypt; and you shall be careful to observe these statutes" (Deut. 16:12), here concerning the proper treatment of slaves. The Israelite is not to imagine what it would be like to be a slave, nor is he or she to recall that previous generations were enslaved in Egypt. Rather, there is a clear existential link in the memory of subsequent generations. Through the covenant, memories are handed down, like the land, from generation to generation. To remember God is a commandment, but likewise so is remembering human beings. "Remember those who are in prison" (Heb. 13:3) and "remember the poor" (Gal. 2:10). The implication is clear, and the history of this century underscores it all too well—it is all too convenient for humans, especially those removed from normal society (as in a nursing home), to be forgotten. Quite appropriately, John Patton's *Pastoral Care in Context: An Introduction to Pastoral Care* places a great emphasis on memory and remembering in pastoral care.

Memory strengthens us not only through reminding us of our duties. An important theme in some Stoic writings is the deep joy which we experience when we recall our own virtuous deeds. Conversely, Christ says in *The Imitation of Christ*, "Remember your sins with deep sorrow and displeasure."[23] By regret, we become better prepared to avoid sin. By recalling both pleasures and pains, then, we strengthen our capacity to live a life pleasing to God. To say that a person has a clean conscience is to say that the person's memories do not contain the knowledge of her own willful evil. The Thomistic conception of cooperating with grace and the infusion of virtuous habits reminds us that habit, like memory, makes past deeds active in the present ethical contexts. For good and for ill, we develop mnemonic habits which shape our conduct.

Forgetting, Sin, and Modernity

Despite the importance of memories for all aspects of our existence, human beings seem to be the most forgetful of creatures. Things "slip our mind" frequently, and we are often looking for car keys. As anyone who has attempted to present an autobiography will recognize, even the memories of many central events in our lives seem uncertain. Rousseau's *Confessions* contain many apologies for his weak memory. Given the sheer amount of sensory impressions we receive at any moment and the data we gather through reading, watching, or listening, it is not surprising that we are unable to recall everything. According to Henri Bergson, we should be glad that one of the functions of the brain is to sort and discard unnecessary data.

More importantly, perhaps, human memory is not only inherently forgetful, it is also fallible.[24] Contemporary studies in the legal profession have demonstrated that memories of witnesses are highly susceptible to alteration and emendation. Interrogators may be able to change a witness' memories by introducing false data concerning a crime scene unobtrusively in early questions and eliciting these bits of information from the witness in subsequent questions: "So, you were standing near the blue Ford when . . . What was the color of the Ford?" The car may have been white, but the witness may now remember it as blue. Moreover, memories can be altered by emotions and personal biases. John Dean's famous detailed Watergate testimony about conversations he had was substantially correct, but later comparisons with the actual tape recordings of the talks reveal that he magnified his own role in his memories. We remember in specific situations, and our egos, emotions, prejudices, and personal narratives greatly affect a supposedly neutral memory of events.

Neurologists describe these problems in terms of the physiological complexity of memory. Impressions from the different senses are stored in different parts of the brain, while the brain's limbic system has the responsibility of integrating such data into a whole. Age is important, too; children's brains are immature and do not retain memories well, and some brain deterioration is normal in old age. Scientists speak of the brain's encoding new data over old bits, and so it becomes possible to imagine how a seemingly simple memory can be altered, lost, or made meaningless as it loses connectedness to the rest of a person. (Many readers' own experiences with fickle computer files and hard drives may illustrate this problem of memory, too.)

More dramatically, the recent cases of "repressed memories" and the alleged recovery of memories of crimes (such as the one involving Cardinal Bernardin of Chicago) complicate our understanding of memory. They plant seeds of uncertainty about our own past. Are memories supposedly recovered through hypnosis and/or the use of the hypnotic drug sodium amytal genuinely a part of who we are? Or are they false memories implanted by quack therapists in violation of a person (or of a whole family, since many of the legal cases involve incest or rape)? Apparently, it is disturbingly easy to plant a false memory which will appear so real as to be indistinguishable from the subject's true memories. The literature on this topic has become enormous; within the last several years many major publishers have come out with major books on the subject. Given the importance of memory in general, and given the legal, professional, and personal issues at stake, we should not be surprised that those who argue both for and against the authenticity of these "memories" become quite passionate.

With Alzheimer's patients who still retain lucidity, memory seems fickle indeed. Sometimes your wife recognizes you, sometimes she does not. Sometimes a caregiver may feel like Socrates the midwife. By asking the right questions diligently, the caregiver helps the patient give birth to the knowledge she already has. The patient crying out to her father may come to remember that he died many years ago. But at the same time, caregivers themselves risk dangers similar to those of therapists recovering repressed memories. When you repeatedly rephrase a question in order to get a patient to answer, are you inadvertently eliciting a true or a false memory? Will the patient suddenly expect her father to enter the room as he did yesterday?

Therapists in the repressed memory debate have been following Freud's lead in believing that traumatic experiences early in life would be repressed only to produce neuroses or hysteria later as the repressed events continued to assert themselves unconsciously. According to Freudian theories of repression, the memory is still there buried somewhere in the unconscious. With Alzheimer's disease, by contrast, damage to the brain may suggest that the memories no longer exist. Human memories may be like computer files—once you destroy the computer's "memory" the data simply no longer exist. (When we consider the soul in chapter 4, we will return to the material or metaphysical basis for human memories.) Regardless of how court cases and psychoanalytical procedures resolve the legitimacy of these practices, the issues raised do highlight the potentially fragile nature of memory. We do forget, repress, or deny parts of our past experiences.

A theological appreciation of memory requires that we consider the forgetfulness and fallibility of memory as it pertains to our religious existence, and such a consideration is most concerned with the relationship between sin and memory. Although academics of all disciplines are holding conferences on memory, rarely do such investigations touch on this crucial relationship. Neurology, in particular, does not seem well suited to investigating how character and memory intersect, since such a linkage presupposes something neurology does not address adequately: the quality and existential significance of our memories. Any attempt to construct a psychology of remembering and forgetting without reference to the effects of "man's first disobedience" (in Milton's phrase) will inevitably fail to do justice to the human condition *coram Deo*.

According to diverse Biblical witnesses, sin is both a cause and effect of forgetting. Despite the Deuteronomist's warning to the Israelites to take heed lest they forget the Lord and sin (Deut. 8:11), the Israelites were quite proficient at not remembering. Israel's idolatry and ingratitude towards the late Gideon's family is interwoven with the fact that "the people of Israel did not remember the LORD their God" (Judg. 8:34). Similar tapestries of forgetfulness and sin are found throughout the prophets (e.g. Neh. 9:17). Likewise, the testimonies of our own forgetfulness are legion. The adulterer forgets the spouse, the rich forget the poor, the friend forgets the friend. We forget the simplest acts of writing thank you and birthday cards. Perhaps we are too busy to remember. Remembering, after all, takes time, and if we follow the rich connotations of the Hebrew *zkr*, remembering also entails distinct responsibilities.

But the psychology of sin and memory is more complicated, as Augustine's penetrating *Confessions* reveal. He describes the way he initially coped with his sins: "I had noticed my iniquity, but I had dissembled it, and contained it, and forgotten it."[25] Our capacity to forget God is exceeded, perhaps, only by our ability to manipulate our own memories so that we can discard our sins mentally. Only God's ability to justify us exceeds our ability to legitimate ourselves. Thus, as we have seen, the *Imitation of Christ*, like Augustine's *Confessions* a perceptive study of spiritual psychology, recommends that we be certain to remember the weakness of our sinful nature, for unless we recall this unfortunate condition we are all too likely to forget the many resolutions we make against sin.[26] Memory *of* sin can be transformed into memory *against* sin. For this reason, it is all the more important that we train ourselves through the church's traditions to strengthen those memories which do contribute to a life of love and virtue, a life pleasing to God.

Because humans seem predisposed to forgetting, Israel and the church have been given a great variety of means for remembering. The Israelites are to wear tassels on the corners of their garments for the sake of remembering the commandments of the Lord (Num. 15:39). As we have already discussed, the pastoral epistles emphasize the importance of regular preaching, and the central act of the church itself, the Eucharist, is an act done in memory. Orthodox liturgies perhaps do a greater service to worshippers as prayers are repeated; such repetition strengthens memory and tempers the soul. The liturgical calendar itself serves as a mnemonic guide for the diversity of religious celebrations and days of remembrance. Our burial practices—tombstones, brass rubbings, sarcophagi, memorial bequests to universities—all express our desire to remember and to be remembered. But the sad reality is that in most cases people are forgotten within a few decades or even years after their death.

That God helps human beings remember (through commanding the Israelites to wear tassels, through sending prophets, or through the institution of the Eucharist) is also one of the central elements of the Biblical witness. Jesus' pedagogical practices—his use of parables, hyperbole, rhetorical questions, etc.—seem designed specifically to promote the remembering of his teachings.[27] In the New Testament, the divine assistance for memory is attributed to, in part, the Holy Spirit. In John 14:25-6, Jesus states, "These things I have spoken to you, while I am still with you. But the Counselor, the Holy Spirit, whom the Father will send in my name, he will teach you all things, and bring to your remembrance all that I have said to you." Throughout the New Testament and Christian tradition, the Paraclete has helped to actualize the past, has aided humans as they seek to remember the divine mercies which have been given in time. Because of the Paraclete, we can have hope for human memory and human faith. We may ask the same rhetorical question asked in the *Imitation of Christ*, "How can I forget You, who have deigned to remember me, even after I was corrupted and lost?"[28]

Emphasizing the divine roles in the process of human memory seems to be needed now more than ever. Although the history of sin from the Old Testament on reveals that humans have been forgetting God for millennia, for many reasons modern Christians seem to have more difficulty in remembering than previous generations. Contemporary Christian understandings of memory do not have the same dense meanings—existential, cognitive, ethical, historical, communal—which were associated with the Hebrew root *zkr*. We would do well to remind ourselves about our modern obstacles to memory and why we need to take great care to appreciate memory theologically. If we are to recover some of the richness of *zkr*—a recovery I believe Alzheimer's provokes us to attempt—then we will need to consider some of the peculiar problems of our age.

In large part, the contemporary problem of memory and faith is the problem of history, or rather, of our time and place in history. Writing his *Democracy in America* over a century and one half ago, Alexis de Tocqueville, at once the herald and critic of the new age of democracy, suggested that democratic peoples would not be as interested in history as previous generations had been. Earlier societies, which he termed aristocratic, were more closely tied to their histories, in part because the aristocratic rulers derived their authority from the past. By contrast, democratic peoples would have their eyes fixed on the present and the future, ever eager to put their pasts behind them, ever desiring to generate new lives and new opportunities for themselves. The past could be a source of knowledge, but rarely of inspiration or authority. Tocqueville was a Frenchman describing America in the 1830s, and for a man who could see the monuments and art produced by centuries of Europeans, America was bound to seem curious and ahistorical. Hannibal, Caesars, Holy Roman Emperors, Napoleon—these men had already crossed the Alps, but what great names had ever crossed the Appalachians or the Rockies at the head of an army to change history?

The peculiar aspects of the American experience led R. W. B. Lewis, in *The American Adam*, to interpret American history, and especially American literature, in terms of the Genesis typology. Each generation of Americans is a new Adam, boundlessly free to make of the American garden what he will, living without a past, capable of choosing afresh between good and evil. This American predisposition has been strengthened by the seductive idea of Progress which we have inherited. Despite the horrors of this most progressive century, our assumptions about progress and the constant improvement of the human condition make us look condescendingly, not devotionally, towards the past. In this regard, Americans are far more Greek (Athenian) than Hebrew. We are democratic, predisposed to shorter historical memories, and ever seeking to be rational and pragmatic. Of the Titans, Americans are Promethean, great makers, and Protean, always capable of change; we are less intimate with another of the Titans, Mnemosyne (memory).

The new American spirit of democracy was, in part, the result of the Enlightenment, an age that combined radically historical and anti-historical elements. Or rather, it placed history in the service of critical reason, detaching the historian from the past as it sought to liberate all humanity from the intellectual and political chains of history, tradition, and authority. This period has weakened the capacity of modern Christians to remember faithfully in four related ways.

Hans Frei's *The Eclipse of the Biblical Narrative* has identified one of the central changes in Christianity in this period which have transformed our ability to *zkr* (if I may refashion a verb). Whereas pre-Enlightenment Christians understood their own worlds through the world of Scripture, theologians and scholars of this era began to locate the meaning of Scripture in terms of their own contemporary worlds. To reformulate the problem in light of this study, whereas to *zkr* could be a logical result of pre-modern exegesis and preaching, there has developed a tendency away from "remembering" the past and making it active in the present. In its place has arisen a habit of locating the present in the past. The Bible is relevant to the extent that it depicts something we already can recognize. Now, human epistemology precedes divine pedagogy.

Along with this transformation strides the most important feature of the Enlightenment for modern Christian memory—the rise, development, and ascendancy of the historical-critical method. This method, despite its apparent historicity, has in fact made the church less historical; over the past two to three centuries, church people have grown less and less confident about their own past. That the

61

historical-critical method has made it harder to remember the past can be seen in one of its greatest exponents, Adolph von Harnack. His anti-dogmatic agenda led him to use history as a tool for distinguishing between the genuine life and teachings of Jesus and ecclesiastical, historical, Christianity. It is hardly surprising that Harnack himself came to espouse Marcionite views about the Old Testament.

The third important Enlightenment legacy for Christian self-understanding which bears directly on the problem of our memories is the emphasis on reason. The quest for an intelligible understanding of the life of the mind, a quest which emphasizes rationality, scientific certainty, and consciousness, enervated the narrative aspects of theology. (This, too, was an important theme for Frei.) But memory and narrative are interwoven, and consequently the memorial elements of theology are enervated as well. Moreover, with the Enlightenment's distrust of received authority and its emphasis on the individual's own rational thinking, the communal aspects of memory—so powerful in Deuteronomy—become diminished as well. In more recent decades in America, the ability to appropriate the story of Israel, the story of a people, has become even weaker in a culture which emphasizes religion as a private matter. (This loss of communal memories is one of the concerns of Robert N. Bellah and other communitarians.)

Finally, human pain and distress, another inextricable part of the Biblical discussions of memory, was not something the Enlightenment could be comfortable with. Memories of human suffering constitute a great threat to the abstract reasonings of philosophers.[29] Enlightenment optimism does not know how to address this since the Enlightenment, informed by the idea of Progress, proceeds from the assumption that suffering is not endemic to the human condition. Presumably, suffering, like superstition, is susceptible to elimination.

Romanticism, another modern strand, one that runs counter to the Enlightenment (while also drawing from its energy), has likewise enervated the modern church's ability to remember. Rousseau's emphasis on feelings and the imagination and Schleiermacher's regrounding religious faith in the experiences and feelings of the believer distanced and separated Christians from their ancestors. The new code words of Romantic discourse—feeling, experience, imagination, spontaneity—are not the code words which easily lend themselves to the memorial apprehension of the past. Rousseau privileges the authenticity of his feelings over the rest of his memories in the *Confessions*—a move which seems akin to privileging general intent over actual deed (we intend the good, whether we act upon that is not so important). Although Romantics frequently turned to the past for their inspiration, histories written under this muse often tell us far more about the author's age than about the historical subjects themselves. The emphasis on the individual, one of the glories of some strains of Romanticism, likewise makes it difficult for modern Christians to appropriate communal memories as their own.

The existential appropriation of the Incarnation which began with Kierkegaard also reduced and circumscribed the God of history (especially when combined with the sophisticated techniques of de-mythologization). God is not remembered from the past but the report of this God is confronted in this present. In its more extreme forms, it almost seems as if we no longer need the historical events themselves. The existential reading of the New Testament at times has a rather unknowable God who appeared briefly on the field of human history only to recede again. God becomes a blip in time. Love, it would seem to me if I read 1 Corinthians 1:13 correctly, would endure, not disappear. Love would stick around through sorrows and sufferings. If God loves, God permeates history. If we love, we should remember.

None of these modern traditions, Enlightenment, Romantic, existential, can make the same memorial appropriation of the past as can the psalmist of Psalm 105 who can remember *all* of the history of Israel as part of God's providential merciful redemptive plan. We need to recover our memories—we need to recover the full memories of God's never-failing presence in the world.

Dynamism and Durée: Modern Contributions to Memory

We have as of yet refrained from attempting to define precisely what the cognitive or epistemological functions of memory might be. This is in part because certain intellectual, cultural, and neurological transformations of the modern period have dramatically altered contemporary understandings of memory. Another obstacle to a working definition of memory is that defining memory requires certain commitments to related concepts such as—habit, idea, sensation, feeling, thought, imagination, consciousness, and in the case of theology, sin. As Jacques Le Goff observes, "The idea of memory is an intersection."[30] Hence, a review of the issues and directions taken by some modern thinkers may help to clarify the difficult task of describing memory. In particular, a theological description of memory will benefit from a concept associated with the work of Henri Bergson: *durée*. As we shall see, his idea of the dynamism of memory and its powerful, often uncontrollable influences on the present will provide us with an important way of thinking about memory theologically.

Before turning to the modern world and its uses of cognitive memory, it will be useful to consider some of the major views prior to the nineteenth century. Christian reflections on the epistemological aspects of memory have tended to follow philosophical or medical leads on what memory actually is. Augustine's reflections on memory in Book X of the *Confessions*, for example, follow Platonic traditions. And Aquinas' *Summa Theologiae* draws heavily for its interpretation of memory on Aristotle. What is perhaps most striking in the writings of both philosophers and theologians before the twentieth century is the relative simplicity of memory. Plato and Aristotle speak of memory as a wax tablet, something which merely records sensory impressions. Augustine describes memory as a great cave, and Locke chooses the metaphor of a storehouse.[31] Regardless of the actual image, the functioning of memory appears, by modern standards, straightforward. The dynamics and cognitive processes of memory appear relatively uncomplicated.

Moreover, the memory in the process of receiving stimuli remains passive—it is a tablet onto which impressions are put. Consequently, remembering itself seems relatively simple. We can imagine Plato searching through his tablets, Augustine rummaging around in his cave, or Locke scanning the shelves of his storehouse in order to find the information concerning what each had for breakfast. Today, perhaps, we would use computer metaphors, and we would be inserting various disks into our mind's computer. Both Aristotle and Aquinas, as might be expected, pay some attention to the problem of organic dysfunctions and the concomitant loss of mnemonic function, but for both men these are merely diversions.

By contrast, philosophers, psychologists, artists, and doctors of the last century have viewed memory as highly problematic, confusing, and not nearly so simple as first imagined. Students of memory now readily distinguish between many different types of remembering as well as of several distinct stages in the process. Semantic memory, for example, refers to factual memory (how many nickels are in a quarter), and it is a type of memory often retained by amnesiac patients. By contrast, episodic or autobiographical memory denotes one's own particular experiences and the capacity to reflect upon them. Generally we think of amnesiac patients as having lost this. Others speak of instrumental memory, the process whereby the elderly enhance their sense of self by recalling past successes.[32] Although I sometimes describe Alzheimer's families' experiences in light of these different categories, I have not thought that these distinctions about types of memory are crucial for a theological discussion of Alzheimer's disease. Eventually a patient comes to lose all of his memories and mnemonic capacities. Hence, it is the nature of memory as a whole which needs theological elucidation.

The dramatic shift in modern thinking about memory occurred in large part because of changes in fundamental categories of existence. In *The Culture of Time and Space*, Stephen Kern examined the transformations wrought by various modern trends on our views of time, space, speed, duration, and memory. The key revolutions for memory were changes in perceptions about time itself. So dramatic was the metamorphosis in thinking that it became possible to identify Bergson as "the first philosopher to take time seriously."[33] Quite naturally, a change in human thinking about temporality makes for alterations in human thinking about memory.

Beginning with the end of the last century, innovations and events such as electric clocks, time cards, the cinema, the development of geology, the standardization of world time by the acceptance of Greenwich Mean Time, even the profound spatial and temporal dislocations of trench warfare—all these and more led to a new awareness of the pervasive problematic character of time. Scholars of various disciplines and artists of all sorts responded with a flurry of new views about time, memory, and the nature of human existence. Examining differing religious calendars, for example, Durkheim argued that time itself was a social construction, that it was qualitative rather than quantitative. Jaspers, too, argued against a universal, abstract, mechanical time, believing that time is primarily subjective (he was especially concerned with the case of the mentally ill).

In their own ways, these moderns were drawing on Kant's rejection of ordered, Newtonian, absolute time in his *Critique of Pure Reason*. Given our biological nature—a nature which admits of problematic perceptual dimensions as well as passions, hopes, and fears—

time simply cannot be experienced as the Englishman had conceived of it. Consequently, Kant argues that the human memory is active when it receives sensory impressions. It cannot be understood as a simple, regularly-ordered storehouse or any such passive metaphor. Both the time card and the simple wax tablet appear to be gross distortions. Any child who, while waiting for the bell to ring, looks at the school clock repeatedly in the last five minutes of the school day, will confirm the fact that mechanical concepts of minutes and seconds are inadequate descriptions of the human experience of time.

Consequently, the number of different theories of memory and time increased dramatically in the decades before and after the turn of the century. William James, Freud, Bergson, Joyce, Proust, Kafka, Nietzsche—all of these and many more offered new visions of what memory is and how it relates to human existence. As the now-common phrase "stream of consciousness" suggests, the rather neatly arranged filing space of the ancients gave way to a construal of memory which was fluid, dynamic, and, like a river, potentially raging and chaotic. As one cannot dissect a stream in the way one can separate a set of shelves, so we cannot distinguish neatly between moments in the flow of consciousness. What comes to the fore in modern discourse is not the way we control the remembering of specific events but the way in which our minds often spontaneously and unpredictably are capable of splashing from one memory to the next—from a baseball game to a library to a poem to a love affair to a snowy evening to a pair of boots. A river seems to have flooded the storehouse and scattered the memories all about.

A consequence of this fluvial construction of memory is a concentration on the dynamism of past and present wherein memories can well up, flood, or pour into consciousness. For Proust, many memories of the protagonists in *Remembrances of Things Past* were spontaneous intrusions into consciousness. The French title of this work is even more suggestive for Alzheimer's patients and their families: *A la Recherche du temps perdu*—or "In Search of Times Lost." Freud's idea of repression and the suppression of events too horrible to think about can also be seen in such watery terms; the pressure from the dammed or repressed memories creates a pounding and stress on the conscious. Memories thus are not always easily compartmentalized. Rather, they impinge on the present, assuming a vitality, almost a life of their own.

For Freud and Proust especially, memories were private. But the work of sociologists, especially Maurice Halbwachs, suggests that human memories have important social dimensions. He spoke of the "social framework of memory" and stressed the social aspects of our recollection and transmission of the past. We retain the past not only individually but also communally. Whereas Proust's and Joyce's protagonists often experience their memories in isolation, most of us share our memories at school reunions, with families, or at any number of different gatherings. That we recall and retell our pasts, often with people who shared the same experiences, suggests that we cannot consider memory as a phenomenon of individuals. Following Stanley Fish's use of the term "interpretive communities" to describe the way groups of people share certain assumptions about how to read a text, Peter Burke understands the collective apprehension of the past through "memory communities."[34] This view of memory would not have seemed new to the Deuteronomist.

Precisely because of the social dimension of human memory, our personal remembrances are subject to distortion, political use, and manipulation. Recent vehement debates about a Smithsonian exhibition on the atomic bomb and about the nature of Polish, Jewish, Soviet, and/or gay memorials at Nazi concentration camps illustrate the significant implications of public remembering. Foucault and his followers have proceeded from the assumption that items from the past represent the attempts of those in power to legitimate their power and dominate the memories of the future. While this may well be an over-generalization for much of humanity's past, certainly this seems to hold true for much of the former Eastern bloc, wherein the State assumed the formal role of historian, or memory-keeper, of the people. Since the eighties, especially with the increasing popularity of works such as Milan Kundera's *The Book of Laughter and Forgetting*, we in the West have become increasingly aware of the precarious attempts of many ordinary people to have their own memories. It is hardly surprising that some Russians, seeking to create space not only for discourse but also for their persons, founded a journal called *Pamyat'*, or *Memory*. Freedom and memory are inseparable. There is a powerful political potential for the manipulation of memories. The first task of a Revolution is to rewrite the past.

There has been, thus, a revolution in memory, but these modern views are sometimes quite different construals of memory from the associations that the root *zkr* exhibits. Indeed, some of these interpretations, one might say obsessions, appear to point in an opposite direction from *zkr*. Joyce, Proust, Nietzsche, and Freud, in particular, emphasize the personal (often self-indulgent), the aesthetic, the free. By contrast, the Hebrew uses of *zkr* and the Christian tradition's own understanding of memory have stressed the communal, the historical, and the ethically responsive.

One aspect of this modern discussion, however, holds great promise for a theological appreciation of memory—Bergson's rich descriptions of *durée*, a term simplified in its translation as "duration." In *Matter and Memory*, *Time and Free Will* and in *Creative Evolution*, his discussions of memory and *durée* become interwoven with a number of other central Bergsonian concepts: intuition and intellect, space/time, the life-force, and creativity.[35] Although we do not need to accept all of Bergson's premises and categories, *durée* does seem to be an accurate description of how God's work both in the past and in the present bears on our lives each moment. Thus, Bergson's ideas of time and memory were highly influential for H. Richard Niebuhr's *The Meaning of Revelation*.[36] In this light, I want to underscore some key points which will be important for the rest of this study.

As already noted, the past for Bergson flows into the present and comes to interpenetrate it. He speaks of "osmosis" as a way of describing how the past endures. The "past" as we commonly understand it, he argues, never really ceases to exist. Moreover, the past has power. To say that something has *durée* is to say that it gnaws and impinges on the present, often without our being aware of it. We do not control our memories as much as we interact with them. Often the sight of something associated with a person or event evokes a powerful response from our memories. Sometimes we enjoy such a serendipitous recollection; at other times, as with Peter and the cock's crowing, the memory is simply too painful. Denial may be possible, but not always.

As a consequence of this understanding of *durée*, Bergson argues, the free person is one who is able to act within the totality of her memories. She acts in continuity with who she is, not in discontinuity or randomness. The dancer becomes more free by being able to utilize the total repertoire of movements she has learned throughout her life. For the Christian, freedom must be considered in the context of God's grace. Hence, this linking of freedom and memory suggests that we can understand the freedom of a Christian as being able to live within the total memory of God's work in Israel and the church. To participate in the communion of the saints is to be able to actualize their memories in one's own life. This total memory includes, of course, memories both of faithfulness and failures.

Following Bergson's notion of *durée*, we can see how memories both of sin and of Christ impinge upon our thought processes without our control, the former sometimes driving us to guilt and the latter shaming us as well as giving hope. Our need for forgiveness is so strong precisely because of the powerful *durée* of sin. At the same time, some memories have increased *durée* because of sin. Human weakness, an integral part of our temporal or narrative existence, creates openings for sinful memories or imaginings. In part because of sin, we do not control all of our conscious thought processes, and the imagination and memory conspire to insert unlawful ideas into our heads. I recall (or imagine) the sin, but I do not regret it; indeed I recall it with some pleasure. Because we do not know how to remember properly—because we do not always interpret these memories or notions in the context of Christ's work—we entertain these thoughts and empower them. We can legitimate ourselves by yielding unfaithfully to *durée*.

At the same time, the grace given through the Holy Spirit enters into our souls through a similar process. It may be that the Spirit helps evoke, in the words of the gospel song, the "Precious memories [which] flood my soul." Why is it that at some times we suddenly find ourselves remembering something Christ said or did? Why is it that Jeremiah discovers that, despite his attempts to forget and deny God, "there is in [his] heart . . . a burning fire" (20:9)? It may be because habit and mnemonic associations assert themselves. It may also be that the Spirit is at work, prodding and eliciting through the memory, strengthening the *durée* of some of our memories.

The need to cooperate with this *durée*—to confess our sins, to discern the Holy Spirit, and to proclaim and obey Christ's lordship—suggests that we need to learn how to remember properly. For this, we need the church and its memories. The conclusion of this chapter now considers how this understanding of *durée* complements a theological appreciation of memory, canonicity, and the church.

A Theological Appreciation of Memory:
Memory as Canon

Building upon some basic lexicographical and historical observations concerning the Hebrew root *zkr*, we have sought to appreciate the complexity and centrality of memory for our existence as religious persons. We have tried to describe the facets of memory—to discern its density and consider how normative or canonical it should be for theological reflection.

I began this chapter with Deuteronomy and God's memory of the covenant as the foundation for our theological memories. A modern historical-critical discussion surrounding the covenant illustrates the similarities between memory and canonicity. Old Testament scholars have debated the role of the covenant in Israel's theology and religion because it appears to be the work largely of the Deuteronomic school.[37] This theme, which is so important for seeing the unity of Old and New Testaments, may be a later interpolation into earlier texts. Similarly, just as we re-remember older events in light of newer ones (Oedipus horribly re-remembers his marriage to Jocasta when he learns whose son he is), so too does canonical acceptance lead to re-remembering the past relations between God and Israel. It is possible for later Israelites to re-remember Abraham in light of their own developing ideas of the covenant. Similarly, Christians remembering Abraham are re-remembering the Old in light of the New. Some memories provide the dominant contexts for reinterpreting other memories of the past. These central memories are, in effect, our canonical memories, the ones which give the primary energy to our identities.

In concluding this chapter it is important to distinguish between memory and imagination; such a distinction further clarifies how we form canonical memories. Memory, in some senses of the word may seem to be grounded in the imaginative, ordering, synthesizing faculties of the mind.[38] Epistemologically, imagination is inseparable from memory, and in the pre-nineteenth-century understanding of mental processes, the relationship was quite clear. In essence, memory stored sensory data, and the imagination was able to use this data for its own free synthesizing and creations. But as memory became more fluvial and assumed its own powers, the memory became more active, and distinguishing between the active imagination and the passive memory of old no longer made much sense. Given the interwoven character of memory and imagination, it may be that the distinction between memory and imagination is a distinction of connotation more than anything else. Still, the different connotations are crucial to the theological implications of the two terms.

The modern affection for the imagination stems from Rousseau, for he imbued the term with all sorts of delightful qualities. Indeed, in *Emile*, the imagination is what bridges the great gap between human beings, linking us all together in sympathy and compassion. "Imagination" currently means different mental processes to different theologians, and it now encompasses many features of what used to go by reason, contemplation, and memory. Imagination as some employ the term is the vehicle for self-understanding, a capacity for employing paradigms to order the world. It thus allows for an aesthetic unifying of life's experiences. It can serve as the basis for the formation of the Christian character, and it can provide directions for the lived life. As discussed by some theologians, the imaginative faculty shares with *zkr* its appropriative, existential functions. The imagination is seen as a "an activity of the psyche as a whole."[39] That is, whereas Deuteronomy might say, "Remember that you were in Egypt" to a generation many decades removed from that experience, we might today say, "Imagine that you, too, were in Egypt."

But a comparison of the two sentences reveals crucial differences. While it may appear that imagination as the appropriation of images and events is the same as *zkr*, to say that "one remembers" suggests that something actually happened and that one submits oneself to the reality of that event and accepts it. To say that "one imagines" leaves so much room for the question of reality. Indeed, for the imagination, the functions of history could be as adequately served by the stage as by the past. The Greek tragedies are not historical, but they do fire the imagination.

Compare likewise these two sentences: Remember that God in Jesus Christ died on the Cross so that human beings might enjoy eternal life. Imagine that God in Jesus Christ died on the Cross so that human beings might enjoy eternal life. The first is open to *durée*. That is, it accepts the fact that this act of remembering inherently will impinge upon the present. It will drive us in certain directions, and we willfully surrender to it. We accept the narrative of the Cross as canonical. The second seems to leave open the question of whether one should accept this reality or not. The imagination, which is derived from the freedom of the creative subject, here remains free.

71

Because Alzheimer's disease exposes this creative subject as vulnerable to dissolution, we learn that what God does for us is crucial. While how we imagine God is important, our salvation lies in remembering not in imagining. Because memory acknowledges and accepts God's prevenience, it is more open to God's present reality than the imagination. Again, this discussion is describing how "memory" and "imagination" connote fundamentally different attitudes, not what each necessarily is.[40] But these connotations are important because they affect our devotional fervor and the energy we bring to loving God and neighbor.

Faith and memory are linked in ways more profound than faith and imagination. Imaginative efforts may provide genuine depth and content to a person's faith. But memory is linked to history, to a belief that certain events did transpire in very specific ways and for specific purposes. We may follow Loyola's injunctions to imagine the details of the nativity of Christ, but when we do so, we give priority to the limits of what we have in the historical narrative. In viewing different paintings of the nativity, we acknowledge the artist's imagination, but we use the Gospel account to set limits for our ability to accept the artist's imaginative construction. Memory considers itself to be relentlessly accurate, relentlessly faithful to God and to the past, especially the past we share with others. By contrast, the imagination entertains its own creativity. Memory accepts God's activity and God's role in history in ways more dramatic than the imagination. Memory, in a way, accepts the irresistibility of God's grace. By contrast, as Hume observed, "Nothing is more free than the imagination of man."[41]

While our imaginations are socially informed, they remain personal in a way that our memories do not. With good reason we speak more readily of shared memories than of shared imaginings (small utopian communities might be the exception that proves the rule). Hence, while the term imagination can adumbrate a number of epistemological functions, it remains more individual than communal. Ecclesiologically, we should prefer memory to imagination. Shared authoritative memories provide a canonical description of our shared identities.

Some who advocate theology as a fundamentally imaginative enterprise openly accept the fabricative connotations of imagination, for above all they intend to underscore the tentative and non-reified nature of theology. Such an approach to theology does little good to

72

those families that have to experience the phenomena of Alzheimer's. If only these events were imaginative. Caregivers come to fear the imaginations of the patients—especially those who become paranoid. Similarly, having to acknowledge the fact that your parent now imagines you to be someone else, perhaps even her parent, is a terrible moment. Consequently, caregivers do not want to dwell upon what goes on in the imaginations of victims, for such contemplation produces only sorrow. Moreover, what caregivers need so desperately to see in patients is some sign that memories do remain. Particularly in the most ambiguous phases of the disease, when a patient requires complete care but is still able to communicate, indications of memory are desperately sought after. No one wants to know that they are forgotten.

It is precisely in the area of pastoral care that theology as primarily an imaginative enterprise seems weakest. It is here where memory and being faithful to memory become crucial. Ultimately, the lonely and the sick are to be remembered not imagined. Even if one grants the imagination to be a "complete act of the psyche" and imbues it with all sorts of rich connotations, it still falls flat. And as *zkr* means to remember with responsibility, so too does remembering the dying prompt us to act, to become faithful caregivers or better friends. Sins and forgetfulness are quite closely linked, and hence cultivating faithful memories becomes necessary.

Perhaps the most important difference between memory and imagination emerges from a consideration of God. We use the phrase "God remembers" as a way of expressing God's omnipotence. How might we use the phrase "God imagines"? Moreover, what would its significance be? God might imagine a way of life pleasing to the divine or might imagine the kingdom of God, but it remains unclear how that might relate to human existence. Some proponents of imagination, such as Gordon Kaufman, have no problem with this issue since for them God is active in human affairs only to the extent that an imaginative construct of human minds can affect human behavior.

Imagination maximizes human freedom, but theology seeks, above all, to maximize human fidelity. And for that task, we need to return to *zkr* as a departure point. As the subsequent chapter will make clear, there are important roles for the imagination. But these creative faculties need to be exercised within the canonical framework which the church's memory provides.

Chapter 3

Method as Memory

Thy Sacred Academie above
Of Doctors, whose paines have unclasp'd, and taught
Both books of life to us . . .
. . . pray for us there
That what they have misdone
Or mis-said, wee to that may not adhere.
Their zeal may be our sinne.
—John Donne, "The Litanie"

This chapter, which discusses theological method, will help explain how I came to believe that orthodox Christianity's dogma—etymologically, "that which seems good"—is the best answer to the dilemmas raised by Alzheimer's. By "answer" I do not mean that dogma solves personal or existential problems. As Flannery O'Connor observes, "A belief in fixed dogma cannot fix what goes on in life or blind the believer to it."[1] Rather, by "answer" I mean not only that which most illuminates my sense of my mother's inextinguishable personhood, my own sinfulness, and God's creative and redemptive love but also that which best strengthens my desire and capacity to be faithful to her and to God. Can non-orthodox or non-Christian "answers" to this disease be found? Of course. But are these responses intellectually coherent and devotionally stimulating? As will becoming increasing clear as this study unfolds, there are contemporary theological agendas which I do not find either logically sustainable, personally moving, or theologically faithful in light of the realities of Alzheimer's disease. The peculiar phenomena of the "Theological Disease" may well come to challenge radically contemporary theology.

One of the aspects of this disease which strikes me most forsefully is how reflecting on it brings me back constantly to orthodoxy (precisely what I mean by this term will emerge through the course of this chapter). I have discovered at every turn that orthodox Christianity's messages repeatedly gave me hope, relieved my doubts, and strengthened my resolve. At times, too, the proclamation of the Good News has been received with fright and sorrow. Accepting the truths of orthodoxy entails accepting the ugliness and significance of one's sins. Moreover, deepening your own sense of the love which God gives in the creation, on the Cross, and through the church means deepening your own sense of just how much a person with Alzheimer's loses as the disease progresses. Still, this sadness and this loss are transfigured by orthodoxy. As it sometimes becomes hard to experience joy and beauty without tears, so does it become hard to cry without feeling a deep reservoir of thanksgiving somewhere inside.

In the first part of the chapter, I will preface the articulation of my theological convictions with a few observations stemming from personal experiences and pastoral needs. I sense that a few words on the following subjects may be useful: the implications of Alzheimer's disease for theological method; sin; the *durée* of doctrine; the reality of orthodoxy today; and the academy as a location for theology. I hope these remarks will help illuminate how pastoral concerns should inform theology and how theology needs to assist those in the parish. The second part of this chapter, the actual discussion of my principles, argues for understanding method as memory. As we shall see, Alzheimer's prompts us to recover the memory of church traditions.

Personal Experience and Pastoral Needs

It is my sincere hope that there will be no theological discoveries in this book, only reminders of theological truths. The loss of personal memories and capacities caused by Alzheimer's disease highlights the fact that Christian hopes are grounded in the past, primarily in events wrought by God nearly two thousand years ago. Moreover, our hopes are grounded in the belief that the apostolic witness of the churches guided by the Holy Spirit have developed and transmitted faithfully the truths of God's work and the proper ways for us to respond. To seek an alternative foundation would be to seek to build on mere human opinion, to build on sand.

Alzheimer's disease brings our choices about orthodoxy into

clear perspective, because watching the irrevocable dissolution caused by this disease may lead us to become skeptical about the ultimate efficacy of human endeavors. Caregivers have no illusions about what humans can and cannot accomplish. We can make a great difference in a patient's life, but we can neither heal nor redeem. One of the harder lessons of caregiving is that we must be humble and aspire to be stewards not saviors. Hence, human opinion, however nicely packaged, becomes suspect if it is unsupported by centuries of apostolic activity. And the teaching tradition of the church, a tradition which recognizes God's ongoing role as teacher, becomes more meaningful, more powerful. If God does love my mother, then he loves Israel and the church, and he has fortified them even as they have been unfaithful.

Because Alzheimer's families confront the presence of irreversible dissolution—the person seems to disintegrate, just as the corpse in the coffin will—they may be particularly aware of the problems of future-oriented theologies, particularly those theologies which proclaim a radical break with the church's traditions. How can a "subversive" reading of the New Testament have something to say for the dying or provide encouragement for caregiving? These families do not have the luxury of waiting for the next annual meeting of the American Academy of Religion to see what's new, and no future political liberation will mean much.

A fresh articulation of God's work can help bring people to Christ, but all such articulations are based on the continuing historical work of God. Barthian neo-Orthodoxy, Liberation Theology, neo-Thomism, Feminist Theology—each of these when it first appeared provided inspiration to many, but none of them could do anything for the dead and very little for the terminally ill. When you love someone even as they disintegrate before your eyes, it heightens an awareness that the churches need to be concerned with the lives of all humans, living, dead, and yet to breathe. A theology, particularly a politically-oriented theology, which offers something to the next generation but which has nothing to say about the lives of previous ones strikes me as myopic. By contrast, a theology grounded in God's ongoing work through time helps bring us into the communion of saints. A new theology becomes efficacious only as it brings people into the trans-temporal body of Christ—and certainly God has something to do with this.

In light of this disease, it becomes clear that what the churches have proclaimed throughout the centuries is our long-term Christian memory. Modern trends are but short-term memories: easily forgettable and in the long run not nearly as important for describing who—and whose—we are. Donne, concluding the stanza from "The Litanie" quoted above, states of the theologians that we may "call them stars, but not the Sunne." Hence my desire is not for a new theological insight or synthesis but for fidelity to the Sun (Son).

There is a peculiar irony in reflecting on method in a theological study of Alzheimer's disease. Such professional discussions presuppose a rational, discerning subject both as readers and as followers, and yet it is precisely this subject which disappears with the development of the disease. Throughout this study, then, we are asking whether modern theology places an undue emphasis on the distinctive powers of a discrete subject. I mention my family's and friends' contributions to this study by name in the text, not in the footnotes as is conventional, precisely to underscore my dependence on others. If I am to suffer from this disease (I may have inherited a genetic predisposition) or from some other form of sustained dissolution, it will be these people who will have to care for me and bear my memories for me. Dementia, pain, doubt, anger, fear—these realities of Alzheimer's disease may well frustrate any cognitive plans we formulate for conceptual clarity.

Theological method needs to take into consideration not only the existence of suffering but also the effect of suffering on real persons. (Arthur C. McGill's *Suffering: A Test of Theological Method* is aptly named.) For those who suffer, the time horizon seems quite short. It is day to day, hour to hour. Caregiving ritualizes time, making it seem cyclical. Each day calls for the same spacing of medications, meals, trips to the bathroom, or exercises, and these rituals are what govern a person's life. Time, therefore, may seem qualitatively to be the same day in and day out. The idea of "progress" seems unthinkable, and planning for one's own future seems impossible. It may appear that God's own crucified suffering seems perennial, just as the caregiver's woes are. The chronological gap between A.D. 33 and the present may diminish as the optimism which we cherish dissolves. When inescapably confronted with the perennial problems of sin, death, love, and forgiveness, the modern world's cultural and technological experiences may provide but a thin, highly permeable membrane between the powerful narratives of the Bible and present existential dilemmas. If the Cross seems more real, then so too may the resurrection, for it becomes clear that "salvation" for an advanced patient can mean only euthanasia, a coma, or life everlasting.

The first chapter of this study sought in part to understand this disease in the context of the breakdown of narrative and language. Some theologians take their cue precisely from a certain modern or post-modern skepticism about language, suggesting that we must in some sense begin with accepting non-literal language and rejecting the (imperialistic) enterprise of linking signs with realities. Sally McFague, for example, suggests that "metaphorical theology . . . is a kind of theology especially well-suited for times of uncertainty and change, when systematic, comprehensive construction seems inappropriate if not impossible."[2] When one has the luxury of being able to live comfortably through a time of uncertainty and change—something not available to the poor, to the dying, or to Alzheimer's caregivers—this may seem to be the case. But when we are confronted with the reality of living cognitive dissolution, we may be inclined towards respecting the integrity of everyday language, something which we had heretofore taken for granted. We may be reminded of how remarkable it is that human beings can communicate directly and that God, having revealed himself in Christ and having used language, does communicate directly as well. Our language about God is grounded in the very Logos of God, in the Second Person of the Trinity. As the Incarnation demonstrated that the material world is not evil, so does it demonstrate that realistic, literal language can be a vehicle for truth and for grace.

Using human language for discussing the truth can be like driving on ice, and it is very easy to demonstrate linguistic slipperiness. Still, when we are careful, human language does get us where we want to go. Both kataphatic and apophatic teachings are part of the church's heritage, and they are best seen as complementary, not contradictory. Apophatic traditions may be particularly appealing for some Alzheimer's families, as the breakdown in a patient's linguistic capabilities may seem to mirror our own inability to grasp concretely the mystery of God; Alzheimer's families know all too well the conceptual emptying of "the dark night of the soul." At the same time, others experiencing this disease may come to cherish kataphatic formulations precisely because they express a certainty to which we cling.

As we will see more directly in chapters 5 and 6, Alzheimer's disease confronts us starkly with the reality of human sin, and sin is one of the central problems for any theological method, both as a difficult subject and as an obstacle to faithful theological reflection. If language or meaning sometimes seems uncertain, sin is not. By sin I mean both original and actual sins. By original sin I mean that none of us had a choice in being born into a deicidal humanity so wretched as to require the Cross for its salvation. This sinful human condition engenders susceptibility to illicit temptations as well as profound weaknesses in our ability to love. Thus, we entice ourselves into actual sins against both God and neighbor, and we commit rebellious and evil acts. (My particular emphasis on the corrupting influence of sin is indebted to the Augustinian heritage; whether this rather strong view of sin is in fact most adequate and/or appropriate in light of the realities of Alzheimer's will be tested through the course of the book.)

If there is one thing I know beyond doubt, it is that I am a sinner. That is, I sin, therefore I cannot doubt that I am (much as I would like to do so sometimes). I sense that Luther is correct in recognizing that faithful Christian theology is the fruit of being judged as a forgiven sinner. My most certain knowledge is thus the source of one of my disappointments with modern discussions of theological method. I remain surprised by the relative lack of concern for the power of sin exhibited in formal discussions of theological method; often a phrase such as "limitation of creatureliness" is preferred, as if these limits can be understood without first confronting sin's corrupting powers.[3]

The effects of sin on the human person, I believe, are profound. Sinful habits inhibit the faithful reading of Scripture in different degrees in each person. Each of us is reluctant to admit certain truths or be open to certain problems. Moreover, sin affects our presentation of theological beliefs so strongly that we are wise to be suspicious of ourselves and our vested interests. Sincerity and truthfulness, after all, are inseparable from fashion, convention, and even vanity. As Dante observes (*Purgatorio*, X.3), sin, particularly pride, "makes the crooked way seem straight." Despite the fact that theological method often serves to keep us honest, it, like most human constructions, has the capacity to mask bad faith.

Hence, "method" construed as a primarily human endeavor does not seem particularly reliable. A primary concern of theological method ought to be to leave God's freedom intact. When our prayers for understanding are answered, when the Holy Spirit is present among us, when we feel God's forgiveness in our hearts, when our hearts are strangely warmed—these are the profound moments which guide our reading of Scripture and recitation of the Creeds. These are moments of God's freedom. These mysteries of sin and grace frustrate carefully delineated theological methods if for no other reason than mystery and method blend about as well as the sweet and the bitter. There is no formula for forgiveness, love, or inspiration. There is no formula for divine activity. While liturgical language expresses these formally, we recognize that they are not automatically operative in our lives.

The Durée of Doctrine

Theological method needs to account for the psychology (literally, "soul-speak") of God's free presence. As the previous chapter suggested, the dynamism of memory allows us to understand how the Holy Spirit does precisely what Jesus promised (John 14:26): "the Holy Spirit, whom the Father will send in my name, he will teach you all things, and bring to your remembrance all that I have said to you." Through the durée of Christian memories, we feel the power of God's merciful presence.

Consequently, we need to consider Christian dogma not as inert propositions but as entities which have durée. Sin, the Cross, suffering, John 3:16—these impinge upon our daily lives whether we like it or not. Moreover, the contrapuntal antinomies at the heart of Christianity—the God who is Three, yet One; the Savior who is fully human, yet fully divine—these are inherently dynamic because they lead us in seemingly different directions. When we find ourselves emphasizing the humanity of Christ, we suddenly remember that he is also divine, and we must reassess our thinking. To echo somewhat unfairly the language of Gregory Palamas, we may consider theological truths more as "energies." Because of the Holy Spirit, the church's teaching tradition, and the dynamism of memory, the grace of God manifest in history can burst into our lives unexpectedly as "water welling up to eternal life" (John 4:14). It becomes the grace of God freely given in the present as we "actualize" the memories of the Cross and make them our own. God's love and the doctrines which proclaim this are percussive; the psychology of revelation is largely a psychology of propulsion, or in H. Richard Niebuhr's term, of "compulsion."[4] The church's transmission of doctrine and the

81

workings of grace, therefore, work similarly, each working with the other, each impinging on our memories.

Because of its seriousness, existential theology, in a way, recognizes the *durée* of doctrine. It acknowledges that we are starkly challenged by powerful memories which the church proclaims and that we must each make a decision about actualizing the kerygma. But I do not think existential theology always does justice to the historical reality of these memories or to the ongoing work of the Spirit. Existential theology's over-emphasis on the subject and consciousness seems incomplete, as it separates Alzheimer's patients from God and all of us from God's work in the soul. As we acknowledge that we are not pure subjects, in complete and free control of our wills and our epistemological experiences, perhaps we can prepare ourselves for God's own freedom. In appreciating God's free graciousness, we give thanks that, in part through the *durée* of doctrine, "He has caused his wonderful works to be remembered" (Ps. 111:4).

I have a special reverence and gratitude for doctrine for two reasons. First, as a historian, I am astounded by its endurance (*durée*, if you will) through the centuries. Many impressive thoughts have not survived, and many that have, have lost all of their power today. Second, and more personally, I am thankful for doctrine because I believe that only through the faithful transmission of the church's traditional teachings is it possible for me to have hope for my mother; for my father, her primary caregiver; and for the rest of the world which suffers each sunrise and sunset. Hence, as I use the term, orthodoxy is not only about doctrine or guiding principles; it also denotes a kind of existence to be desired in itself. Orthodoxy is a deep longing to align one's own life and memories with the life and memories of the church. (This fundamental communal orientation lies at the heart of David S. Yeago's useful description of a "generous orthodoxy," a phrase he learned from Hans Frei.)[5] The current fractured condition of the church makes this a harder goal to realize, but it should not quench the desire itself.

Hence, it will not be surprising that, to quote a Walker Percy character, I believe "the whole business: God, the Jews, Christ, the Church, grace, and the forgiveness of sins."[6] That is, I strive to be faithful to orthodoxy as revealed in Scripture, as elaborated in the Creeds, and as witnessed to in apostolic history. Yes, this includes those embarrassing miracles (which are really about God's freedom).

And yes, it also means taking seriously the Greek metaphysical context for the formulation of the Creeds. My beliefs also include the reality of the soul, the *imago Dei*, the beatific vision, and the resurrection. While these fundamental doctrines are bracketed in many theological endeavors, I believe we must return to them not only in the case of Alzheimer's but in all considerations of what it means to live and die.

With Augustine, and more recently with Stanley Hauerwas, I agree that we believe not through a classroom or on our own, but through a worshiping community grounded in history. That is, try as we might, we cannot separate Jesus from his church. Or to phrase it in the language of the mystical tradition, we cannot separate Jesus from his body. That his ecclesiastical body is now as violently fractured as his human body was on the Cross does not seem to be without significance. We are, I suspect, intended to experience some of his suffering in our painful experiences of a divided church catholic.

Because I recognize that any hope for my family outside the church would be ephemeral or naïve were I to come up with it on my own, I believe that I have little choice in the matter. Unless I have very, very good reasons I should defer to the church. After all, I cannot redeem anyone. I cannot resurrect anyone. The church as a living, historical whole, not individuals acting as individuals, can help bring people into the Kingdom of God. I accept this "ecclesiastical maximalism," and I am grateful for it. Thus, I am willing to defer to Paul's profound experiences of suffering when I confront my own problems.

It has become a commonplace in some theological circles to argue that universal, exclusive truth-claims are inherently an act of violence, or at least of marginalization, against those who do not agree with the propositions. We all, presumably, have equal rights before God. But I believe that the Jews are the chosen people of God and that they are called to graver responsibilities than non-Jews. Similarly, Christians are called to proclaim truths which are not entirely pleasant for all. Moreover, we are called to live by these truths responsibly in the spirit of charity. Obviously, the church's record as a whole is a highly imperfect one, and obviously, we will answer for the abuses we commit in the name of truth. We do proclaim a confrontational truth—we should not expect something universally uplifting from a God nailed to a tree. And as we recognize that our

83

mission is embedded in our sinfulness, we do experience fear and trembling. We should be ashamed of our sins, not our *Kyrie Eleison*.

Like most people, I find that there is much that I cannot grasp in Scripture and the tradition. But I do not assume that I have the right to understand everything. Indeed, I am glad that there is much I find vexing, for if it all became so familiar, the Word of God would be so domesticated as to be useless. John 3:16 is the mysterious bedrock of our existence, and accepting this makes it easy for me to have confidence in the church's teachings. That is, our lives and our hopes are grounded not so much on pure reason, intelligibility, or justice, but on enduring, gracious love. Hence, I feel free to adopt the principle of my grandmother, Elizabeth Keck. She confesses that "If I don't understand a part of the Bible, I let it be." In other words, she respects God's freedom to be mysterious. This seems to be a sign of her spiritual maturity. As Margaret Somerville, director of the McGill Centre for Medical Ethics and Law, notes in the context of the challenging debate over physician-assisted suicide, "We're frightened by mysteries, and to deal with this fear, we convert mysteries to problems, because we can control problems."[7] Consequently, I do not feel a compelling need to work out in great logical detail answers to all the Christian conundra which have been accumulating since the first century before I try to live faithfully.

While there is much that seems difficult to fathom, I believe that at the Resurrection, all of my questions will be answered. Indeed, I will then know what the right questions actually are. For now, the main question has been answered, and I prefer slavery to Christ to slavery to sin. I have found that the habits of caregiving teach the patience that is conducive to faith. In both caregiving and theology, I suspect, steady, patient loving is more faithful than a desire for a definitive resolution to the problem. My dear friend Russ Martin wisely compares our apprehension of the church's teachings to a two-year-old's trying to play with a toy made for a ten-year-old: we play with it clumsily. If we do not break the gift fumbling with it, or if we do not forget it in some closet, we will eventually mature and enjoy it fully.

Confidence is important because theology cannot be separated from faith. There are few artistic experiences as awful as listening to a symphony orchestra which is unsure of its notes. Theological discourse which hems and haws about the truth of the Creeds, a discourse which looks for ways to make the faith seem more acceptable to the sophisticated mind, will not do any good for Alzheimer's families. Theologians who "blink" when discussing the basics of faith are about as trustworthy as a used car salesman who hesitates when asked, "Is this car reliable?" A family witnessing the dissolution of a loved one does not need careful intellectual conceptualization but a person saying without hesitation, "Yes it is true! God so loved the world that he gave his only Son for our sakes so that we might have eternal life!" This emphasis on the importance of gut-felt personal proclamation is to underscore that there are few things as powerful as a person in whom faith blossoms and produces great fruits. The Good News requires confident messengers to be believable, as the title of my father's *The Church Confident* suggests.

Traditional Christianity and the Church/Academy Problem

At the time of this writing (who knows in what condition she will be when you read this), my mother's favorite music is a CD performed by the Hee Haw Gospel Quartet. Nothing can transform as quickly her disoriented agitation into peace, into tranquil rhythmic clapping. This CD contains traditional Gospel hymns—"Amazing Grace," "Dust on the Bible," "Where Could I Go But to the Lord"— and I cannot help thinking that there is something to be learned about theological method from the Hee Haw Gospel Quartet. These hymns present the Gospel in everyday situations and with everyday metaphors. The reality of God is down to earth, and these folks are singing about it joyfully. Better still, God is not just down to earth, rather he is, as the Incarnation suggests, both immanent and transcendent, and this reality makes it possible for God to be present and yet mysterious at every moment. Even in the sadder songs, songs which do not hide the suffering of the world, there remains a clear sense of praise and hope. As a faithful, no nonsense, tell-it-like-it-is proclamation of the Good News, these are hard to beat.

What is striking is that this theology is all about daily lives, and it is a historical curiosity that Christians living their daily lives prove to be a great contradiction of academic theologians. Bultmann's entire theological agenda is predicated on his dictum that modern people listening to radios could not possibly believe in traditional Christianity (hence the legitimation of demythologization). The existence of traditional hymns on CD technology suggests that Bultmann was fundamentally wrong (cf. the hymn "Turn Your Radio

85

On"), but a more powerful refutation of Bultmann comes from the Internet.

Each day, Orthodox Christians all across the planet log into the Orthodox discussion group, and each day this vibrant exchange concerning Orthodox theology, liturgy, and devotional practices demonstrates that high-tech humanity can believe. The members of this group are priests and laypeople, mostly professionals, and some of them even belong to secular universities. The Orthodox Jews who run 47th Street Photo in New York City are just as powerful a reminder that the modern world does not preclude orthodoxy. Similarly, when I was in college, many of the most traditionally oriented Christians were science majors. Of course, modernity is not just science, but Bultmann's own formulation suggests that technological change and scientific discoveries have been major factors in supposedly weakening our ability to believe. These living contradictions of academic ambiguity should make us think twice about what people can and cannot believe.

I would hope that one of the lessons of multiculturalism will be that the imperialistic, universal "we" of modern theology—as in discussions of "where we are" in theology—simply does not exist. There is no abstract "any contemporary Westerner" who embodies and limits the capacities for "our" beliefs. All too often, it seems to me, theologians invoke this creature in order to legitimate an anti-traditional theology, but we should recognize that this creature is little more than a duck decoy. It does not live and breathe even though it sometimes attracts others who do.[8] The reality of pluralism means that traditional beliefs are not beholden to what any given segment of a society can or cannot believe. Recognizing the diversity of modern America entails, therefore, recognizing that traditional orthodox Christianity is possible today.

A final consideration for theological method is location. As many multicultural theologians observe, we do not come to theological reflection from a neutral vantage point. We are creatures of different historical and biological circumstances. We bring to theology our particular cultural habits, oftentimes the cultural habits of the academy. As I write, I am a member of a university, but I suspect that my most faithful efforts have more to do with trying to see myself in a pew rather than in a classroom, trying to see myself listening to God's Word rather than speaking my own. I believe theology's home is properly in the church and in the home, both in and beside the wheelchair, but it seems that these days, like it or not, its work is done in the university. I suspect that this may be part of the problem facing us.

One of my chief objections to formal discussions of theological method also applies to many forms of religious scholarship. Academics, it seems, have an inordinate confidence in future academic production. We are in the habit of looking for new methods of exegesis, fresh examinations of the sources, new conceptualizations of old problems, etc. just as we are in the habit of looking for new low-fat products or faster cars. We search for a new consensus, but as Paul Holmer is said to have quipped, "You know where 'consensus' comes from? Fatigue." A history of modern Christian thought can easily give the impression that academics are passing from one fad to the next, often to the detriment of apostolic teaching or pastoral work. As Holmer observes, having dozens of theologies floating around is a real problem: "All one seems to get is points of view and not knowledge of God."[9] Although we are more enlightened on some issues, is the church as a whole really better off than it was ten, twenty, or a hundred years ago? Are more people brought to Christ or are becoming more Christ-like? One does not have to agree with all of Thomas Oden's recent critique of mainline seminaries to feel that it is legitimate to question the fidelity and spiritual efficacy of contemporary and future academic theology.

Academic theological production requires this confidence about future scholarship. But David Damrosch's We Scholars suggests that theology as a churched enterprise and the academy may be in fundamental contradiction. This sociological analysis of the academy demonstrates that the most learned practitioners of theological method are socialized, in part, in a system of natural selection which chooses its survivors according to the principles of "alienation and aggression."[10] It is not hard to see that the socialization process of publications, academic disputation, and tenure-hunting is not necessarily conducive to instilling Christian charity. When we are not engaged in disputation (which is what "dialogue" often really is), the learned hermeneutic of suspicion and irony, not a vibrant faith, are the highly regarded marks of academic sophistication. Because tenure—not charity, forgiveness, or fidelity—becomes the most-valued prize, we all too easily confuse the freedom of tenure with the freedom of a Christian.

A theological consideration of Alzheimer's disease illuminates the regrettable tendency for discussions of theological method to be separated from the needs of pastoral theology. (This need not be surprising: as Damrosch observes, the academy is an institution driven by people working as isolated individuals, not as members of a community; by contrast, pastoral theology presupposes the interaction of at least two people, ideally a whole community.)[11] I suspect, wrongly in some cases perhaps, that a concern for a proper theological method is related to a certain anticlericalism and/or antisacramentalism. Rigorous distinctions between first-, second-, etc.-order theological language seem particularly well-suited to preserving the privileges of the academic theologian. But theology needs to have populist dimensions and applications else it becomes little more than obtuse scribalism. Theology belongs to all the people of God, not just to the privileged. Here, the Orthodox communities' tradition of calling a person a theologian only when it is formally determined that a person speaks for the whole church seems much more sound than the academic habit of calling people theologians simply because they have received a doctoral degree in theology.

Ministers, priests, caregivers—they all must adopt the Nike sports approach to theology: as the commercials say, "Just Do It." These people do have to manifest faith, hope, and love, because if they do not, their charges will suffer. Too many discussions of theological method seem to be turgid prolegomena completely separated from sin, love, and the Cross—as if these could ever be bracketed. It is perhaps easier to be less concerned about the refinements of theological method if one already believes in the first place. As my father observes in the second chapter of his *Church Confident*, so much of today's academic theology resembles not faith seeking understanding, but rather understanding seeking faith. People often speak of method when they are wary about substance.

Theological Convictions

I have chosen to use the word "convictions" here because "conviction" can mean both something which you espouse as well as something which happens to you. Because doctrine has *durée*, theological beliefs are hardly passive. Because of the Holy Spirit, our personal beliefs are empowered by "external stimulation." To echo one of Donne's wonderful sonnets, at times the doctrines of the "Three-person'd God" batter our hearts and break, blow, burn, and even ravish us. It may well be arrogant to claim that the Holy Spirit can be involved in our mnemonic processes. But we should remember that because God respects our freedom, the Paraclete's presence does not guarantee that we will interpret Scripture or discern the Spirit correctly. We remain just as responsible and just as liable to commit errors. As Peter understood when the cock crowed, our recognition of sin is precisely when God's Word batters us most. Moreover, the formation of our convictions is not exclusively theological. All of our experiences flow together, as the fluvial character of memory suggests, and in different combinations they exercise their *durée* and shape our beliefs. What, then, are the main convictions of this study?

God is found primarily on the Cross—not dead, but dying. God, as he has chosen to reveal himself, is, before all else, suffering and redeeming love. While the doctrines of creation, providence, and omnipotence might seem conceptually or temporally to precede the Cross, there is no doubt in my mind that we should approach these mysteries only after we have sought to become matured in the mystery of the Cross. All too often, the initial problematic of Alzheimer's disease, or of any form of suffering, is of God's omnipotence and human misery. The theological question which friends have most frequently posed to me is why God allows this disease to happen. This natural but naive question seems to me to miss the point entirely. My father refuses to ask, Why does this happen to her? because he realizes that he could just as easily ask, Why should it not happen to her or to me? Where are we promised that we are spared life's sufferings? We need to consider rather this question: Why should any of us be spared when God himself was whipped and murdered? Hence, the initial problematic should be, in my opinion, divine love and human sin. We find God—more accurately, God comes to us—on the Cross, not on a throne. (That other encounter is reserved for the end of history.)

Reflections on God's work on the Cross and in the cosmos must *always seek to fortify our faith, hope, and love*. At different times in the course of caregiving, each of these becomes difficult. We become tired, and, being generally less circumspect than Job, we are found wanting. We need help, and hence we need to keep praise high on our list of concerns as well. It is all too easy to become angry when confronted with this disease. What has been so painful for all of us in the family has been seeing ourselves grow angry with my mother as she does not stand up, open her mouth, or simply be quiet when we need her to. There is no reason for this anger, except our own weakness. We know all to well that there is ugliness in the world, and we need to learn how to meet it with charity and praise. Theological reflection here can help us if it unfailingly reminds us of whose we are, why we love, and for what we hope. Praise can be a struggle—we need help. But, ultimately, to be able to praise is to triumph, because being able to praise God means living in the triumph of the Cross.

This study needs to distinguish between orthodox truths (dogmas) as embedded particularly in Scripture's narratives and the Creeds (such as the Trinity, the two natures of Christ) and *licit devotional speculations* to which the broader traditions of the churches bear witness (such as meditations on the beatific vision). The former, of course, set the proper boundaries for the latter. The latter will be particularly important because the inculcation of Christian habits requires devotional speculation about heaven, the soul (both as the metaphysical basis of personhood and as the locus of God's work in us), and the Kingdom of God. Faith is not just a cognitive assent to dogma, but also a persistent loyalty in both the light and the shadow of the Cross. And this loyalty is nurtured by proper speculation. Especially when confronting a dissolving personality, we wonder about the person's metaphysical reality both now and in the future. Our hopes are expressed in credal formulations which are often terse; by wondering we can give these realities a "thickness" (to borrow from Clifford Geertz), and this thickness, like a good piece of lumber, helps give us strength. At times, then, I hope to delineate what we can consider to be possible, likely, or badly needed as we consider the problems raised by Alzheimer's disease.

In this sense, *we need to cultivate orthodox imaginations.* I am uncomfortable with the word reimagining since it suggests, to me at least, a desire to start over. As I have tried to suggest, starting over or creating afresh is not likely to do Alzheimer's families any good. We may have ultimate confidence in something which has always been true, but when we must resign our hopes for our own lives in order to care for a patient, we will be less likely to believe something which has come along only this century. (As a historian, I am particularly sensitive to the transience of twentieth-century theological fads; a "neo-" will always stagnate and eventually yield to a "post-.") An orthodox imagination, I hope to suggest, will be much like a Gospel song. That is, it will explore creatively within the bounds of orthodox traditions what it means to anticipate that time "when the roll is called up yonder"; what it is to anticipate that there will be "no tears in heaven"; or to live with that sweet saving power of "amazing grace."

At times, especially when discussing the soul, *this study will need to have recourse to the metaphorical language* that Sally McFague describes as being "unsubstitutable" or part of a "strategy of desperation."[12] Some theological mysteries do require these kinds of elliptical approaches, and we will at times need to turn to the poets for assistance. In this enterprise, we need to remember that there is a great difference between seeking new metaphorical or poetic ways of expressing perennial realities and striking out to create so-called new realities. Metaphors, if they are successful, also may strengthen our memories as they provide striking descriptions which are easy to recollect. At the same time, metaphor, I believe, cannot be the primary basis for theological discourse since the most powerful theological statements—the Incarnation and the Cross—are, like the Holocaust, poverty, and death, primarily literal, historical, and tangible, not only metaphoric or symbolic. As with Aquinas' view of the traditional four-fold scheme of medieval exegesis, the figurative senses of language and our devotional speculations must be grounded in the literal sense and in dogma.

When considering the realities of Alzheimer's disease, *the vicarious elements in theological reflection and church practice need particular emphasis*. Because the patient seems to lose all capacities of subjecthood, it is the work done by others for him which becomes crucial. As the community accepts the responsibility of believing for a newly-baptized infant, so too at the end of life does the church accept this task for those in end-stage dementia. Just as my two grandmothers' prayers were influential in promoting my relationship with God, so too do we now pray for my mother's relationship with her Creator. Consequently, we come to see that ultimately it is God's vicarious work—especially the vicarious atonement—which is crucial for her salvation and our ability to participate in the Kingdom of God.

This study is an "intramural" study in the sense that it presupposes Christian dogmas. Another study, equally important but addressing a different audience, would have much to say "extramurally," and I hope that this text would be useful for that work in some respect. Christians need to engage audiences of all types, each according to its capacity for hearing the Gospel. Naturally, this means different approaches and appeals to different criteria. The church has been doing this since the earliest days, and there is every reason to continue. The work of Hans Frei, George Lindbeck, and what is sometimes called the "Yale school" of theology has underscored the importance of the intramural theological description of Christianity. This approach is central here because the challenge of Alzheimer's is not, properly speaking, an extramural challenge (a challenge posed by external, non-Christian claims about reality). I have written this as an intramural study because with Alzheimer's I sense that we are not on the Areopagus with Paul as much as we are in the darkness of the lion's den with Daniel. Stephen G. Post's attempt to develop an ethics of dementia for a broad audience demonstrates just how difficult it is to speak meaningfully of Alzheimer's with people and communities who do not share certain ideas about God, humanity, the marginalized, and compassion.[13]

Regrettably, *this study is ecumenical.* I say regrettably because I sense—though I may be quite in error—that the divisions of Christendom are indeed horrible. (It may well be the case that the different churches are necessary in a mystical sense for embodying different aspects of Christ's unified Lordship.) We profess the church to be catholic, but it is not, and this is sorrowful. I say regrettably also because an ecumenical presentation precludes the detailed exploration of many topics. Doctrinal, sacramental, and liturgical differences are real, and each church must unfold the implications of its own doctrines differently. There is, to be sure, a great wealth of shared beliefs, and this study draws on them. But this work must also remain satisfied at times merely to point the different churches in certain directions.

Orthodoxy, defined broadly as being faithful to the Creeds and Ecumenical Councils, is crucial because it *describes the framework within which we can proceed confidently with faith, hope, and love.* There are many faithful witnesses in the Christian churches (as well as many heterodox and heretical ones), and there are many theologies which seem either to diverge widely or even to contradict each other. The *Doctores Ecclesiae* offer different emphases and contributions, and yet they are, by and large, orthodox, and they would concur on the importance of orthodoxy itself. Narrative theology and mystical traditions both have significant contributions to make, and both apologetics and confessional theology can be helpful.[14] The important point is that within our diversity we converge on certain matters which we share not only with each other but also with the apostolic past. If we abandon our communion with the past, we diminish our capacities for the three theological virtues; we weaken the foundations of our hope and praise.

This emphasis on an open-ended orthodoxy means that despite the temptation to determine a univocal method for "how theology must proceed," we should remain open to a number of approaches. While I often argue for the *theologia crucis* over the *theologia gloriae*, it is altogether possible for a different person confronting Alzheimer's to experience the reality of God's love through meditations on Christ Pantocrator. The mysteries of God are manifold, and he draws us to himself through differing means, through different charisms, ideas, or historical events. Thus, we need to balance our own freedom to worship and imagine God in different liturgies, poems, or gospel songs with an honest awareness of God's own reality and desires for us. Orthodoxy guides such fidelity for the idea of orthodoxy is itself an acknowledgment that our work is in service to a Lord. It is an acknowledgment that his work is prevenient and our work is responsive. Orthodoxy instills gratitude not just to God but also to our ancestors in the church as well.

An important criterion for many theologies is social justice. Unfortunately, *social justice cannot be a criterion for this study* since it is impossible for families of Alzheimer's disease to be liberated politically or benefit from social equality. As we have seen in the first chapter, this disease is an equal opportunity destroyer. Alzheimer's disease may strike each of us as if we are angels in heaven, neither white nor of color, neither male nor female, neither rich nor poor. We could consider recommendations for more equitably distributing the burdens of caregiving, but that would not be a matter of theology *per se* but of public policy, charity, and common sense. Ultimately, death and disease scandalously overcome us all.

Theological problems are inherently social (as the great questions of life, death, love, and forgiveness are), *but they are not inherently political.* The perpetual confusion of the social and the political, while legitimating the church's role in politics and creating an illusion of "relevance," seems highly suspect in light of this disease. Alzheimer's has important social dimensions since it isolates victims and their families. Moreover, it often divides families, as they disagree over questions of care and duty. Despite these important social or com-

93

munal aspects, the theological consideration of the disease has few direct political dimensions (the exceptions being certain questions of public funding for research and Medicare, as well as the question of legalizing assisted suicide). The church's great work here is to be done by families and local church communities in the homes of patients, not in the streets, on Capitol Hill, or in some New World Order. If anything, then, this study will suggest that Alzheimer's disease teaches us not to look to the political arena but to the Cross for our liberation.

As Allan Bloom illustrates throughout his *Love and Friendship*, the arbiter of truth for a lover is not a political order nor a society, but rather the beloved. That is, the lover cares less for other people's opinions than what his or her beloved thinks. Hence, *our ultimate criterion for theology must surely be whether it pleases the Triune God whom we love.* Admittedly, determining this is not easy, but I do not think that we can have any choice in the matter. Does a study manifest the love of God? Is it faithful to God's work in Christ? Can it help others love and serve the Lord? Can it help others love their neighbors? These are the primary questions. When we aspire to be orthodox and faithful to God's love, we hope to place ourselves firmly within the totality of the history of Christian witness without undue concern for the particular type of theology we preach. We aspire to love God with the full communion of all the saints.

Method as Memory

Throughout this study, I emphasize the Christian tradition because the characteristics of Alzheimer's disease are a reminder both of its riches and of the past's ever-precarious existence. When watching a patient struggle to recall her own past, it becomes clear how little of our own lives actually remain in our memories. What did I eat for lunch sixteen days ago? At what time did I eat? Was I alone? Was I fearful? About what or whom was I thinking? Who went hungry that day? As I contemplate how much there is even in my own past, so do I realize that there is sufficient wealth in the Christian past for many, many lifetimes. And just as there are evils in the memories of my own sins, so too does the church's history bear witness to human evil—and to the need for Christ.

Throughout this study, therefore, I have drawn from a wide variety of sources. Both the Hee Haw Gospel Quartet and St. Thomas

Aquinas have something to tell us. Confronting the dissolution of memory which is Alzheimer's leads us to recognize that we have a special calling to recover the memory of the church's traditions throughout the entire history of the church and Israel. By remembering Augustine's, Luther's, and Barth's readings of Romans, we remember all three—and we can refresh our souls with Paul, the Law, and the unity of the Old and New Testaments as well. Seeing "Precious Memories" evaporate before our eyes should help us to recognize the importance of exercising such Christian memories. Thinking of method as memory emphasizes that we need to include not just the Biblical stories or canonical statements of the church in our theological reflections but also the great variety of churches' expressions of faith.

This study's use of both eclectic and canonical sources according to a "hermeneutic of affirmation" is one attempt to do so. My father has described this interpretive habit as "a persistent but pained loyalty to a heritage, which, though flawed, nonetheless has given us what faith we have and which is supple enough to survive what we will do to it."[15] We are responsible for remembering the canonical, and we have the pleasure of discovering the more peculiar and personal. I hope that the texts I invoke here, many of which friends have suggested to me, will be both familiar and relatively unknown. By discovering the past riches of the tradition which the grace of Christ and the Holy Ghost have inspired, we may feel more strongly the reality of the communion of the saints. The only person on whom we build is Christ, though we construct our houses from many different materials. (In this sense, theologies which build primarily on the work of single persons, be these giants Barth, Heidegger, or Aquinas, seem prematurely foreshortened.) There are many witnesses pleasing to God, each emphasizing different parts of the whole, each more or less likely to resonate powerfully with you or with me.

The exercise of Christian memory is not simply the preservation of the past; it is also strengthening for the present and the future. By reading Bunyan's *Pilgrim's Progress*, we fortify ourselves through the exercise of Christian imagination and hope. Let us allow the diverse witnesses of the past to impress us and stir us to fidelity. Let the beauty of Christian poetry, music, and painting add strength to our memory, faith, and love. At the same time, by not forgetting the Holocaust, the Inquisition, or the New England witch hunts, let us remind ourselves of our own sinfulness and our own capacity for evil. Fluttering above our proud helmets as we recall "Onward Christian Soldiers" is a grotesque banner of sin.

A pastoral study of people with dementia underscores the importance of Christian traditions, particularly liturgical traditions, for sustaining our relationship with God. Working at a predominantly Methodist nursing home, James W. Ellor, John Stettner, and Helen Spath discovered that senile patients were able to participate in a liturgy which was constructed around familiar Bible passages, hymns, prayers, and liturgical responses. Because they had heard the 23rd Psalm many times, patients were able to repeat it when given "no more direction than a pastor would give an average group" even though individually they could not remember it on their own.[16] It was not the new which sustained these people but the old, the oft-repeated. It seems hard to remain connected to a community of worship which is always changing, and this seems especially true of Alzheimer's patients. Liturgical or theological innovation may seem appealing, but can they preserve us throughout our lifetimes? Can they provide us with the memories we need? As the liturgy is the central vehicle for our faithful remembering of God, I can think of no better way to conclude this chapter on method as memory than with this illustration of how the church's liturgical memories allow us to remain worshipers even as our minds degenerate.

Chapter 4

The Soul and Its Grammar

For God alone my soul waits in silence;
from him comes my salvation.
— Psalm 62:1

The essay on "Soul" (*Ame*) in Voltaire's *Philosophical Dictionary* parodies many different conceptions of the soul. He catalogues debates about the soul's substance (fire, ether, atoms, spirit, God), its location (the organs of reproduction, the *corpus callosum*), its operations (thinking, feeling, heartbeats), and what happens to it after death (whether the soul of a madman will still be insane). He even addresses questions of the seemingly inconsistent Biblical views of the soul and the afterlife. But he reserves his greatest disdain for those who try to prove the existence and nature of the soul apart from revelation, for he himself concludes that "You cannot know it except through faith."

Indeed, in several thousand years, the soul has accumulated quite a number of curious meanings and problematic definitions, yet it remained for the *philosophe* an irreducible component of human existence. (He was a vigorous opponent of materialism throughout the last decades of his life.) An alphabetical accident in the *Dictionary* places *Ame* in the immediate company of *Adam*, *Amitie*, and *Amour*, which, as we shall see, is a felicitous accident indeed. The soul may be not only a breath of life (as in the Hebrew *nephesh*), but also a central component in our recovery from the Fall and our sharing of friendship and love. The soul may not only help describe who we are but also how God works in us.

Because the church has a responsibility to consider exactly what happens to a patient who suffers from Alzheimer's disease, the phenomena of this affliction evoke a theological consideration of the basic stuff of human beings. Of what, precisely, are we made? Is there more to a human being than neurological processes, blood, tendons, and bone? Is there indeed a non-material (or perhaps non-corporeal) principle of life, as the Biblical witnesses suggest? What do neurological processes reveal about human existence and about the great questions of life, freedom, and love?

The church needs to continue bearing witness to the non-corporeal nature of our existence—that which is not subject to bodily disease and dissolution and which is subject to the workings of God's grace. Without this witness, there will be very little for the church to say, not only to Alzheimer's patients and their families but also to many, many others who face death each day. Alzheimer's disease, in this respect, is a revealing instance of the larger problem of human suffering and death. It is a decisive example of a death which deprives humans of their capacity to experience the Kingdom of God as it might be manifest in this world. By exposing our reliance on self-consciousness and "leading full, rewarding lives," it raises questions about the adequacy of Christian existentialism or political theologies. In short, the realities of Alzheimer's suggest that the alternatives to transcendence, "soul-speak," and the resurrection which many theologians now proclaim are incapable of addressing many of the ultimate sufferings and miseries of this world.

Although it would perhaps be more appropriate to begin Christian anthropology with the subject of the resurrection, I begin with the soul and its relationship to human corporeality, because it is precisely the relationship between body, mind, and soul which caring for an Alzheimer's patient compels us to examine. We are led to contemplate the non-materiality of our humanity, because Alzheimer's is a physiological affliction which incapacitates the mental functions traditionally associated with the soul. Hence we begin with one distinct aspect of the psychosomatic unity of human beings. Although, as we shall see, the doctrine of the resurrection is the strongest Christian argument in favor of the soul (a soul is all but required as the basis of personal continuity between death and the resurrection), caregivers may not be able to wait until the resurrection for a confirmation of the personhood of their patients. They need to know now that the souls of their loved ones are very much alive, even as their patients seem incapable of speech. Hence, this chapter precedes the chapter on the resurrection.

The first section of this chapter describes the traditional teachings of the church concerning the soul, teachings which centered on how the soul may be said to be the locus of God's work in us. The second section examines how a series of philosophical, theological, scientific, and political transformations from Descartes through the present have produced an atmosphere in which serious considerations of the soul have become rare. The third section engages the problems of materialist and neurological doctrines and establishes the reasons why modern folks need not feel silly, outmoded, or *passé* if they believe in a human soul. The final section demonstrates why Christians must proclaim the soul's existence if they are to remain faithful to the Gospel promises, to the work of Christ, and to the mission of the church.

The conclusion describes my own sense of what Christians can say about the relationship between soul and body. Here, what I will refer to as "integrative dualism" will be discussed. I take this phrase from Charles Taliaferro, and I owe much to his own discussion of the soul.[1] He employs this phrase to suggest that our two aspects of body and soul are always interacting and are completely integrated in the unity of our lives. While we can think of the two as distinct, they almost always exist and function together; the survival of the soul prior to the resurrection is the exception, not the rule. To quote Karl Rahner, "created spirituality is quite unthinkable without reference to materiality as a condition of its possibility."[2] Taken as a whole, this chapter constitutes "A Grammar of the Soul." Its purpose is to describe the ways in which the soul functions in the inner context of the Christian world of meaning. It is this devotional mode, not the modes of metaphysics, phenomenology, or existentialism, which is most appropriate to the great mystery of the soul.

The Passive-Voice Soul

Because the subject of the soul invites humans to fathom the great mysteries of life, mind, freedom, and love, we should expect that there would be a certain amount of variety in Christian witness concerning the subject. Indeed, in over twenty centuries there have been some significant disagreements as to the nature of the soul, what its origins might be, and many other such matters. What seems important for our purposes is first to identify the points of consensus and the shared assumptions which diverse authors exhibit. Second, we should describe the ways in which the soul is not just an integral part of metaphysics and epistemology but also an inextricable element of the much broader doctrinal, sacramental, and devotional life of the church. Ultimately, we need to remember that the soul reveals more about what God does than what we can achieve through our natural powers. Hence, the title of this section emphasizes the soul not as an active agent, but rather as a creature which God acts upon.

From the outset we should suggest some caution. Although scholastic theologians tended to be more bold in their analysis of the soul, other members of the tradition bear witness to the great deference to be paid the mystery of the soul. Many early theologians, for example, recognized that God's creation of the soul is a crucial part of the doctrine of creation, but they confessed their inability to fathom how God actually creates the soul in human beings.[3] Despite significant differences, the Christian tradition prior to the onset of modernity bears common witness to a crucial convergence of beliefs regarding the stuff of human beings. This convergence of beliefs was a product of history. The origins of psychology (literally "soul-speak," from *psyche* and *logos*) lie in Old Testament anthropology, but the full elaboration of the church's teachings would incorporate the New Testament as well as Greek philosophical concepts. As with the doctrines of the Trinity and the Incarnation, a clear sense of what an orthodox Christian understanding of body and soul might be was not to emerge for several centuries after the resurrection and after several decisive encounters with philosophers and heretics. More importantly, a vision of the ways in which the soul is related to the complex, diverse activities of the church and its members developed only with time, only as the church's life unfolded in diverse contexts with different members.

Ernst Käsemann's study of the problem of searching the Bible for *the* biblical view of anything as complex and multifaceted as humanity should remind us not to expect a coherent, consistent view of the soul throughout Scripture. In Barth's phrasing, the biblical authors often exhibit a "carefree inexactness."[4] Nevertheless, some general points of agreement are manifest. Old Testament anthropology concentrated on human beings in the totality of the existence. As the term *nephesh* (originally "breath") suggests, there is an animating principle in us which is an integral part of both human beings and animals. The term *nephesh* can be translated in various ways, including life, soul, a living being, etc. Although there is no dualism of any modern variety explicit in the Old Testament, neither is life reduced to purely material or biological considerations. Significantly, the developing tradition of *sheol* and the idea of an afterlife bears witness to continuous personal existence after the death of the body (see, for example, Ps. 86:13 and 139:8).

The New Testament witness concerning human beings and the soul is more complicated. As with *nephesh*, the term *psyche* exhibits several possible meanings (principle of life, life itself, a living entity), and there remains an absence of sustained reflection on it. Matthew 10:28 seems to suggest a duality of body and soul (though the parallel of Luke 12:4 does diminish this possible reading). Revelation 6:9 and 20:4 also describes an immortal soul, but on the whole the New Testament speaks of immortality through the resurrection rather than in the context of an outright dualism of soul and body. Paul seems to prefer the triad body, soul, and spirit, but it is far from clear what he means precisely (as would be indicated by the different ways in which these terms are translated in various English editions). In short, we and the church Fathers inherit from the witnesses of Scripture an undeveloped anthropology which, at the least, rejects materialism of any modern variety, and at the most does suggest that patristic anthropology, which on the whole viewed human beings as a natural union of body and soul, is in accordance with Scripture.[5]

But the terms *nephesh* and *psyche* encompass more than life in itself. The terms are also linked to the fullness of life. The soul loves (Mark 12:30, citing Deut. 6:4-5), experiences sorrow and fear (Ps. 42:5, Acts 2:43), can be in need of God's healing (Ps. 41:4), and expresses the human capacity for community and friendship (1 Sam. 18:1 and Num. 15:30). At the same time, the reality of sin, the darkness of life, is understood through the soul's need for purification (1 Pet. 1:22). Moreover, as Psalm 42 makes clear (as would an allegorical reading of Song of Songs 3:4), the soul is always striving for God, for a soul apart from God would be as a hart who must search the wilderness without the refreshment of a flowing stream. Similarly, Paul's statement about the law's requirements being written on our hearts (Rom. 2:15) and Deuteronomy's promise that "the Lord your God will circumcise your heart" testify to God's working in the person. Such passages figuratively suggest what *psyche* literally refers to: a locus of God's activity in the person which is mysterious, encompassing the total person, and is not limited to specific organs such as the brain.

Thanks to the influence of Greek philosophy, the Fathers and most of their theological opponents all assumed that human beings are, in some way, made of both body and soul. (And thanks to

101

Scripture and the Fathers, so too did the Reformers largely assume the body-soul duality.)[6] Many philosophical traditions accepted a notion of a soul precisely because it was possible to see in the soul the locus of reasoning and willing, of understanding and morality, the two unique traits of human beings. The issue for the Fathers was thus not the immortality of the soul—rather the issues were whether this immortality was natural or divinely given and the status of the resurrection of the body. Consequently, the Nicene and Apostle's Creeds do not mention the soul, though they do affirm the resurrection of the body. Still, the devoured flesh of the martyrs was a clear indication that the body would not be the ground of personal continuity between death and the resurrection.

Against Platonic, Gnostic, and Manichaean views of the body as a prison for the soul, the Fathers saw that the Incarnation was the vindication of the body. The flesh that Christ assumed was both natural and good. Souls were not enjoying a blissful pre-existence for they are created to be united with bodies—the separation of the two which occurs at death is merely transitional. Conceptually, Christology and the body-soul problem were easily related. Clement of Alexandria compared the divine and human natures in Christ to the soul and its body. Many centuries later, Luther would see in the soul's permeation of the body a way of understanding how Christ could be present in the physical elements of the Eucharist.[7] Reflections on the metaphysical understanding of the soul's reality evolved through the centuries as theologians and churches embraced or rejected particular philosophical terms and concepts. For the Roman Catholic Church, the Council of Vienne (1311–12) followed the terminology of Aristotle and the medieval scholastics and condemned those who declared that the "substance of the rational or intellectual soul is not itself and essentially the form of the human body."[8]

Significantly for a consideration of Alzheimer's disease, relatively little attention was paid to the relationship between the soul and the brain. Gregory of Nyssa's *On the Making of Man* does not engage what is now labeled the mind-body problem, even though he does acknowledge that damage to the brain can affect human capacities.[9] Following Aristotle's interest in the bodily realm, Aquinas raised the question of the brain's relationship to the soul, but because of his Aristotelian metaphysics, the relationship between the two did not receive as extensive an examination as we might prefer. The problem we face now in the case of Alzheimer's was a problem which could receive only cursory attention, in large part because of the limitations of biology and non-existence of neurology.

Despite different metaphysical construals of the soul and fleeting considerations of the mind-body problem, the ontological link between the soul and God remained prominent in understanding the nature and function of the soul. The meditations on being created in the *imago Dei* (Genesis 1:26-7) centered on the soul since the image of God could hardly be corporeal. In particular, for many of the major figures in the Christian tradition, the understanding of the thinking, rational element of the soul was the central locus of the *imago*.[10] Reason, memory, consciousness, the moral conscience, the will, the capacity to love, the mental life of a person—these are the distinguishing features of the image of God in humanity.

Such reflections underscore humans as thinking and feeling subjects, but the crucial question regarding the *imago Dei* raised by Alzheimer's is not what this image accomplishes on its own, but how it is that God reforms this image, an image distorted by sin. The recognition of human sinfulness prevented theologians from blithely equating our human minds with the image of God. Citing Colossians 3:10 and 2 Corinthians 3:18, Calvin, for example, stresses that the imperfect image we now bear is to be reformed and regenerated through the work of Christ and the Holy Spirit.[11] Thus, the consideration of the soul as an image of God is absolutely incomplete without a consideration of the entire Christian life in the church, the sacraments, prayer, and grace. Although the thinking self dominated many discussions of the soul as the image of God, theologians refused to limit the discussion to the mental faculties. Herein lies the great divide between philosophical considerations of the soul and Christian reflections on the soul: in the former the soul (or mind, or however it is construed) is heroically self-sufficient, but in the latter the soul becomes the locus of God's work in us. The soul becomes an admission of insufficiency.

The medieval *Imitation of Christ* bears witness to the diverse aspects of the life of the soul. Despite great differences in metaphysics, epistemology, and soteriology, there is a general consensus in the pre-modern tradition that the soul is the primary locus of God's work in us, and this text provides a good illustration of the depth and variety of Christian "soul-speak." Thomas à Kempis' work, a decidedly anti-scholastic, anti-academic devotional text, eschews many philosophical considerations. It addresses the devotional and spiri-

103

tual needs of human beings. Not surprisingly, the soul suffuses his text just as his own soul once suffused his body (and will do so again). "God of Israel, zealous lover of souls . . . Christ, the spouse of the soul . . . the Physician of souls . . . the Guardian of the soul"—these are the epithets which Kempis employs to describe the multifaceted relationship between the soul and God. God provides food for the soul both through Scripture and the Eucharist.[12] The soul, and God's illumination of the soul, thus is the pre-condition for reading Scripture faithfully and profiting from its mysteries.

Kempis, and many others, see spiritual life not as a mere modality (simply eschewing the desires of the material world) but as an ontologically different existence. The person literally changes as the soul grows in strength, power, and the virtues. Vatican II still affirms the Holy Spirit's ongoing enriching of the soul with diverse gifts and talents.[13] Language of God's working in and strengthening the soul is not limited to a Catholic understanding of sanctification. Luther, for whom talk of sanctifying grace infused into the soul was anathema, speaks of the growth of righteousness in us, in our soul. Calvin follows traditions similar to Kempis when he writes of the illumination of the soul and the Holy Spirit's vivifying of souls at baptism and throughout life.[14] Although theologians use many terms as the locus of God's work in humans (the mind, heart, spirit, will, etc.), they ground these different expressions in a soul.

Significantly for Alzheimer's patients, Kempis writes frequently of the immediacy of the God-soul relationship. God speaks within a person's soul; he opens human hearts to his mercies and gifts; he provides comfort for the soul, strengthening it in its weariness; and echoing Genesis 1:2, Kempis declares, "Until your light illuminates my soul, I am dull earth, formless and empty" (Glenn Weaver uses this same language to describe patients with dementia). The grounding of the soul in God's work is complete. Kempis hails Christ, "All things are in your power, and you always long to bring souls to perfection."[15] The soul is thus seen teleologically—it cannot be considered apart from its final resting place. Until we get there, we are reminded that even in a demented person, God's Spirit can be present to the soul. (John of the Cross' *Dark Night of the Soul* suggests perhaps that dementia-like states and a seeming isolation from God are not alien to the purgatorial trials of mysticism.)

What emerges from this overview is the significance of what might be called the "passive-voice soul"—the soul as an object of

God's work, neither the subject nor author of its nature and destiny. For while theologians stress the soul's capacity in terms of what we now call a subject, they also stress the character of the soul as something which desperately needs to be acted upon. As Kempis writes, "Unless a man's soul *is raised* . . . and wholly united to God, neither his knowledge nor his possessions are of any value."[16] The fate of these dense spiritual traditions is the subject of the next section.

The Deactivation of the Active-Voice Soul

Although a natural union of body and soul was an integral part of traditional Christian anthropologies in the main Catholic and Protestant traditions, the modern era has a relative dearth of discussions of the human soul. As Allan Bloom's posthumous *Love and Friendship* reveals, modern Platonists, too, are distressed by this lack of "soul-speak."[17] The reasons for the modern world's reluctance to engage in considerations of the soul are numerous and complex, and this section can attempt only to underscore some of the crucial developments.[18] As a result of these transformations, even those who do use the term "soul" do so in ways which the phenomena of Alzheimer's disease make suspect.

Although both Protestant antipathy towards indulgences for the souls of the dead and criticism of "soul-speak" as irresponsibly otherworldly have led theologians away from developing teachings on the soul, philosophical developments have been even more important for theology's reluctance to consider this topic. In particular, the philosophical debate more frequently known as the mind-body problem has been decisive. Descartes has become one of the favorite whipping boys of recent times, for he managed not only to set up many of the terms for the mind-body debate but also to reach conclusions which almost no one shares.[19] Two elements of his work on the soul are crucial. First, as the preface to his *Discourse on Method* indicates, he attempts to prove the existence of the human soul (as well as of God). Thus, argument replaced faith, and certainty supplanted belief as criteria for discussions of the soul. Second, despite his attempt to serve Christianity, Descartes returned to the thorough dualism which the Christian tradition had fought so hard to reject. Humans were now composed of a non-mechanical thinking substance, the soul, and a mechanical (Newtonian) extended substance, the body. The thinking part of the human (which became the definition of the soul) was thus separated from the living, breathing, tear-forming body. Descartes and his successors were fascinated by the soul's twin aspects—thinker, and object of thought. Unfortunately they paid less attention to the crucial issue raised in light of Alzheimer's—the soul as a vehicle for God's work, the soul's life in Christ and the Holy Spirit. Descartes and Thomas à Kempis could hardly be further apart.

The British tradition of empiricism produced a certain skepticism in Locke, and culminated in a flat rejection of the concept of the soul by Hume. Many, perhaps most, modern theologians follow Hume in his shift from talk of a soul to concentration on a "self." This "self" becomes the referent of bundles of impressions, ideas, and thoughts which exhibit continuity over time in each person's own consciousness. It is this "self" which is now often used in philosophical discussions of surrogate decision-making or of the ethics of maintaining life support for the demented and impaired. Focusing on such a "self," it may be argued, encourages us to think about our lives in terms of our own powers and not in terms of how a person truly is God's. (Recall that the church's opposition to suicide has often centered on the fact that we are not independent and autonomous, we belong to God.) As we are seeing, Alzheimer's disease might suggest that we should be skeptical about this "self" as the ultimate locus of human identity and existence.

Kant's rigorous assault on metaphysics and the absolute dividing line he drew between the phenomenal and noumenal realms ended the Cartesian project to prove the soul's existence. Kant's examination of consciousness led him to conclude that such consciousness is outside the realm of knowable objects (hence it lies beyond proof). As a consequence the thinking person becomes much more of a subject with a much clearer picture of what she can perceive as a proper object. The "turn to the subject" (the concentration on the thinking subject as the locus of authority and arbiter of truth) seems complete. Similarly, Hegel's interest in consciousness, immanence, and process have continued to exercise an influence in modern theology. Such emphases are not conducive to speaking of a transcendent God who works through the soul. Although Schleiermacher himself does speak of a human soul (he does so largely because Jesus seems to have been comfortable with souls and spirits, particularly his own), it is hardly surprising that followers of Schleiermacher exhibit such a disinclination towards thinking about souls.[20] Human consciousness of God, rather than the presence or actual workings of God in the person, becomes the central category for theological reflection.

Another important figure for theologians (particularly political theologians), Marx, simply had no room in his system for anything non-material. The soul for him was an ideological illusion, one which legitimated existing class structures. Freud, who has been more important for pastoral theologians, provided an alternative system of concepts, categories, and techniques for thinking about the human person and responding to psychological needs. Physiology rather than metaphysics, it is suggested, is the groundwork of "soul-speak." Although Hobbes was the first major modern figure in the Christian era to advocate a thorough-going materialism, it has been only in the last two centuries with the increasing discoveries of medicine, neurology, and computers that the materialist position in the mind-body problem has gained wide-spread currency. In different ways, Marx and Freud emphasized matter, and many modern philosophers, particularly the neo-positivists, are inclined towards what they feel to be the certitude of the brain over the indeterminacy of the soul. Computer-based artificial intelligence can now mimic many of what were once seen as the unique workings of the human mind. By describing the soul nearly exclusively as an "active-voice soul," by imagining it in terms of its thinking powers, we have prepared the way for the deactivation of the idea of the soul itself.

While some modern authors, notably some phenomenologists and existentialists, have responded to materialism's claims in favor of a distinctive existence for humanity, they have, on the whole, done so in thoroughly Cartesian, subjective terms. Although many in this group avoid the term "self" or "subject" (often preferring a hyphenated combination of "being" and some other words), they nevertheless remain mentalists. The mind-body problem is often side-stepped as a non-issue, since the terms and categories for describing consciousness do not admit of a philosophical exploration of the relationship between brain and thought. Fergus Kerr's *Theology after Wittgenstein*, a work to which we will return, demonstrates the thorough Cartesianism of most modern theologians, and his observations about the centrality of the thinking subject hold true for philosophers as well. The "turn to the subject" does seem decisive.

It is hardly surprising that modern theologians have been subject to these same philosophical influences. (For many of them, the historical-critical method and the predilection for demythologizing Scripture and the tradition have rendered anything prior to nineteenth-century criticism problematic at best.) Hence, David Kelsey identifies the starting point for theological reflection on human beings as the "autonomy, historicity, and self-constitutingness of persons as subjects."[21] Kelsey and Thomas à Kempis could hardly be further apart. The extent to which contemporary theologians as a whole do or do not take the soul seriously cannot be determined here (and each reader will already have some sense of this), but my impression is that even those who do employ the soul as a central category do so in Cartesian, subject-centered ways.[22]

To take but one example, Charles Gerkin does try to reclaim the soul, but his preference for a thorough-going immanence to the exclusion of transcendence already means that his soul will be rather different from the soul of the pre-modern church. In *The Living Human Document*, he takes as his "core image, the image of the self as interpreter of its own experience." Hence, the "life of the soul is a continuous life of interpretation."[23] Despite his complex nuances regarding differences between the ego, the self, and the soul, it seems that his position is grounded almost exclusively in a human thinking subject. Because of his focus on immanence and self-interpretation, there seems to be very little room for the mysterious in-breaking of grace and illumination, and it becomes difficult to see how one can speak meaningfully about a merciful God who can be present in and vitalize a person with Alzheimer's. Similarly, theologians drawing heavily on phenomenology may speak of a soul, but such a soul is linked more with our consciousness than with God's work within us. Those who defend the reality of the soul in a theistic context or in a discussion of the philosophy of mind still concentrate on the soul's epistemological and metaphysical aspects, often bracketing the moral, devotional, and spiritual aspects which are crucial for the full, rich life of the soul. Although Barth does include a sustained discussion of the soul in his *Church Dogmatics*, his treatment here, as with his writings on other subjects in the modern world, appears as a rear-guard action, one often outflanked.[24]

The culmination of these modern developments, then, seems to be the grounding of theology and philosophy in a nebulous entity, "consciousness," an entity which may slowly disintegrate, an entity which is no longer present in the latter stages of Alzheimer's disease.

At this time, consciousness itself appears to deactivate. The Enlightenment impulse of liberating humanity from prejudices and thereby empowering humanity, has, it seems, made it much harder for the church to understand how it is that these powerless patients can be empowered by God. I do not believe we should be satisfied with such an unfortunate conclusion.

Materialism and "Soul-Speak"

The purpose of this section is to provide some reasons and arguments which might make it possible, or at least easier, for us to be more congenially disposed to "soul-speak." For three reasons, much of this section is set in explicitly non-theological language. First, the debate about a non-corporeal part of humanity has been a debate carried on in non-Christian circles. Second, the central challenges to a Christian soul have often come from those outside the communion of the saints. Currently, materialism both implicitly and explicitly is the dominant anthropology. Consequently, to make "soul-speak" more comfortable, we need to engage the secular world on its own terms and see how materialism might be inadequate. The third reason for the use of non-theological language is perhaps more encouraging. As we shall see, there are still defenders of the church under the porch of the Stoa.

In *The Varieties of Religious Experience*, William James identified this modern problematic with the title of his first chapter, "Religion and Neurology." He noted and sought to refute the medical materialism that he saw as threatening the legitimacy of religious experience. Modern neurology has progressed quite rapidly from the days when James took his degree in physiology at Harvard, and the issues are perhaps more acute now than they were then. However, the challenge to Christians raised by the scientific study of the body is much older. Indeed, it may be recalled that in Bunyan's *Pilgrim's Progress*, when Christian proclaims his desire to seek the Celestial City, Obstinate calls him a "brain-sick fellow" and even his family thinks that "some frenzy distemper had got into his head."[25] The issue of materialist explanations for religious experience and indeed all human experience has become a perennial one, and perhaps we would do well to address the problem squarely. As the title of one of Voltaire's anti-materialist tracts suggests, *We Must Take Sides*.

Materialism, of course, has as many different meanings as there are materialists. "Matter" has been replaced by "mass" and other concepts, and is a category no longer used by scientists. Nevertheless, materialism as a historical concept still suggests what the fundamental issues are. The term may refer to economic or political theories; to a philosophical or neurological approach to the mind-body problem; or even to theoretical physics and quantum mechanics. For the purposes of this review of materialism, however, these theories may be grouped together and classified negatively in that they share significant beliefs concerning what reality is not.

For the materialist, reality is to be described wholly in nonspiritual terms. That is, the cascading droplets of a waterfall are, in all likelihood, of the same general type of phenomenon as motion along an inclined plane and as the working of the human brain. These events (and "event," too, is now a loaded term) differ more in degree than in kind. There are no things or events or substances which lie outside the realm of material investigation and explanation. Consciousness is to be described in purely biological or physical terms. Criteria for inquiry and evaluation differ from materialist to materialist. There is a general respect for the mathematically describable and the repeatable (and hence the predictive). There is also a certain desire for the elimination of the role of the subject in observation (though many argue that relativity theory shows that this is, strictly speaking, impossible). The water descends exactly as it does from the higher to the lower regardless of whether you or I or Socrates is watching.[26]

For our purposes, the most important of the materialist claims center around the mind-body problem, hence around neurology and not sub-atomic theory. Can Christians maintain their traditional anthropological claims about the soul in light of modern discoveries? This is not the place to examine the different versions of dualism and materialism which the marketplace of ideas now offers. A fine introduction to the doctrines and various arguments in the current debate can be found in Paul M. Churchland's *Matter and Consciousness*, and much of this section comes from his analysis.[27] He sketches the distinctions between several different varieties of dualism and materialism (there are at least ten options available), and analyzes the strengths and weaknesses of each. A review of the philosophical, psychological, and neurological evidence on the question of the soul and the mind-body problem reveals four important subjects for our consideration: the inconclusive results of these disciplines; materialism's tendency towards reductionism; the problem of *qualia*; and the mystery of meaning.

One of the reasons why the results are inconclusive is that the problem itself is enormous—what set of theories, laws of nature, chemical processes, etc., can account adequately for the great variety of mental activities? How can you study an organ made up of as many as one hundred billion neurons? Although he himself is far from being a dualist, Churchland admits that the problem of mind is far from being answered. While the explanatory powers of neurology tend to favor certain varieties of materialism, no theories seem to explain adequately the great range of mental phenomena. "Despite this general advance, a central mystery remains largely a mystery: the nature of conscious intelligence. . . . Neither dualism nor materialism can yet explain all of the phenomena to be explained."[28] Curiously, almost all sides in this debate look to the future for vindication—either in an afterlife for dualists (though dualists do not necessarily have to believe in one) or to new and improved scientific breakthroughs for the materialists. No one claims to have solved all the problems, and speculation is endemic to all theories.

One of the more unfortunate aspects of materialism is the way in which brain studies tend to reduce human experience to discrete, measurable chemical, or physical events. A passage from Dickens' *Hard Times*, a novel set in the middle of the industrialization of England and the English, illustrates the danger of a too-scientific view of things. A young girl, Sissy Jupe, is commanded by the schoolmaster, Thomas Gradgrind, to provide a definition for a horse. Although she is familiar with the noble creatures, she is thrown into "alarm" by this. The model pupil of this society, Bitzer, provides the correct definition:

> Quadruped. Graminivorous. Forty teeth, namely, twenty-four grinders, four eye-teeth, and twelve incisive. Sheds coat in the spring; in marshy countries, sheds hoofs, too. Hoofs hard, but requiring to be shod with iron. Age known by marks in mouth.

The students subsequently learn from a "gentleman visitor" that they are never to paper the walls of their houses with horses because you never "see horses walking up and down the sides of rooms in reality—in fact." Further, Sissy and the rest of the children are told, "You are never to fancy. . . . Fact, fact, fact! . . . You are to be in all things regulated and governed . . . by fact."[29]

Materialism *per se* is not necessarily reductionistic (seeing consciousness as an "emergent property" of the brain in its nondissectable totality avoids this), but I believe that a materialist outlook ultimately does encourage the compartmentalizing of both thought and life. Science, in this sense, obfuscates and cheapens our lives as human persons just as Gradgrind's school cheapened the horse (and the students). Mystery, the sublime, the eternal, the transcendent, the irreducible—these words, hardly scientific, are the words of human beings.

A particularly challenging version of materialism, eliminative materialism, suggests that states such as joy and love are simply misnomers, terms which will one day be seen as inadequate representations of neurochemical processes. What we now call love will be understood more accurately as specific patterns of neural synapses. There are profound implications for our lives in each of the answers to the mind-body problem. Moreover, there are profound implications for Christology. Richard Rorty's famous pronouncement that the "science of the future" may tell us that our supposed feelings of pain should be understood scientifically as neural brain processes and nothing else suggests that Christ's suffering on the Cross was but a brain event.[30] Indeed, we may have to conclude that only the human brain of Jesus experienced neural firings while the divine nature, if it is immaterial, was not capable of experiencing anything at all. Can a religion which starts with the primacy of a suffering God accept a worldview like eliminative materialism?

This, then, is one of the strongest arguments in favor of dualism, one which Churchland advertises—the fact that humans experience not only data, but also quality, not only a quadruped but also a fiery beast laden with many possible connotations of sexuality, war, nobility, swiftness, and divinity.[31] Indeed, just as *nephesh* and *psyche* resonate with much more than life *per se*, so do our lives vibrate with much more than sensory input. For many, materialism seems simply unable to address what is called the problem of *qualia*. Quite literally, these are the things that animate our *animas*. Such an inability to account for quality bears witness to A. N. Whitehead's observation about the bifurcation of nature characteristic of modern thought, the separation of experience into qualitative (subjective) and quantitative (physical, scientific) categories. Our experiences in an opera house or a meadow do not "mesh" with our sense of physics; rarely do we describe a voice or a flower's petals in terms of wavelengths.

112

In part because of this quality to our experiences and God's, Richard Swinburne, a theist, has defended the existence of the special human soul. In *The Evolution of the Soul*, Swinburne takes evolution quite seriously and argues that what has evolved in the human being is qualitatively different from the rest of the physical world (much like a turtle is qualitatively different from a rock).[32] Charles Arthur Campbell had defended the legitimacy of the soul according to natural theology and philosophy, but Swinburne engages modern materialists, and he develops his arguments in greater detail.[33]

Swinburne provides an interesting counter-argument to the confident, scientific expectations of the materialists. Quantum theory, he observes, suggests that there will be no way to account for the human will in mechanical terms. The variables and the levels of complexity confirm, if anything, the irreducibility of the human (chaos theory adds support to the unpredictability of mental phenomena—and without the element of predictability, materialism loses much of its explanatory power). His use of quantum theory as an illustration of the impossibility of a purely materialist reckoning of human existence echoes Roger Penrose's recent book, *Shadows of the Mind*. Significantly, Swinburne's discussion of quantum theory occurs in a chapter entitled "The Freedom of the Will." Although he does not connect his own discussion to a church or to God, he does remind us that the traditional construction of arguments for the soul have been (too) limited to human cognitive processes. (Penrose himself explicitly disavows a specific interest in "ethics, morality, and aesthetics" for his work.)[34] Much more is at work inside a soul than thinking itself. We choose, we love, we sin. Can materialism and neurology do justice to the ugliness of sin? When we pray for God's gift of peace, does God cause synapses to fire in the brain, or does he release some "feel-good" chemicals, such as endorphins?

Related to the question of the quality of our experiences is another issue which Churchland and Swinburne note as supportive of some sort of dualism: the mystery of meaning. Human beings seem to have the habit of ascribing meaning to things, events, images, sensations, and thoughts. Can neurology account for meaning? It is, perhaps, in recognition of the fact that human meaning transcends the material world that Thomas Moore's recent book *The Care of the Soul* and its imitators have been so phenomenally successful at bookstores. Though Moore himself does not view the soul in the same way as Gregory of Nyssa, it is clear that he is not sympathetic to materialism. Despite the lack of interest exhibited by many professional theologians, many lay people are deeply interested in the question of their souls and the meaning of their experiences. Our daily language and our liturgies speak of spirituality, and one wonders where this spirituality is to be grounded if there is no spirit or soul, if there is only a spiritual modality. In the patristic era, Modalism was rejected in the orthodox definition of the Trinity for good reason, for it is not just a matter of what and how God and humans do certain things, but also what we are in our essences.

If the physiological evidence for either dualism or materialism is inconclusive, can we find another way of proceeding? In 1788, just over two centuries before my mother was diagnosed with Alzheimer's disease, Kant produced his *Critique of Practical Reason*. Though many today would disagree with him on many points, his critiques may help prepare the way of the soul. While his distinction between the phenomenal (things as they appear, that which the human mind can investigate) and the noumenal (things-in-themselves, that which lies beyond human knowledge) has inclined many towards the phenomenal, towards knowledge, and away from the soul, the distinction can also serve to underscore that the Christian claims about the noumenal are statements of faith.[35] The question for Kant, and for us moderns of weak faith, is: Are these statements about noumenal reality, about the soul, "reasonable," are they "believable"? As he suggests in his famous preface to his *Critique of Pure Reason*, the answer for him will be yes: he declares that he had "found it necessary to deny knowledge in order to make room for faith."

Kant exhibited a strong sense of the limits of empiricism and science, of humanity as observer, and of humans as actors. Thus, in his first critique, *The Critique of Pure Reason*, he stressed that far from being passive, the mind itself is active, bringing to its investigations certain *a priori* categories, categories such as "space" which precede and arrange sensory impressions. Moreover, a human is also a moral actor, a person whose existence is laden with moral value and meaning. We do far more than know or explain. In his *Critique of Judgment*, he observes that morality and a sense of the beautiful are linked. The realm of Kant's reflections is extensive and quite rich, and it is characteristic of his thought (and in contrast to some materialists), that humans can hardly be considered apart from morality.

As Kant works his way through a consideration of human morality in his *Critique of Practical Reason*, he reaches some important

114

conclusions regarding the soul, freedom, and God. Morality, which for him was the given, suggests that claims about what a person *ought* to do implies what a person *can* do. Thus he demonstrates the existence of human freedom, something which is not, properly speaking, an object of knowledge. (Whether or not he takes sin seriously enough is a separate question.) Further, morality implies that people are rewarded according to their virtues and vices. Yet as any reading of history, Greek tragedy, or current events reveals, the virtuous are often overwhelmed by the wicked, by forces of nature, or by simple circumstance. And the wicked often seem quite happy in their vices. Consequently, humanity's moral sensibility requires the existence of an immortal soul, a soul which will be able to progress in virtue and happiness (or justly experience the opposite). Similarly, God is required for this to be possible, specifically a God whose will and power are causally connected to morality, to rewards and to punishments. Kant does not call this a proof for the existence of the soul. Rather, he calls the soul, freedom, and God rational postulates required for moral existence. Without these postulates, morality becomes a cruel farce of a concept. God's work and the soul are non-empirical, but they are not beyond reason. He states that these postulates, though not proven, are real, because morality demands the reality of its beliefs.

What does this suggest for our current dilemma about the soul? Kant's work provides a possible way to ground Christian belief about the soul. First, in its conformity with the ignorance of neurology regarding the mind, freedom, and the possible existence of the soul, it suggests that considerations of the soul are really primarily moral matters and are most properly in the realm of faith. Second, it demonstrates that while the soul is a transcendental topic, it is nevertheless quite a reasonable transcendental topic (that is, if one accepts morality as a premise). Thus, the work of Kant, taken together with the work of Swinburne, the warning of Dickens, and the very real limits of materialism, suggests that the burden of "proof" rests not with Christianity but with the secular world. (I might add that the testimony of most of the world's religions also would lend widespread support to the reality of the soul.) The real issue of the soul is not epistemology but life itself in all its fullness, in all its pleasures, agonies, and responsibilities. In other words, the soul's grammatical context includes freedom, morality, a bleeding God, God's works in us, and many other terms in addition to life and

115

consciousness. Ultimately, can we have freedom, morality, and the spiritual richness of our hymnody in a purely materialist world?

Calvin and Hobbes

I refer here not to the famous comic strip characters, the precocious boy and his pet tiger, but rather to the option which confronts Christianity, the choice between Calvin (belief in a soul) and Hobbes (materialism). I believe that this consideration of the soul evoked by the phenomena of Alzheimer's disease puts into a clear relief the issues and implications involved. I also believe that for the churches of Christendom to remain true to their callings, to remain faithful to God's work in history both in Christ and the Holy Spirit, the churches must proclaim vigorously the life of the soul. The other major options available for modern folk, materialism and mentalism (the focus on the self-conscious subject as the ground of religious thought and existence), are inadequate, as I now hope to show, in the light of Alzheimer's disease.

The Hobbesian alternative should make it clear that materialism is inadequate and that Christians must affirm at the very least some non-material principle of life. Thomas Hobbes, the seventeenth-century philosopher, amanuensis to Francis Bacon, and tutor to the future Charles II of England, provided moderns with the first thorough exposition of materialist anthropology. In *Leviathan* and in *Questions Concerning Liberty, Necessity, and Chance,* Hobbes sought to explain human functioning in purely natural, scientific terms. There would be no soul for humanity in his work. If there had been significant advances in the materialist point of view, there would be little point in considering Hobbes and his system. But, by and large, there have been only technical, neurological advances (his system was Newtonian physics), and the materialist position remains largely Hobbesian today. For our purposes, Hobbes has the advantage of being more broad-minded than most materialists, for his materialism is linked to his politics, and it is in the broader implications of materialism as an exclusivist doctrine that Christians must find offense.

Hobbes, the son of an ill-trained and incompetent vicar, begins with the now-conventional doctrine of materialism, that ideas, feelings, thought, and imaginings are but events in the brain. The conundrum for previous materialists, particularly the Epicureans, had been how to account for what appears to be free will and voluntary action. These Greek atomists posited that the mind of human beings had some atoms which could swerve around spontaneously, and this swerving, not being subject to the laws of matter and science, accounted for the will. Not a very satisfying solution, but a solution. Hobbes rejects even this attempt to account for such freedom in humans. For him, and for most materialists, everything we do is causally determined by material events in the brain, sensory organs, and the rest of the body. Modern studies of brain-damaged persons show that moral *behavior* does depend on certain sections of the brain, but does human freedom itself? Alzheimer's disease forces us to take the body quite seriously, but it does not compel us to become thoroughgoing materialists.

What does Hobbes say about freedom? Liberty is simply the absence of external constraints. The will can be fully caused and free at the same time. Freedom is acting in accordance with nature and the intrinsic quality of the agent. Thus an unclogged stream is free when it flows down hill, for it is in the nature of water to flow from higher to lower. The crucial category of "freedom for" which has been a central Christian problem since Paul, is to him nonsense, since it presupposes an uncaused agent. Human decisions are made according to a balancing and contrasting of aversions and desires, which are themselves the product of physical processes.

Hobbes' materialism in the seventeenth century and, most drastically, eliminative materialism in the twentieth both expound doctrines which, in effect, obfuscate freedom and moral responsibility. Although some have construed an understanding of materialism, causality, and freedom in such a way that one can speak of "freedom" in a materialist world, these tortured construals are certainly unable to account for, as the title of one of Luther's treatises proclaims, *The Freedom of a Christian* (we could also cite Calvin's lengthy consideration of freedom in the *Institutes*).[36] Christian freedom extends to far more, indeed evokes from us far more, than simply an unconstrained choice between ginger snaps and graham crackers. Hence, Christians should consider under what circumstances their concept of freedom may or may not be in accord with their views of neurology and the brain. The ancient understanding of the soul as the locus of freedom of the will and moral responsibility reasserts itself. That neurochemical processes do affect our ability to will, love, and forgive is clear, but that they also determine them is not.

117

Hobbes explicitly observes, then, that the distinction between desire and love is quite simple: desire pertains to the object when absent, love when it is present.[37] The difference between the love of Romeo and Juliet and having enough potato chips to eat while watching television is a difference of degree, not kind. Hobbes' materialistic presentation seems incapable of doing justice to the role of the imagination in love or to the intense way in which the joy of love itself increases our desire for greater and more intense love. This way of speaking about the simultaneously satisfying and ever-desiring aspects of love has been familiar to "soul-speakers" since Plato. As one might expect, "good" and "evil" are relative to a person's own desires and aversions. (Nietzsche appears rather pedantic after reading Hobbes.) And in the realm of politics, the consequences are no less bleak. Hobbes' defense of the political absolutism of the sovereign should come as no surprise in light of his materialist, determinist anthropology. But, one may well ask what all the political fuss is about, since human beings are no longer particularly noble creatures. We might ask Hobbes, "What is man that thou are mindful of him?"

One of the deep antipathies to "soul-speak" in the modern world has come from a concern for the political realm and the manifest cruelties which some inflict, others endure. But remembering the soul may be integral to political responsibility. The soul distinguishes us from irrational beasts and, by forgetting the soul, we may be blurring the "distinction between humans and animals, which in turn may lead, and often has led, to the worst forms of biologism, racism, or naturalism. The Nazi *Lebensphilosophie*, to cite an egregious example, explicitly assimilated human strivings to the impulses of animal instinct."[38] Many of those regimes which, following Marx, proclaimed an explicit materialist anthropology have collapsed in recent years. While Cuba has not imploded, the country did, in July 1992, amend the constitution to indicate that Cuba is no longer a country based on Marxist-Leninist philosophical materialism. The popular evaluation of the significance of the end of the Cold War, Francis Fukuyama's *The End of History and the Last Man*, relies in part on a consideration of the soul (derived ultimately from Plato) and the irreducibility of the soul and human spiritedness, a spiritedness which cannot be accounted for materially.

It is impossible to predict what directions international events will take. But if the end of Marxist regimes (and the rise of capitalism in others) does make it possible for individuals, religious organizations, and nations to work for greater respect for human rights across the planet, then we may wonder where the metaphysical or ontological basis for human rights will be located. Vatican II was explicit on this point—human equality and human rights are grounded in the fact that all humans possess a rational soul and are created in the image of God. Luther, even with his now unfashionable reading of Romans 13, likewise argued that the existence of the human soul was above all what set clear limits to the powers of the prince over his people. And Barth's discussion of the soul occurs in the context of his discussion of "Respect for Life."[39] Considerations of freedom and responsibility, both moral and political, may well be inseparable from reflections on the soul.

Tocqueville's *Democracy in America* anticipated this recent collapse of materialist societies (as well as Weber's linking of spiritual values and material well-being in his exposition of the Protestant work ethic). He clearly foresaw the continual dangers of capitalism, too. For the French aristocrat, the materialism of American capitalism needed, above all, a regular preaching of the soul and the spiritual life of humanity. In his own attack on materialism—which he was seeing in practice all around him—Tocqueville observes its vicious cycle:

> Democracy encourages a taste for physical gratification; this taste, if it become excessive, soon disposes men to believe that all is matter only; and materialism, in its turn, hurries them on with mad impatience to these same delights; such is the fatal circle within which democratic nations are driven round.

The immortality of the soul, he went on to argue, was the greatest defense against the materialist malaise. For this teaching provides us with an eye for the eternal, a capacity to overcome base desires, and the foundation of our freedom and morality. Such spiritual benefits were necessary for a healthy political and economic body. "There is a closer tie than is commonly supposed between the improvement of the soul and the amelioration of what belongs to the body."[40]

Tocqueville had read Rousseau and other Romantics, and it is perhaps from their respect for the powers and dignity of the human soul that he derived his understanding of the role of the soul in the life of a people. The Romantic soul, capable of great selfishness, was also capable of eschewing simple material pleasures; it was given to striving for human excellence and to a willingness to forgo the

119

"delights" Tocqueville observed occupying the early Americans. As caregivers will tell us readily, their work requires that they forgo delights; their souls have to grow strong if they are to succeed.

Materialism is not the only major option confronting us. As observed in the second section of this chapter, there is now a preference in some, perhaps most, theologians for grounding theology in the self-conscious subject. Thus, as noted above, David Kelsey argues that the agenda for modern theology is now grounded in the "autonomy, historicity, and self-constitutingness of persons as subjects."[41] He subsequently traces several possible approaches to reconciling this anthropological foundation with the problem of knowing and being redeemed by God. Such approaches include categories of self-choosing, self-making, and authenticity. (One may confess that in a theology of such a mighty subject the need for being redeemed is no longer apparent.)

This approach, which on the whole side-steps the fundamental questions raised by the mind-body question, does have the advantage of moving us away from materialism's problems. It does stress human freedom and responsibility, and it does recognize the peculiar qualities and meanings which make us alive, not merely functional. In some respects, then it does appear to be adequate. But the phenomena of Alzheimer's inform us that "subjecthood" does not include millions of mentally-impaired people. Hence, we need now to critique the role of the "subject" in theology in order to see how the soul, as the locus of God's work, not ours, needs to be at the center of our anthropological reflections.

From a Wittgensteinian point of view, Fergus Kerr has critiqued (and parodied) modern theology's "turn to the subject" as seen in the work of Rahner, Küng, Don Cupitt, Schubert Ogden, Timothy O'Connell, Gordon Kaufman, and even Barth.[42] Seeing them all as heirs to Descartes (the soul as a thinking mental ego), not as heirs to the Christian spiritual tradition as a whole (the soul thinks, acts, and is transformed by God), Kerr argues that the ultimate result of this line of inquiry is a human being detached from the world and from other people, stuck inside a mind, trying valiantly to make sense of it all, imbuing meaning when and where it needs to. These theologians, he contends, are seeking a pure, genuine, infallible, knowing self, and their obsession with subject-centered epistemologies reveals a desire for scientific certainty and a certain spiritual purity. Kerr himself argues that Wittgenstein's respect for the bodiliness and creatureliness of humanity is the proper antidote for this decayed Cartesianism.

Although his parodies and analysis may not be entirely accurate, they do underscore the dilemmas inherent in the turn to the subject. In particular, it becomes very difficult to see how all our rather autonomous, self-construing selves can possibly hope to get along in an ecclesiastical setting, let alone at a sporting event or in a hot, crowded supermarket. Kelsey, following the lead of liberation theologians, himself cites a more difficult critique of the subject: "Is not the concept 'subject' in modern theology fatally flawed for the purposes of Christian theology precisely because it reflects a Western, male, bourgeois status that has the requisite surplus of time beyond what is needed to sustain life, but only as the fruit of other people's oppression?"[43] While we may prefer to see the category of subjecthood primarily in terms of consciousness and an epistemology which we all share, being able to be a subject in the first place requires social, economic, and cognitive capacities not available to all.

The Cartesian subject, as Kerr notes, is deeply ingrained in theology. Although Reinhold Niebuhr rejects Cartesian dualism, he too, in his effort to hold together the body, mind, and spirit, speaks of the "self's capacity for self-transcendence." The self remains the being doing the transcending. The tendency to draw on certain varieties of existentialism and phenomenology (for Niebuhr, this means Heidegger and Scheler) has exacerbated theology's emphasis on the subject.[44] Similarly, David Tracy's debt to phenomenology likewise deepens his commitment to grounding theological work in human consciousness. The unfortunate fact, however, is that what Tracy describes as the central disclosure of the New Testament, a new mode of being-in-the-world, may also apply to the experience of patients with Alzheimer's. They, too, particularly in the early stages, experience what is for them a new mode of being-in-the-world. The categories suggested by Kelsey in his review of modern theological options, especially the category of "authenticity" seem inadequate for a description of what happens to a patient with this disease.

It should be apparent now that the phenomena of Alzheimer's render the self-conscious subject as the ground of theological and religious life highly suspect. Because the real experiences of patients are so contrary to the experiences of consciousness, it is simply unclear how these types of theologies can address adequately the theological dimensions of dementia without compromising their own assumptions. Because the turn to the subject in most of its manifestations presupposes some sort of mind-body unity there appears to be no place to turn when the body so viciously renders the mind problematic. Kelsey, like Churchland, acknowledges the dangers to the subject posed by behaviorism and neurology, but it remains unclear how modern theologies might proceed to respond to the challenge of dementia in a way which is faithful to God's work, the church's mission, and the dignity of patients and caregivers.[45]

Significantly, Stanley Hauerwas has addressed the theological issues of the mentally disabled and the deaths of children. For him, we do not come at these folks after we have engaged in theological self-consciousness. Rather, we begin our work in the context of human mental insufficiency, incapacity, and suffering. As David H. Smith has phrased it, "[T]he problem of loss of control and suffering belongs at the *beginning* of religious thought rather than the end. That is—one should not construct a theology and then confront the problem of dementia."[46] Starting, as we have here, with the fact of Alzheimer's, we can see why the subject seems so unsteady a foundation. Certainly not the rock which Jesus recommended for building a house (Matt. 7:24-7). We can learn, therefore, from both the psalmist and the Alzheimer' patient as they each say (Ps. 62:1), "For God alone my soul waits in silence."

Ultimately, God is the most important reason why we must speak of the soul regularly, for as Charles Taliaferro argues (following Augustine's *On the Trinity*), our ideas about God and humanity are interrelated. When we imagine an immaterial God who loves, reasons, and acts, we can better comprehend an immaterial soul which does likewise. Similarly, by asserting the spiritual dimension of human existence we affirm that God is not material. By contrast, if we are nothing but matter, will that not also affect our notions of God, particularly of the Incarnate Lord? If we deny our soul, we implicitly may be denying our God, and we certainly make it more difficult for us to imagine how God can work inside us. While Rahner stresses that God's spirituality and our spirituality are related only analogously (our souls require matter; God does not), this analogous relationship sheds light on how the Spirit dwells within us (as Paul states in Rom. 8:9).[47] And by imagining the Spirit within us, we can also imagine our souls suffusing our bodies. Finally, "soul-speak" is crucial for our thinking about God because of the doctrine of creation. By affirming the reality of the soul, we remind ourselves that God gives us our lives. Sperm and egg cells form the body, but the soul is created by God. Alzheimer's may urge us to contemplate the soul's relationship to aging and dementia, but the creation leads us to appreciate how the soul is related to life itself.

The Heart-Body Mystery

Offering some remarks to the ongoing Christian exploration of the mystery of the soul and how it interacts with our body is the task of this concluding section. While the philosopher's tendency is to phrase discussions of the soul in terms of the mind-body problem, the church may be better served if it reformulates its explorations of the soul into the heart-body mystery. The question of the soul is not just a question of cognitive capacities but also a question of love, of meaning, of freedom, and of chest-thumping faith. After all, we may speak of the Sacred Heart of Jesus, but we do not speak of his Sacred Brain. As God is love, not just mind, the subjects we normally express in terms of the "heart," particularly love, courage, and "hardness of the heart," become central to theology. Hence, speaking of "The Heart-Body Mystery" reminds us that the soul is concerned with all of the broader matters that help describe life's fullness.

Voltaire understood that we approach the question of the soul through faith. This does not mean that we ignore science. It is important to underscore that this is an ongoing speculative enterprise, one which properly respects the discoveries of contemporary science as well as its limits. Brain research is useful as it helps many people recover from injuries and illness, and it also helps us all to appreciate the mysteries of the creation. While I sometimes may seem to oppose science to theology, science may also end up supporting the church's claims; recent empirical investigations into mystical states may well support evidence of a "transcendental ground of self beyond the phenomenal ego."[48] Modern advances in neurology and genetics remind us that we are not pure spirits. Our cognitive and affective lives are interwoven with synapses and molecular strands of DNA. What we call habits are perhaps both pathways of brain neurons established by experience and trained inclinations of the soul. Things do happen in our brain when we fall in love, and these things are supposed to happen because we are psychosomatic unities. Our bodies have been given to us as a gift of the Creator. While some may be envious of the angels, the angels, too, may be envious of our particular joys.

As I have argued above, our will and many of our volitional and thought processes are grounded in the soul, though we cannot exercise our freedom or think apart from our brains—indeed apart from the rest of the organs necessary for life. I believe that because the soul is a desiring soul created for fellowship with God and other creatures, our motivations to love are grounded at least in part here. (God's creative providence works through the body, too, and we may expect that corporeal drives, hormonal secretions, and the like, are also part of how we may enjoy the gifts of God and do his service.) The soul is created in the image of the Triune God, and this nature of self-communicating love seems to describe how our souls were originally meant to direct us. We long to share, to communicate, to give, to receive. Sin, no doubt, has weakened this image and diminished its impelling power. Indeed, in many cases, sin has perverted these inclinations and redirected them to unlawful purposes. Sin is more powerful, I fear, than neurochemistry itself is capable of suggesting.

Of particular concern for a consideration of Alzheimer's disease is the relationship between the soul and memory. As the soul is integral to our identities and to our cognitive functions, it must be also a crucial element of our mnemonic capacities. The case of Alzheimer's patients is instructive for us as we consider how brain and soul interact to form our memories. Currently, we see a person's memories deteriorating because of brain tissue decay. At the same time, we believe that all our memories will be perfected at the resurrection (it will hardly be a resurrection worth praising if the Alzheimer's patient is resurrected in end-stage dementia). Consequently, we see that in this world where our bodies are subject to decay, the mnemonic capacities of the soul must intersect with an imperfect, unreliable corporeal mechanism. At the eschaton, we will experience no such difficulties. Until then, however, we may also hope for divine aid.

Jesus promises that the Holy Spirit will strengthen our memories of his teachings (John 14:26, cf. also 2 Tim. 1:14). Similarly, we pray to God for peace, guidance, and strength. How are we to understand these divine workings? Does the Spirit fire synapses or release chemicals in our brains? Or does the Spirit stir us through the soul, perhaps the way bright sunlight transforms a candle-lit room? The candle of our soul, it may seem, is given increased capacity, an increased capacity from a power which resembles its own nature. (Whether we actually discern the origin of this light correctly and cooperate with this gift or whether we turn our eyes from it are different matters; still, spiritual discernment would seem to be an important issue for hermeneutics.) Metaphors like these are needed to describe the soul's workings since mathematical or literal formulations of the soul may be quite beyond us in this life.

A description of the soul needs to consider not only these discrete affective, moral, and cognitive roles of the soul but also the existence of the soul in its totality. Bruno Bettelheim has shown that the near-systematic mistranslation of Freud's work has obscured Freud's own respect for the *Seele*.[49] To be sure, Freud does not speak of the soul as Gregory of Nyssa does, but he does employ "soul" to indicate the irreducible unity of our rational, mnemonic, willful, and affective lives. Because, perhaps, it is not located in a specific part of the hippocampus or in a certain gland, the *nephesh* or *psyche* describes our lives in a rich, comprehensive unity. But while some may prefer to retain "soul" simply as a metaphor, I believe that we need to acknowledge the soul's actual substantial existence.

Returning to Aristotle may be helpful here, not in order to reestablish a specific metaphysical doctrine of the cosmos, but to remember what is at stake in the notion of such a substantial soul. Aristotle spoke metaphysically of a creature's soul in order to underscore the importance of seeing the creature in its totality as it persists through time. All things experience change, but their substance is what endures (this notion should resonate with the endurance of *durée*). Unlike his predecessors, he refused to reduce living organism to component parts, either to atoms or to the four elements. Rather, his talk of the soul, like his use of natures and essences, was a way of describing the unity and continuity of existence. The soul does naturally interact with and depend upon the brain, intestines, and feet for its vitality, but human personhood is not capable of being dissected completely into discrete parts precisely because of the soul's substantial unifying reality.[50] In his own way, Aristotle is engaging the traditional problem of flux and continuity. Heraclitus had approached this problem through considering whether we can ever enter the same river twice. As we have seen, fluvial imagery has also become central to studies of memory. Rivers and memories change, overflow, recede, become dry. Does our very existence do so as well, or do we persist through time, even through death's sting?

The importance of remembering the soul as a substantial entity is highlighted by the doctrine of the resurrection. Our bodies are to be resurrected, and somehow these perfected bodies will be related to our current ones (beyond what Paul suggests in 1 Corinthians 15, I do not profess to know how). But what happens to us until the resurrection? Do we cease to exist except in the mind of God? Will God recreate Janice Keck *ex nihilo* in her perfected state? Would such a recreated creature truly be the same person? It seems to make much more sense to say that our souls do continue to exist substantially after our deaths. Our memories, which seem to be the primary existential content of who we are, are preserved in the soul. For if each of us is to endure as a distinct person, then our memories will endure as well.

Whether the soul of a deceased person flies off to the bosom of Abraham, or whether prior to the resurrection it clings to atoms of the body like a shipwrecked sailor clings to driftwood until he is rescued (the image is from Gregory of Nyssa), remains a mystery. The next chapter more fully explores death, resurrection, and spiritual survival, but for now I hope that this brief reflection indicates the importance of imagining the substantial soul as the locus of our continuity after death. Indeed, if we look at the Alzheimer's patient in this light, we see that his soul, while currently constrained by a decaying brain, still retains the fullness of his life. His memories have not been lost; they are still part of him. Moreover, we may also wonder if the soul of even an end-stage patient still perceives its environment as you or I would, even if he cannot communicate this, act upon it, or even be aware of it in this life; the implications for caregivers are enormous.

Ultimately, how are we to understand the "integrative dualism" which I believe best describes the psychosomatic unity of humanity? There are many options, each of which might well prove to be faithful. For some, the quantum world and its discovery of the vast amounts of "space" in the cosmos may create a vehicle for understanding the nexus of a non-material soul and the corporeal body. Harvey Cox thus suggests that African traditions and their "primal spirituality" may be more in line with quantum theory than "Western critical theology." The Orthodox, who seem not to have been as influenced by a radical distinction between the "natural" and "supernatural" realms as the West, may also provide help. For them, the spiritual and material are seen as parts of a continuous reality not discontinuous segments. Hence, Taliaferro acknowledges his kinship with the church Fathers in his discussion of the "interrelated but distinct realities of both the material and the immaterial." Similarly, Rahner speaks of spirit and matter as "mutually correlative, nonseparable constitutive elements of the one created reality" which are linked both in the creation, in history itself, and in the resurrection.[51]

I do not believe that we need to be precise in our conception of the soul and its relationship to the physical world. Metaphors may be particularly useful since a good metaphor will be evocative. As I have tried to show, imagining the soul is important devotionally, and our devotional lives need all the stirring they can receive. Some may wish to think of the soul in terms of energy or electrical charges. Some may prefer to conjure the image of a ghost, a phantasm which looks like us but is ethereal. Light, too, suggests itself, especially because of its rich links to illumination, warmth, and stimulation. However we construe the soul, it needs to incorporate many, many aspects of our lives and our relationship to God.

Ultimately, if we understood in precise detail how the soul and body interact, we would understand the mysteries of our freedom, love, and sin. As the title of the chapter suggests, the heart-body mystery may better be seen more as a matter of grammar than of science. That is, we want to know how our souls as part of the substantial basis of our personhood are integrated with our loving, forgiving, knowing, and doing. I hope that this chapter has suggested the grammatical relations of the soul. More importantly, we need to remember how the soul is the locus of God's own loving, sustaining, healing, and resurrecting. For when we speak of the special human soul, it is not our powers that we celebrate, but the gifts of God which we praise.

Chapter 5

Death and Resurrection, Praise and Paradise

> For I am sure that neither death, nor life, nor angels,
> nor principalities . . . will be able to separate us
> from the love of God in Christ Jesus our Lord.
> — Romans 8:38-39

Julius Caesar, who suffered from what had been called the "sacred disease" (epilepsy), was said to have had his wish fulfilled when he received a swift death, albeit at the hands of the hostile Senators and his erstwhile friend, Brutus. According to Suetonius, his last gesture was to cover himself with his robe so that "he would die with both legs decently covered."[1] By contrast, the dying of Alzheimer's patients is a prolonged process of continual deterioration and the loss of any such Cesarean dignity and self-awareness. What does the church have to say about this form of death and dying? Indeed, what does it have to say about all of our deaths? Moreover, how is the church to respond not only to death but also to the caregiver's prolonged experience of the dying? As I have tried to confront the disease as it ravages my mother, there is one subject which continually seizes my spirit and shakes me as violently as the spasms shake her. It is the subject which is the basis for my hope for her, indeed for all of us, and it is the subject which makes it possible for me to write this work at all. It is the resurrection.

In many different personal expressions, Christian writers on death bear witness to the centrality of the resurrection. Offering an evocative metaphor, Henri Nouwen states that "To write about death and dying without mentioning the resurrection is like writing about sailing without mentioning the wind."[2] But the wind is an uneven and unpredictable creature, and Nouwen himself suggests that the resurrection of Jesus is difficult both to fathom and to preach. Although Nicholas Wolterstorff in his *Lament for a Son* declares that he did not find much consolation in the resurrection, it is clear that his work, too, could not have been written without this teaching of the church. Indeed he himself looks forward to embracing his son once again, and he anticipates being able to share and ask for forgiveness with us all.[3] The lesson seems clear—despite the difficulties and ambivalence which many of us face, the resurrection remains, in the language of 1 Peter 3:15, the basis for our account of the hope that is in us. This chapter, then, considers this basis in the specific context of the challenges of Alzheimer's disease.

The first section, "Resurrection, Present and Past," provides both a review of the fundamental teachings of the church concerning the resurrection and also a brief assessment of where the subject is now in contemporary Christian thought. There are many theologians today who write about sailing without mentioning the wind, and it will be of some use to examine why this is so and how the church might best respond. The second section, "Caregiving and Resurrection," examines how the resurrection is crucial for understanding caregiving. The third section, "Death, Dying, and Alzheimer's Disease," seeks to describe what the church can and ought to be saying about dying and death. The church does have a unique, central reference point for discussing these mysteries. Unlike Julius Caesar, the man who died on the Cross (nailed to the wood by Romans and betrayed by an erstwhile friend) died a slow, agonizing death. Like many who die in nursing homes, he, in the language of Isaiah 53:3, died despised and rejected, and this is not without significance for us all. The fourth section, "Death, Praise, and the Church," considers dying and death from the perspective of the caregivers. How can the church minister to the caregivers in such a situation? How can the church's teachings about death and resurrection fortify caregivers?

Oddly, perhaps, through praise. Wolterstorff stresses the importance of respecting the "dynamics of each person's sorrow" and of not blithely proclaiming God's goodness to a grieving parent. Comfort for him would come from shared presence on his mourning bench. For my part, I feel slightly differently. I cannot help but confess that as I experience my mother's deterioration what I long for most is to hear the message of joy and glad tidings. I can only hope that my call for active, vigorous church proclamation and praise will be found to be useful for some. When celebrating the horrible event of the Cross, we all become—especially as we cry our Hosannas—members of "the company of mourners" who share one great bench.[4]

Caesar's death led first to a brutal civil war, and then to the rule of Caesar Augustus (who declared the enrollment which brought Joseph and Mary to Bethlehem). By contrast, Christ's imprisonment and death evoked denial, desolation, and doubt, and his resurrection led to quite a different rule. When confronted with the challenges of Alzheimer's, how can we not praise the Easter event and proclaim its promise?

To conclude our treatment of what the church can and should say about dying and death in Alzheimer's disease, we must consider what actually happens to patients after they die. Julius Caesar was deified after his death by an imperial cult eager to legitimate its rule. In language more familiar to the Orthodox, we, too, are to be deified, though our deification is wrought by him who needs no justification.[5] Hence, one of the central sources of the caregiver's strength may well be her expectations and hopes for paradise. An imaginative exploration of what the next life might be like is not a theological discourse but a useful devotional exercise. It is exercise just as lifting weights and running are; it strengthens the person and prepares her for greater feats. Because end-stage Alzheimer's patients are deprived of the ability to confront their own deaths with dignity and faith, caregivers and the church need to do the dying vicariously for the patients. For this task, they need the strength that comes from imagining the resurrection and its glories.

Resurrection, Present and Past

Describing his seminary days at the beginning of the century, Reinhold Niebuhr in *Beyond Tragedy* states that the credal formulations about the resurrection of body were "an offense and a stumbling block to young theologians."[6] Despite the fact that Johannes Weiss' and Albert Schweitzer's insights regarding the eschatological character of Jesus' own ministry have been widely accepted, traditional eschatology, now seen to belong essentially to primitive Christianity, "appears unintelligible to the modern mind."[7] Hans Küng's *Eternal Life?* reads as a painful, sustained, uphill struggle to make its subject matter even vaguely fathomable. A disinterest in the resurrection is especially sad in the case of pastoral theology, since one would expect that pastoral theologians would have the most to say to Alzheimer's patients and caregivers. Thus John Patton, in his treatment of death in *Pastoral Care in Context*, is able to read Barth and

131

the church Fathers in such a way as to ignore completely their treatment of the resurrection.[8] Because the Kingdom of God is sometimes understood in purely this-worldly terms, "resurrection" can be interpreted in purely political categories. For Carter Heyward, resurrection "is a relational movement, the revolutionary carrying-on of a spirit of love and justice that does not and will not die."[9] Glenn Weaver wisely sees that senile dementia evokes a renewed emphasis on the resurrection, but, in my opinion, he backs away from the crucial eschatological dimension of the doctrine.[10] I find myself to be like the professor in C. S. Lewis' *The Lion, the Witch, and the Wardrobe* as he asked, "What are they teaching them in the schools these days?"

It is hardly surprising that people might have doubts about the resurrection since, as Paul Hessert has argued in *Christ and the End of Meaning*, the idea of resurrection may well entail a rejection of all of our easily-accepted, socially-conditioned ways of thinking. Since the resurrection may lead us to a mode-of-being not yet experienced (to borrow a phrasing from the phenomenologists), should we not be open to the fact that our criteria of meaning and importance might be thoroughly inadequate? The resurrection is a stripping away of all of life's accretions and acquisitions. It is a reminder that we do not have the boundless freedom to make and remake the cosmos and ourselves according to the *Zeitgeist*. It entails a redefinition of poverty and personhood—that we become persons when we acknowledge our abject poverty apart from God.[11] No wonder the resurrection is unpopular. No wonder we should approach this mystery with a certain amount of trepidation.

Modern theologians of different inclinations have been arguing over the historical bodily resurrection of Jesus for quite some time now, and the issues have become fairly clear. The differences between Barth, Bultmann, Pannenberg, and others can be discovered in the original texts or in briefer reviews.[12] One of the insights from these modern debates, however, suggests that our modern problem of doubt and disbelief (and its concomitant reformulation of eschatological themes) is not a modern problem at all. In response to Bultmann's assertion that Christian faith preceded the resurrection, Barth argued that the context of the apostolic experience of the resurrection was anything but faith.[13] Rather when their Lord reappeared, they were agonizing over what to do now that Jesus had been taken from them and crucified. The very first resurrection was a resurrection in the midst of doubt. Similarly, Paul's reception at

Athens, as described in Acts 17:32, suggests that from earliest times, the doctrine of the resurrection of the body received mockery. Even some of the earliest Christian communities expressed serious reservations about this teaching, as 1 Corinthians 15 reveals.

Paul clearly understood the issues and implications involved in the historical resurrection of Christ and the promised resurrection of the faithful. He understood that no amount of sophistication or equivocation can avoid the fundamental, humbling either/or of the resurrection. There is no doubt for him that a Christian's faith entirely depends on the resurrection of Jesus and the resurrection of believers:

> But if there is no resurrection of the dead, then Christ has not been raised; if Christ has not been raised, then our preaching is in vain and your faith is in vain. We are even found to be misrepresenting God, because we testified of God that he raised Christ, whom he did not raise if it is true that the dead are not raised. . . . If Christ has not been raised, your faith is futile and you are still in your sins. Then those who have fallen asleep in Christ have perished. If for this life only we have hoped in Christ, we are of all men most to be pitied. (1 Cor. 15:13-19)

Why are we to be so pitied? We remain unredeemed from sins; death's sting still triumphs; we have blasphemed; and, as Paul reminds by quoting Isaiah 22:13 ("Let us eat and drink, for tomorrow we die" [15:32]), we have been wasting our precious time. There are other belief systems and ways of living, and without the resurrection of Christ, would-be Christians have no particularly compelling reason to follow a rather pathetic figure like Jesus. That Paul approaches this subject negatively—through a discussion of the consequences of denying it—suggests that it is not simple to believe. Still, the terms for the Corinthians may resonate with Alzheimer's families. If there was no resurrection of Jesus and there will be no resurrection of the dead, what then can we say about what will happen to Alzheimer's patients? Only after the resurrection of the body has been confirmed in the epistle can Paul ask, "O, Death, where is thy victory? O, Death, where is thy sting?" (1 Cor. 15:55).

Not only does Paul's framing of the problem seem accurate for Christian belief as a whole, but his formulation also seems particularly true for a Christian consideration of the Kingdom of God. Any attempts to construct an exclusively this-worldly Kingdom of God or eschatology seem incapable of addressing the phenomena of

133

Alzheimer's disease. It is hard for me to see how a person who has lost the capacity to speak, feed herself, and go to the bathroom can be said to be experiencing or participating in the Kingdom of God. Political and existential theologies are in need of modification for people who do not meet the criteria for their theologies, and these criteria include self-consciousness and agency, things which are not available to all. Being called into the present Kingdom of God does describe caregiving. Those who articulate the immanence of the Kingdom do recognize that we can participate in God's reign even now. As Peter Carnley stresses, belief in the resurrection is part of our present experience of the living Christ.[14] But the immanent present remains inadequate for patients.

But we have yet to answer the question, When faced with fundamental teachings which are not easily accepted by contemporaries, what then should Christians and the church do? At these times, more than ever, it seems to me that Christians should strive to proclaim the fullness, the depth, and the richness of the great Gospel message. In his survey of modern views of the resurrection, Gerald O'Collins uses the term "underbelief" to describe the way in which teachings are altered into acceptability. "Rather than what they appear to mean, these propositions must mean something which *can* be believed—something less than a personal resurrection for Jesus himself."[15] As the term underbelief suggests, approaches such as Bultmann's simply leave so much out. I imagine underbelief concerning the resurrections of Christ and the dead to be similar to a performance of Handel's "Hallelujah Chorus" in which only the alto part is sung. There are no deep basses, no high sopranos, and the booming horns and vigorous strings are also absent. The same words are there, but the presentation would be clearly inadequate.

In light of Alzheimer's we come to recognize that we sometimes must do the believing for others. As we assume this heavy responsibility, we should consider that we have a particular responsibility not to underbelieve. That is, as we bear the fullness of a person through the last years of dementia, so too should we bear the abundance of the resurrection and God's work for us. Not everyone can bear this plenitude—as either a caregiver or a Christian—but, as caregivers strive to sustain the fullness of a person, so should the body of Christ seek to bear the fullness of his work. As the church encourages the caregivers in their labors, so too should the church encourage believers in their faith in the resurrection.

Caregiving and Resurrection

The Christian idea of resurrection has implications beyond propositions about what happens to the dead. This belief requires that we are faithful only when we view and respond to resurrection in all its dimensions.[16] Whenever we struggle against the ever-threatening victory of sin and death, such as when we become caregivers, we are participating properly in the work of God. Considering caregiving in the light of both the resurrection and Alzheimer's disease, however, suggests that there are certain aspects of the resurrection which become particularly important. In this disease, especially in the later stages, we too readily see the patient as non-person (to paraphrase the title of one of Paul Ramsey's books). The distinctive appearances of individual personhood dissolve, and increasingly we ask what capacities the creature still has. Can she still feed herself? Can she still read? And all of this because of a deterioration of the body. This disease makes the second-century taunt of Celsus that Christians are "philosomatics" (lovers of the body) seem cruel indeed.

Thus, the central motif of the resurrection which is striking for Alzheimer's disease is not liberation, or the struggle against death's power, or the in-breaking of the Kingdom of God (though these are all important). Rather, it is what the resurrection says about the body itself. Both this doctrine and the idea of the Incarnation reveal that Christians are to have a profound respect for our physical stuff. As anyone who looks in the mirror after holiday bingeing or before going out on a date understands, bodiliness is not always an easy thing to accept. As Carolyn Walker Bynum argues, the duality between body as "locus of pain and limitation, and body as locus not merely of pleasure but of personhood itself" is a "duality in the Western tradition more profound than gender."[17] It is hardly surprising the Christian tradition exhibits both aspects of this tension.

The resurrection is not only about our current bodies but also about human futurity. To paraphrase an Orthodox theologian, human beings are creatures whose roots are in the future.[18] That is, we cannot understand humanity apart from our resurrected corporeal, glorified state. As the inescapable realities of Alzheimer's and birth defects underscore, the bodiliness of all human persons as a gift from God cannot be conceived apart from the new bodies given to us in the resurrection. The martyrs, I think, understood this quite well, and they have been willing to endure torture, dismemberment, and death because they anticipate a new, incorruptible body. Although we do not yet experience this glorification and our incorruptible bodies, we are to recognize that our anticipations impinge on our present. As Paul writes in Romans 6:3-11, being baptized into Christ's death and resurrection means being baptized into both a future resurrection and present responsibilities. Thus, when we seek to understand caregiving for Alzheimer's patients, we must look backwards from the perspective of our future bodies to the present state of seeking to live our new lives in the body of Christ which is part of human history.

Reinhold Niebuhr argued that the doctrine of the resurrection and the body provided the crucial link between Christianity and history and human society. The contrasting Greek worldview which stressed the immortality of the soul led to a bifurcation between the spiritual and the social or political. It is in the body-soul unity, he argued, that humans could recognize and participate in the dialectic between now and eternity. Christians anticipated immortality but only as they participated responsibly in the particular cultures in which they found themselves.[19] But the body of an Alzheimer's patient is what is inexorably separating them from history and society. It is the deterioration of the brain that makes it impossible for the patient to even know what the year is or who their friends are. Hence, the task for caregiving is in part to commit oneself to the losing struggle to keep the patient within history and in her personal community for as long as possible. Just as Christ devoted his whole life and body to us, this endeavor of keeping the person in contact with the world can overwhelm the Alzheimer's caregiver totally and in practice force them to endure lives in seclusion.

In providing for an Alzheimer's patient, the caregiver ultimately will assume nearly complete responsibilities for the patient's body. The patient is no longer able to perform the basic functions of corporeal life, and the responsibility for maintaining this body devolves to someone else. As with a babe, every physical detail of the person becomes your responsibility—combing the hair, choosing clothes, brushing teeth, even physical therapy, all this and more. As a problem particularly well-known to those who have accepted many difficult responsibilities of caregiving illustrates, maintaining the dignity of the body with Alzheimer's cases can be a frightening challenge. When feeding a patient, her spasms or disorientation could make her spit out her food. Although bibs catch most of it, inevitably some stains her garments. Since such a simple task as changing a shirt can produce anxiety or even pain in a patient, a caregiver must decide at what point a change of clothes is appropriate for a person's appearance. Such appearance is not merely cosmetic. Rather it is an issue of the dignity of the person. Hence, there may be a literal struggle to sustain a person's dignity if she does not or cannot cooperate in changing clothes.

As the patient's faculties decline and as the person is less seen by the public, it becomes "easier" to be less attentive to detail, and yet it is clear that this is precisely where the loving attention to detail is so important. Christ's commandment to love even enemies at times may seem easier (they, at least, will respond) than delicately arranging the hair of someone who appears not to notice. Because of the commandments to love and honor our fathers and mothers, we cannot simply accept the duties of caregiving with a resigned Stoicism. The love that accompanies the act of feeding is as important as the perfunctory performance of the task itself. But how can this be sustained in the face of apparent dissolution, hostility, paranoia, or even indifference? It may be that we need to anticipate their future expressions of love and thanksgiving, something we will experience only when we, too, die.

Supporting this Herculean (or better, Samsonian) task of the caregivers is one of the ways in which non-caregivers can most clearly fulfill their call to join the body of Christ. In 1 Corinthians 12, Paul describes the diversity of the body's parts as a way of describing the different gifts of the Spirit and tasks of diverse Christians. So too can we see that those who come by for visits with caregivers, perhaps bringing home-made soup, or who serve as part-time caregivers in their different roles help to form the body of Christ into which Christians are baptized. These seemingly simple tasks (which require so much effort and are not done so frequently) help make us one, just as the pumping of the heart and each action of the digits, glands, and cells make each body one. Christian life and doctrines are not just about individual lives but lives lived together. With good reason, Schleiermacher considered the resurrection not only from the standpoint of individual personal survival but also from the corporate perspective, from the perspective of the "consummation of the church."[20]

Death, Dying, and Alzheimer's Disease

What is death? What happens when we die? How should we die? These are crucial questions for patients and caregivers, questions which need good answers. But discussing death is not easy today. The replacement of the traditional Christian understanding of death (death as the wages of sin) by death as a purely natural process is one of the most important reasons why it is harder today to speak theologically of death and dying. (I will return to the crucial link between sin and mortality in the next chapter.) In several works (e.g., *Suffering Presence*), Stanley Hauerwas has argued that American medical science, despite its revitalization of the field of ethics, has made it particularly difficult for Christians to write about death, and hence also about life. Because of our modern obsession with technological cures and our absolutizing of the sanctity of life, death becomes harder and harder to accept. That people now die more frequently in hospitals and nursing homes also tends to distance us from the process of dying; we hide from our eyes this seemingly alien phenomenon.[21] I cannot remember ever hearing a sermon about how to die well.

Still, the Christian tradition does have great resources for talking about death and dying. For example, the medieval period, a period sensitive to the fact that popes and peasants both would join the Dance of Death, produced many treatises on the art of dying. Modern authors, too, have valuable words. Küng, for example, concentrates on the theme of death with dignity. In particular, because of Christ's work, men and women no longer need to fear the end of their mortal lives. The struggle for health can be maintained without torment and desperation. Indeed, confidence, freedom, and prayer replace anxiety, bondage, and technology.[22] Similarly, Hauerwas examines the "Christian way of death" and observes that a dying person, too, has obligations to die well. That is, a person should recognize that "death creates the economy that makes life worthwhile."[23] Because of our mortality, we must learn to accept the responsibility for valuing some things higher than others. Consequently, when we recognize the new relationship to death brought about by Christ, we can recognize that the way we die should be, in some sense, a profession of faith, trust, and love.

But such options are not available to the end-stage Alzheimer's patient. Dignity is hardly a word which comes to mind when viewing a person in the extreme stages of the disease, and such a person can hardly be able to die responsibly. At least one Alzheimer's patient turned to Jack Kevorkian, and it is easy to see why. No one wants to deteriorate, and no one wants to see their families endure such horror. The slow end to consciousness which Alzheimer's brings evokes a desire to end consciousness swiftly. In considering death and dying with this disease, then, we are faced with the same dilemma confronting philosophers and theologians who are doing their work entrapped by the turn to the subject. Our language about death and dying well assumes a rational, responsible subject, and that is something we can hardly assume here.

Consequently, the Christian communities of the patients have to do the dying for them. Just as a person is baptized in the presence of the entire church and just as the congregation may be asked to assume religious responsibilities for the babe, so too may Alzheimer's caregivers rightly ask that a congregation accept responsibility for helping the person die well. As in infant baptism, the powerlessness of the babe (or here, the patient) is just as we all are before God. Responsibility for our families' bodies and persons can be total, and *having responsibility for* is inseparable from *being at one with*. Luther, in a synthetic exegetical insight, links the union of two bodies in marriage (Gen. 2:24) with the possession of Christ's righteousness by the sinner.[24] Caregivers tending to their spouses are already one flesh, just as we are all united in one body in Christ, just as the sinner possesses Christ's righteousness. Seen in these terms, it becomes possible to see how we can die for others by vicariously helping them to die well; we are already living for others and for Christ.

It may seem curious that the many different types of death which Christians face—accidents, disease, war, famine, aging—should all be related to the singular death of one man. Still, we are all, as Paul observes in Romans 6:3, baptized into Christ's death. (It may seem, too, that Alzheimer's patients and many others who die "despised and rejected" have a particular claim to dying with Christ.) It is important to underscore the diversity of the Gospel accounts of Christ's passion and death—for in this one death of the New Adam can be seen many aspects of our different deaths. As we cannot appreciate a Rodin statue from any one perspective, as we have to move around it and see the ways in which the interplay of bronze, texture, and light affects the sculpture, so too should we read the four Gospel accounts together in their totality if we are to begin to fathom this singular event.

So many different themes become woven together in these narratives—the completion of Christ's teaching; the glorification of the Father; the political dimension of Jesus' claims; the Eucharist; the fulfillment of prophecies; betrayal—that it would be a bit much for us to expect any one narrative to incorporate them all. These different aspects of the passion and death are perhaps better seen as expansively suggestive rather than as a cause for historical-critical concern. Suetonius and Plutarch provide different accounts of Julius Caesar's death, but since he became a god only after he died, we have no need to view the discrepancies as having any theological significance.

The different dimensions which I find so striking are the accounts of the last words Jesus speaks on the Cross. In Mark and Matthew Jesus is deeply human, uttering a cry of desolation. In Luke, having promised the crucified robber Paradise, he is fully trusting of the Father—his cry is loud but it is not of despair. That Luke includes the eclipse of the sun suggests that the cosmos is not indifferent to Christ's death (and ours). In John, too, he reveals his humanity. Only this time, he exhibits his love for others with his words to those at his feet. When he gives up his Spirit, he does so fully cognizant that his work has been done. He is not a Stoic, but he exhibits a profound acceptance even as he continues to fulfill prophecies. Together these diverse accounts bear witness to the fullness of Jesus' humanity and to the possibility of our being baptized into his singular death. The particular deaths of the rest of us are encompassed in the death of the New Adam. Thus, artistic depictions of the crucifixion vary enormously, from an El Greco painting of a pallorous Jesus to Byzantine mosaics worked in gold.

A Christian proclamation of death begins here. Here we see fully the horror and despair of dying; we see the importance of trusting God as we close our eyes for the last time; we see our responsibilities to our families and loved ones as they behold us; and we recognize the centrality of Christ's work for our own ability to die. These aspects of death appear contradictory, as the accounts do. But as the church accepted these narratives as her own, so too did it accept the fullness of Jesus' witness to death. As we accept these accounts we also accept, in the words of Flannery O'Connor "our own slow participation" in Christ's death.[25] Because the church has embraced these narratives, we embrace gratefully Christ's willingness to die well, and we recognize our own responsibility, too. Christ's faithful death makes ours possible. It also makes it possible to do the dying for another. Thus, at Christmas time, families may give presents to each other in the name of patients. Caregivers bear the person's presence, doing things the patient would have done if he were able.

We are left, then, with the problem of what actually happens in death. Hauerwas, following Paul Ramsey's lead, argues that theologically, the church has no real definition of the moment of death (similarly, Pius XII in "The Prolongation of Life" declared that doctors properly were to determine this).[26] The important theological and ethical problem is not of establishing precisely the moment of death but of proclaiming what happens next. The whole point of our shared Christian story is that life does not end on the Cross, a hospital bed, a battlefield, or indeed anywhere. Hauerwas concentrates on the fundamental revelation of God's nature. He follows Romans 8:35-9 and observes that the Christian message says quite forcefully that nothing, not even death, can separate us from the love of God.[27] Much follows from this, especially our continued existence.

If it is hard for us to imagine what happens when we die, it is harder to imagine that God's eternal love for his creation will be like the way we might remember a dear uncle: "He was a great guy when he was around. I miss him." God's eternal love has real, existent beings as its object—us, and consequently through Christ he makes us immortal. God's enduring love will not be frustrated, not even by human sin, not even by death. In the conclusion of this chapter, we will offer some suggestive descriptions of what God's sustaining love has prepared for us in the life to come. We will seek not so much formal, dogmatic propositions but rather "stimulating expressions" of Christian beliefs which will fortify us in the times of weakness which Alzheimer's brings.[28] But first, we must remind ourselves of why the church can preach glad tidings even to those who suffer and grieve.

Death, Praise, and Church Preaching

The source of the churches' capacity to preach about death with gratitude, joy, and praise lies primarily in the resurrection of Jesus Christ, but preaching about this subject to a grieving family can be difficult, even counter-productive. Several authors have observed that the resurrection of Jesus as an exercise of omnipotence too easily fails to do justice to the suffering produced by mortality, a witness to impotence.[29] A cold corpse seems more tangible, more wrenching, than talk of an empty tomb.

At the same time, the grievers' sense of guilt and sinfulness regarding their failures to love the deceased are a potent force wracking suffering spirits. In the case of Alzheimer's caregivers, this may well be heightened, as the loved one may have died in a cold, alien institution. Even during regular visits, the unfeigned love which Paul commends as a mark of a servant of God in 2 Corinthians 6:6 may seem impossible. Although Jesus seems to have been capable of loving those who did not return his love, this is not easy for all. Caregivers may feel that indeed "fault may be found with our ministry" (2 Cor. 6:3). Now, especially, the churches' proclamations about the work of the Cross and the tomb—the great work of love, forgiveness, and reconciliation—are needed.

The question becomes: How can Christians help make it possible for sufferers to hear this Good News? How can the church maintain its mission of praise and worship in the midst of death and suffering? The Cross provides a focal point for reflection on human suffering; the empty tomb offers a message of the end of grief and death. And the Christian message requires us to contemplate the two together. Similarly, the Trinitarian confessions of the church require us to keep in mind not only Jesus but also his Father and the Spirit. By holding these events and divine Persons in mind simultaneously—by refusing to concentrate single-mindedly on any one of these, the church's message about death can become communicable to contemporary men and women of sorrows. It is primarily through the recognition of the grief and the loss of the Father that the churches can preach the message of the resurrection without being glib. Moreover, the church, too, has experienced the loss of a beloved. The disciples lost Jesus, indeed we all lost our Lord, and hence the church preaches as fellow-mourners

Several books have already developed these themes quite well. Arthur C. McGill's *Suffering: A Test of Theological Method* returns to the controversy between Athanasius and the Arians over the Trinity and argues that this debate reveals the basis for understanding God's love, salvific work, and indeed his salvific grief.[30] The Arians held that the essence of divinity was absoluteness, omnipotence, and a certain impassivity. Athanasius (and ultimately the church) rejected these arguments because he recognized the decisive characteristic of divinity was total, self-giving love. Such a God could not be solitary.

Such a God required a plurality of Persons who could each give and share this love. Although God is indeed omnipotent, it is the Triune dynamic of mutual love and giving that forms the true basis for vitality and existence. As a consequence of this view of divinity, Jesus' mission becomes a mission of service not power. As the Son loves and serves the Father, so too does he love and serve humanity. And as the Father loves humanity, so is he willing to allow the Son to die for our sakes. The passion and crucifixion become an interruption in the dynamism of divine love and sharing. As we feel emptied when a beloved dies, so should we remember the great emptiness of the Father and Spirit, an emptiness willingly undertaken for our sakes.

Nicholas Wolterstorff's loss of his own son led him to recognize the suffering of the loving God for the first time. He says that he had always confessed that the man on the Cross was "very God from very God," but that he had never really seen, never fully fathomed what this means: "Instead of explaining our suffering, God shares it." This is a profound insight into the Triune God who not only became the Man of Sorrows for our sakes but who also suffers through the daily exercise of our fallenness. Toward the end of his *Lament*, Wolterstorff ponders what the resurrection might be like and how, indeed whether, God will be able to pull it off. In an admission of the divine suffering of the Father, Wolterstorff is able to imagine God saying to him, "But remember, I made all this and raised my Son from the dead, so. . . ."[31] The divine loss of Jesus' death and the divine love in his resurrection become the basis for making the resurrection credible. We shall see shortly that God's word "remember" is central to this preaching of the resurrection at times of grief.

Nicholas Peter Harvey's *Death's Gift* examines the grief of the apostles as the key to preaching the Christian message about death, bereavement, and hope. Written in the context of this fundamental concern for how to make the church's teachings relevant to mourners, Harvey's book mines the Gospel accounts for a vision of how Mary and the disciples responded to that great loss. In their stories we can see that the Cross and resurrection story is not simply the narrative of God's work but also of human bereavement. Harvey speculates,

> How many people . . . have been bruised or repelled by being glibly told that all is well because the Lord is risen, without any suggestion of either the heights or depths through which the disciples went in

being brought to the point where they could joyfully make that salvific proclamation.[32]

In the first section of this chapter, we noted that the resurrected Lord did not appear to eager Christians. Rather, he appeared to a confused and despairing group. Most of us are like Thomas when we confront the death of someone we love: at that moment, more than ever, we want to put our finger on the wound of the resurrected Lord. Many of us need that, and we need to recognize that.

It is in the context of the grieving Father and the bereaved disciples and Mary that the church can undertake the ministry to those who lose someone they love. As Harvey and McGill have shown, the church is a community which should understand itself fundamentally in terms of both grief and joy. Moreover, the proclamation of the Kingdom of God is a reminder that death is not a private but a communal affair.[33] As such, its mission to the grieving is not an alien mission, but one at which the church and the grieving should feel at home.

There are many different forms of ministry for Christians in times of mourning. The simplest acts of individual people are often the most powerful. Bringing home-cooked food to the bereaved family has always struck me as a quietly beautiful deed. It reaffirms the love between friends and provides some small but distinct opportunity for pleasure and relief. It affords an occasion for the grieving to say, should they want to, "Please, have a seat." This simple act says forcefully to the mourners, "You are remembered." But in addition to the many other possible acts individuals can do, I want to address two central roles for the church as an institution: remembering and praise.

As the church is understood through its own memory of Christ's work, so too is the mission to the grieving a mission of memory. Especially in the case of Alzheimer's disease, the church should feel rather sharply the importance of remembering the person. The most significant vehicle for remembering the dead is prayer. At my school, Ateneo de Manila University, I am struck by the way in which announcements about a person's death conclude: "Please offer a prayer for the repose of her soul." The members of the community, which is essentially Roman Catholic, are asked to give some moments of their time for the deceased just as we are asked to pray for people while they are sick. Through the continued prayer for a deceased person, the church affirms that the person is still alive. However we understand the beatific vision or the resurrection, I believe we can be confident that the dead will come to know of our prayers for them and be comforted. Such prayer affirms that our responsibilities as caregivers do not cease. Prayer then is not just a mental act of memory and commemoration. It is a real work of the soul which links the living, the dead, and their God. It is a real work of caregiving. (We may add, that in the churches which believe in intercessory saints, caregiving prayer is offered both for the dead and by the dead—the deceased, too, are caregivers.)

The second role for the church which I wish to highlight is its most fundamental role of proclamation and praise. For Jesus' passion, death, and resurrection are not only models for understanding and sharing grief, they are also the means whereby God reconciles us with himself. Our story of ultimate sorrows is inseparable from our story of joy and gratitude. The phenomena of Alzheimer's, as I have argued, make our own sinfulness and limitations quite apparent. It can render the caregiver helpless before a demented mother or father. In the latter stages of the disease, it becomes clear that no human reconciliation will be possible. Then more than ever the caregiver needs to hear what the church has to say about sin and death, love and reconciliation. But how can the Gospel call to praise be preached if it is so hard to hear in the midst of grief?

Formulating the question in this way may be part of the problem. William James' observations about the "sick soul" and melancholy suggest that grief, anxiety, uncertainty are some of the sources of our most profound religious experiences.[34] When we are no longer satisfied with quotidian answers to mysterious problems, we become capable of fathoming mysterious answers. Suffering, loss, and disorientation may not be so much obstacles to hearing as sources for understanding. James contrasted the sick soul with the religion of healthy-mindedness, an optimistic religious mentality incapable of bearing sustained suffering. The sick soul describes a person who cannot experience joy, a person overwhelmed by sorrow, sinfulness, and fear. Such persons "cannot swiftly throw off the burden of the consciousness of evil but are congenitally fated to suffer from its presence."[35] Such a description applies to many Alzheimer's caregivers. For years, they will witness the apparent evil of human dissolution in their beloveds, and they will come to know all too well their own mortal limits and sinfulness. They may recognize that despite its appeal, the religion of healthy-mindedness is inadequate. They are in a position to tell us that a pastoral theology of healthy-mindedness—a theology and a church life which does not admit of the reality of sin, suffering, evil, and death—may not be well received.

James observed that while the pessimism of the sick soul was deep, so too was its capacity for joy and rapture—for such a soul has (to paraphrase John 1:7) born witness to the darkness before it sees that (to quote John 1:5 directly), "The light shines in the darkness, and the darkness has not overcome it." Perhaps it is because of this intimate tie between human sorrow and comprehension of the Triune God's love that many Gospel songs are able to sing about human wretchedness so joyfully. The songwriters have learned that because of God's work, sin and death cannot be separated from life or from jubilation. Grieving, suffering souls may no longer be satisfied with what Gerald O'Collins has labeled "underbelief." Such persons, by contrast, may be prepared to pass from a healthy-minded underbelief to the plenitude of Christian belief.

It is when I contemplate what is happening to my mother and my own sinfulness that I most want to hear the church praising God for his terrible redemptive work. When I contemplate the dissolution of my mother's memories and the apparent disintegration of her person, I want to hear all about the resurrection. I also want to hear about what paradise might be like. I want to know how my mother's voice will add to the Hosannas of the angelic chorus; I want to know what she will be sharing. In some sense, it is easier for me to hear about her salvation through the Cross when I am suffering than when I am not. For when I am suffering, I sense that the Man of Sorrows' pains humble me—both because his were greater and because they were for my sake. When I am in a pleasant mood, it is hard for me to hear of the Cross, for then I am shamed. But whether I feel shame or humility, I seek to make my next response one of gratitude, for I should not wallow in my own emotions but recognize that God's suffering evokes something from me. That is, I sense infidelity—which is worse than being humbled or shamed—when I fail to praise God for what he has wrought. I desperately need help praising God for these things; this to me is clear. This is where I sense most clearly my need for the church's praise and proclamation. My voice of praise is weakened by grief—can the church not help strengthen it? Can I not find solace in knowing that even as my voice falters in church, the community's singing of the Hallelujah Chorus continues?

These—praise, God's own suffering and death, the church as a sustaining and grieving community—are the central contexts for the churches' proclamations to Alzheimer's caregivers and, in many respects, to us all. As Wolterstorff testifies, as I myself have experienced in limited ways, and as Harvey records for many others—it is through the loss of a loved one that we sometimes begin to understand what we mean when we recite the creeds. Harvey observes,

> The issue is the life-giving, releasing, affirmatory quality of dying, of death and of bereavement in the spirit of Christ. Each person being unique, each death and each bereavement accepted in his spirit becomes a contribution to the building-up of the body of Christ. This acceptance has nothing to do with mere resignation, everything to do with the creative power of God "bringing into being the things that are not," both in the dying and the bereaved.[36]

Bereavement in the spirit of Christ brings about new understandings just as the resurrection of Christ brought about new understandings of Jesus and his teachings to the disciples (John 2:19-22). As Paul recognized, when we are baptized into Christ, we can no longer look at things from a purely human point of view. This is true, too, when we do the dying for others with Christ.

That the proclamation of Christ's saving work needs to be preached powerfully, vigorously, is underscored by William James' observation about the salvation of the sick soul—"the deliverance must come in as strong a form as the complaint."[37] The Gospel narratives *are* powerful, but do churches do justice to the grief of the Father, the Holy Spirit, Mary, and the disciples? In the language developed in chapter 2, how can the churches help us to *zkr* or "actualize" their sorrow? There I observed that Biblical writers recognized the importance of exercising our flawed memories so that we may be capable not only of remembering God's past work but also of perceiving God's activities in the present. The memories of God's covenant with Abraham, his deliverance from Egypt, his gift of his Son, all of these and more may fill our minds and souls unexpectedly, each one reminding us of God's love, his presence, and his mercies. The church prepares us also to rejoice in our hope-filled sufferings through the formation of our mnemonic habits. Paul's seemingly masochistic claim that "we rejoice in our sufferings" (Rom. 5:3) is encapsulated in a series of developments of the person. Through suffering, we grow in endurance, character, and hope. We can con-

147

front our sufferings, and we triumph over them because we can recall vividly Christ's own passion and resurrection. The memories borne by the church contain the power to transmute suffering to joy. Wolterstorff imagined God telling him to remember whom he had lost and what he had done. God does remind us, for as we have seen, his memory is faithful, and he works through our memories. So, too, should the church minister to our memories.

If this rich, dynamic understanding of memory is accurate, then the question becomes less "How does the church respond to grief when it happens?" and more "How does the church at all times prepare people for suffering, death, and grief?" It would seem that we should not pull out talk of death and eternal life just when someone dies, as we might dust off a tuxedo only for certain occasions. Rather, the ministry of proclamation and praise about Jesus' reconciling work, his death, and resurrection need to be at the heart of the church's ongoing work. For through such ongoing preaching and singing, our memories become increasingly capable of perceiving the presence of God in all things. We become capable of constantly living faithful lives even unto death, and we become prepared to do the dying for others. To recall David H. Smith's insightful phrasing, "The problem of loss of control and suffering belongs at the *beginning* of religious thought rather than at the end."[38] We might well add that these problems belong at the beginning of the church's work, too.

In 1 Corinthians 15, Paul speaks of the resurrected body through the analogy of a seed. Similarly, we may speak of the church's proclamation of the resurrected Lord as a seed which is planted in our memories and which needs constant nourishment, a seed which waits to burst forth from the dark soil and to reach into the heavenly sunlight. Once it breaks through, it needs constant tending if it is to bear the sweetest fruit, provide the richest shade, or blossom into the most spectacular flower. How can the churches help our memories? The church must nourish Christian memories as gardeners cultivate their plants.

Liturgical regularity, both in the weekly services and in the annual cycle, transforms the singularity of historical memories into a vitally experienced, real dynamism of Gospel promise and fulfillment, a dynamism which evokes praise, gratitude, and joy. In a liturgical setting, our memories are also our hopes. Each week, we remember the previous Sunday (not always with the same degree of pleasure), and each week we hopefully anticipate the next Day of the

Lord. While the historical events of the Cross and the resurrection themselves remain singular and past, the experience of them as preached in the church makes them multiple, ever-present, and ever-future. As we remember the past work of Christ, we experience it in the present—especially in the Eucharist—and we anticipate it for our futures.

Streets of Gold and the Beatific Vision

I remember my father's reading of the new heaven and the new earth from the Book of Revelation during the funeral of my mother's mother. The water of life, the holy city of Jerusalem, the crystalline glory of God, the pearly gates, the streets of gold—however and whatever it is, all this is spectacularly beautiful. My grandmother, as you might expect of a good Christian from West Virginia, understood this perfectly well. She said before she died, "Don't wish me back. I'll be in a better place." It is a better place, but her daughter's degenerative disease prevents the daughter from anticipating it with the mother's hope. The church needs to contemplate these visions of hope on behalf of patients like my mother; part of dying well for someone is meditating faithfully on what will happen to them next.

One of the reasons why Jonathan Edwards spoke so frequently about heaven and hell was that he recognized the importance of the role of the affections in the life of faith.[39] That is, he realized that we are stirred by words, concepts, and images, and he knew that we need all the help we can get when we seek to follow Christ. He understood that if we do not refresh our hearts with eschatological thoughts, the promised kingdom will seem like little more than a plant we have long-forgotten to water. We will give it up for dead and buy something new.

This subject of what can be called the beatific vision is particularly difficult to discuss in an ecumenical context since doctrines of merit, purgatory, the intercession of the saints, and other issues are inseparable from the understanding of the afterlife. Moreover, for many Christians it is by no means certain that departed souls will experience anything other than a sort of sleep until the resurrection. We are psychosomatic unities, and speaking of heaven apart from the resurrection is not entirely adequate. Even in the Middle Ages, however, when the doctrine of purgatory developed and when a disembodied existence prior to the resurrection was widely assumed, writers were careful to describe the separated souls as desiring the return of their bodies.[40] Talk of a beatific vision does not do an injustice to the body, rather it provides an occasion for reflecting on the very necessity of the body.

As long as we keep in mind the particularities of each ecclesial community's doctrines, the imaginative exploration of what paradise might be like can proceed in broad terms. There are many images and ways of expressing these realities which the Christian tradition offers, and they are all, in their own ways, potentially quite useful. The reflections offered here are merely general. Hence, important but contentious matters such as heaven's "locality," a possible hierarchy of bliss (as suggested by Paul's reference to the third heaven), or the possibility of progress in our joy I will not explore. Despite great differences between visions of the afterlife, there are also great agreements in the Christian tradition, and I hope that this presentation will be within the proper boundaries of an orthodox imagination.

When I refer to the beatific vision or paradise, I wish to include both a possible experience of paradise before the resurrection (as suggested by Jesus' promise to the penitent thief) and the resurrected life itself. I have chosen to employ the beatific vision over heaven or paradise as the central phrase here because this *amor intellectualis Dei* seems most suitable in the context of Alzheimer's disease. The emphasis on the soul's glorious apprehension of the divine reality is needed at a time when the mind appears to dissolve and the reality of God seems so far away. I have no knowledge of how we will actually experience paradise, but I believe that by attempting to imagine the ineffable, we may grow in desire, love, faith, and hope.

As with most aspects of theology and devotional life, we need help from the church's resources which at different times and in different contexts have opened Christian ears or stirred Christian hearts. In particular, I would like to concentrate on Dante's *Paradiso*, a poem exhibiting a rare combination of arrogant originality and faithful honesty.[41] This text offers a great number of reminders for our own consideration of heaven, for our desire for God's glorious presence, and for affirming our hope of wholeness even as we behold the dissolution of Alzheimer's disease. Dante is not a Biblical authority, and I do not invoke him as such. Rather, his poetic genius is a witness to Christian reflection on what the afterlife might be like in light of orthodox teaching. As Vergil and Beatrice were his guides, so can he escort our contemplations.

The *Divine Comedy*, like all great works of theology, is deeply personal, deeply embedded in history, and thus his poem includes concerns which readers in a different era simply do not share. I trust that modern readers of Dante will be sufficiently enlightened to be able discern in medieval poetry which calls for a white, male, Holy Roman Emperor not just hegemonic verse but also deep insights into the hopes Christianity promises. In reading a human portrayal of the mysteries of heaven, we need to read with charity and circumspection. We need charity for the excesses and faults of an author in her own particular circumstances. And we require circumspection, for the stakes are quite high (the *Paradiso* opens with God's glory) and the theological and social dangers are quite real.

Central to Dante's imaginative exploration of the beatific vision is the reality that God is love. In a remarkable transfiguration of Aristotle's Prime Mover, the Christian poet refers to God as the Prime Lover (IV.118). In one phrase, he has encapsulated the essence of Christianity's metaphysical, epistemological, soteriological, and historical basis. God's love is not the initial push of Aristotle's mover but a perpetual permeation and stirring of the cosmos itself. Thus, Dante describes the conclusion of his long voyage, "But now my desire and will, like a wheel which spins with even motion, were revolved by the love that moves the sun and the other stars" (XXXIII.143-5). His desire and love are simultaneously excited and fulfilled. The psalmist had understood that the human soul is a needy, desiring, seeking soul (cf. Psalms 42 and 73), and the New Testament revelation that God is love provides us with the language to express more fully the *telos* of this desire. By acknowledging our desire for God's presence and our hope to be with Love, we anticipate what Alzheimer's patients lose the capacity to anticipate. We should hope for them, just as we feed them or pay their bills.

Dante's own use of language reminds us to be very careful when we speak of heaven's mysteries. As with the apophatic mystics, the poet consistently protests the inadequacy of his soul, of his memory, and of language itself. Although it is limited, reason can guide us. But it is also fallible. Dante provides the striking image of a bird which "beat[s] [its] wings in downward flight" as a metaphor for the misuse of reason—that which could aid our ascent we all too often use to bear ourselves down (XI.3). Paradise, he tells us, is a free gift of God's grace (here experienced in the form of his new guide, Beatrice). Neither nature nor art can possibly hope to do justice to the divine splendor (XXVII.88–96). He also repeatedly underscores the deficiencies of his memory. But although the poet's memory of that realm remains weak, we may expect the memories of Alzheimer's patients to be restored there. Indeed, we may hope that they are preserved in our souls even as we grow older and more senile.

One of the driving forces of the poem is Dante's recognition of the power of what we have been calling *durée*. "Like him that sees in a dream and after the dream the passion wrought by it remains and the rest returns not to his mind, such am I; for my vision almost wholly fades, and still there drops within my heart the sweetness that was born of it" (XXXIII.58–63). The experience of God exerts an influence on the poet even if he cannot be fully conscious of it later. Indeed, we may wonder if it is possible for someone to have experiences of God's presence and not desire to share them with others, just as the Triune God who is self-communicating love seeks to share his love with his creation.

Dante also suggests that in heaven, the *durée* of sin—the powerful self-condemnations we carry inside us—will be overcome just as death was defeated. When a soul would otherwise recall its sins, such recollections yield immediately to thoughts of God, God's providence, and the beauty of creation and redemption (IX.103–8). So powerful is the love of God that there we will experience no suffering and we will be cleansed of all sins just as Baptism cleanses us of original sin. If we consider Freudian terminology in the light of the beatific vision, we might wonder if the suffusion of grace and love we hope for will make it possible for us to confront the guilt associated with the memories we seek to repress. Because we are certain of the totality of forgiveness, we can remember the totality of our sins even though this remembering will entail no sorrow.

Dante's poetic vision, while singular, is not solitary. His experience is a churched experience, as he signals in canto XXIV when he offers his creedal profession of faith. The reality of the temporal church's mission is not superseded by his own private revelation; rather, special grace confirms Dante's knowledge of the vehicle of all humanity's salvation. Dante reminds us that theological disagreements will be resolved in heaven. Not only will we find out what is true theology and what is false opinion—for then our knowledge will exceed our present weakness—but also we will apprehend such truths as we experience the power of the love of God and the saints. Charity will prepare us for what might otherwise be an unpleasant experience of God's truth. In one of my favorite passages in the *Divine Comedy*, Dante portrays Gregory the Great as he discovers that he was incorrect in his teachings about the angels: "As soon as he opened his eyes in this heaven [the heaven of the angels] he smiled at himself" (XXVIII.134-5). Given the acerbity which sometimes accompanies theological "dialogue" in this life, we may all hope that our future discoveries of our interlocutors' correctness will produce a similarly benevolent result. Disagreement will yield to communion, gratitude, and worship.

Certain doctrines, significantly, are not fully comprehensible to humans (as divine election so remains in canto XIX). The beatific vision itself defies complete cognitive understanding—even as it is being experienced. Dante confesses that he could not grasp the hymn of praise sung by souls in the shape of the Cross (canto XIV). Although much will be clearer when we get there, Dante reminds us that much will remain a mystery even then. Poetry, imagery, wonder, awe, beauty, silence—all these will endure. Moreover, adoration, an act which presupposes a certain awe before the incomprehensible will be central to our lives. Both Thomas Aquinas and a stillborn infant will adore God in his infinite, ineffable glory. Perhaps each of these will share with the other, the former his knowledge, the latter his innocence. I suspect that all of us will be sharing the unique experiences and existence which we each contribute to the body of Christ.

We may hope to encounter not only God's love. Dante reminds us that the communion of saints will be a perpetual increase of love. (He differs from Thomas à Kempis, whose *Imitation of Christ* presents the blessed as being exclusively attentive to Christ.) The joys of the beatific vision which the dead know are hardly static. In canto V, Dante portrays the increase in the joys of heaven that come from shared communion. Love begets further love, and joy perpetually increases. In *Purgatorio* XV, Dante provides the image of souls as mirrors reflecting love back at each other, each new soul and each reflection increasing the love in paradise. Here, however we are to understand it, the church is consummated. Schleiermacher had recognized that some sort of afterlife was "needed" in order for the church to be realized, as Edwards emphasized that heaven would ultimately reveal the perfection of Christ's work. Not only was Paul right in seeing our lives as being in vain without the resurrection, so too is Christ's sacrifice in vain if there is no triumph over death and no vindication for the righteous martyrs of history.

In this communion of saints in the presence of the resurrected Alpha and Omega, the whole of human history is manifest. The famous and the unknown commingle in love and gratitude. Dante recognizes Florentines we would not know—and perhaps we may one day introduce our own friends to Dante. At the resurrection, when history is completed, we will have the opportunity to love all of those from whom we are separated by time and space. What is striking in Dante's account is the eagerness the departed souls exhibit as they converse with the poet and share their confessions of God's glorious work. Moreover, from this perspective of the loving church triumphant, the church militant is critiqued. Aquinas and Bonaventure castigate their respective orders for their failures to live according to the examples of Dominic and Francis. Still, despite the sorrow evoked from the review of the church's crimes (which Dante details at greater length in the *Inferno*), the ultimate perspective on the church and church history is the perspective of love, of charity, and of gratitude. (We will return to the importance of love for the study of history in the final chapter of this study.) Before we can begin to understand both the triumphs and the sins of the church, the poet suggests, we must be "matured in the flame of love" (VII.60).

Love needs no vindication. But the love which caregivers feel for their patients undergoes great trials. It appears to be love unrequited, at times love wasted and turned bitter. Dante's representation of the beatific vision reminds us, however, that no faithful loves will be unrequited. Because we love someone who will be made immortal, our loves will endure forever, and our joys will grow. In Pauline terms, when we share the beatific vision and when we hug each other at the resurrection, we will be "face to face" with those who were once demented, and their faces will be radiant with knowledge and love.

Chapter 6

Sin, Alzheimer's Apocalyptic, and Forgiveness

Therefore a curse devours the earth, and its inhabitants
suffer for their guilt.
— Isaiah 24:6a

A theological consideration of Alzheimer's disease requires an examination of human sinfulness and God's mercy because many caregivers confront their own sin and its manifestations daily.[1] At different times and in differing degrees in each person, three distinct, but often related, dispositions towards sin may dominate caregivers' lives. Understanding the first two of these, acedia (weariness in well-doing) and guilt, is crucial for appreciating how caregivers may view themselves and their work. The third of these, something which could be called an Alzheimer's apocalyptic, will be discussed at somewhat greater length. Here we will see how the doctrines of sin and the Cross are necessary for transmuting angry apocalyptic intimations. Apocalypticism, in contrast to acedia and guilt, derives its strength not from an awareness of sin but from the opposite, a forgetting of one's own sinfulness—a forgetting which has dangerous implications. A consideration of all three of these is needed if the church is to preach forgiveness amid the complex spiritual struggles engendered by caregiving for an Alzheimer's patient. Before exploring these three powerful conditions, however, we need first to consider the subject of sin itself.

It may be objected that "sin" is the wrong category for considering caregivers' feelings of anger and guilt. After all, caregivers are only human and many of them are models of filial piety in their caregiving. Perhaps better terms might be inadequacy, selfishness, or limitation. But these other words fail to do justice to the depth of the anxieties aroused by the processes of this disease. The stakes are quite high; they are nothing less than whether one loves God and family properly. If we are overwhelmed by failure here, what other success in our lives could be meaningful? The wickedness of our thoughts and behavior strikes us in the depths of our being and our ugliness becomes overwhelming. Hence, it is precisely the reality of sin as revealed in its full awfulness on the Cross that makes it possible for us to confront our distress. By acknowledging our sin in the context of the forgiveness of Jesus Christ, we can leave the burdens of sin behind as did Christian in *The Pilgrim's Progress*. The acedia and guilt of caregiving are real, and their awful effects on the soul are profound. But so, too, are the Cross and the resurrection real and so, too, are their effects on the soul beyond measure.

Are we capable of taking sin seriously these days? William James, in describing the religion of his era, particularly liberal Protestantism, suggested that the increasingly popular "religion of healthy-mindedness" would eclipse the idea of sin. He described the healthy-minded religious as a person with "a constitutional incapacity for prolonged suffering."[2] Such persons, and this describes many of us, avoid thinking about vexing matters and are reluctant to probe the conscience for sin. Because new therapies for old problems seem so promising, and because humans seem to be moving forward with such progress, sin no longer seems to be a reality or a very useful category. In optimistic theologies, sin even becomes a burdensome obstacle to our happiness and self-satisfaction. Those Israelites of old may seem quite unfamiliar, since for them, sin was understood to mean rebellion against God (indeed even hatred of him), and their sin both saddened and angered a mighty God. Sin expressed a much darker side of humanity than many people today want to accept.

Modern categories for interpreting the Biblical story of the fall and sin include finitude, limitation, frailty, restriction, and loss of self-control.[3] It is easy to see why such guilt-free terms are appealing if in fact the locus of modern theological reflection is the autonomous, self-constituting subject, as I argued in chapter 4. For such a being, "sin" seems out of place. In chapter 5, I observed that death, too, has become a problematic concept for moderns. Without the link between sin and death, there seems to be no intelligible reason why a creature as wondrous as the autonomous subject should ever die at all. If anything, as my father observes, we may be more likely to feel that we sin because we are mortal. Reversing Paul's understanding that we die because we sin, we may "exploit, suppress, and kill" in a vain attempt to "assure our immortality."[4] It is not surprising that some more traditional thinkers, such as Karl Menninger, find themselves writing books with titles such as *Whatever Happened to Sin?*

If recent generations have inherited an enervated notion of sin—a shallower apprehension of our deep sinful capacities to displease God—then it may be the case that we are indeed ill-prepared for the long-term suffering of Alzheimer's, not only of the patients but also of the caregivers who must struggle with their sins. Although today's rather plural situation makes it almost impossible to generalize about the status of any doctrine in the church catholic, it may be the case that as with other aspects of the "Theological Disease," a disease about forgetting, we have forgotten precisely the doctrines and practices which we need now.

Sin: A Glutinous Conviction

As Theseus required a ball of string to retrace his past steps in order to emerge from the labyrinth, so too may we be in need of history's threads in order to emerge from our present dilemmas. In particular, we need to remember how sin has been a "glutinous" doctrine. The historical and ontological trajectory of sin, human death, God's death, and human salvation at the heart of the Christian message is like the gluten in bread dough—it help keep all the other ingredients together. Without a firm understanding of the magnitude and consequences of human sinfulness, the Christian narrative begins to fall apart conceptually. In addition to being glutinous, sin is also a "conviction" in the sense of the word presented in chapter 3. Sinfulness both is something which Christians believe as a doctrine and is something of which Christians stand convicted.

The reality of humanity's sinfulness permeates both Testaments as sin itself comes to permeate our entire lives. The Old Testament in particular contains a great deal about the history of human estrangement from God, and we should not be surprised that there are many different Hebrew words for sin. So traumatic is sin that even the natural world has been transformed from the original creation. "Cursed is the ground" (Gen. 3:14) because of Adam and Eve, and the flood and the plagues of Egypt are brought on by human wickedness. In Paul's terms, God has subjected nature itself to the "bondage of decay" because of sin (Rom. 8:21). So rotten does the entropic cosmos become that God promises "new heavens and a new earth" (Isa. 65:17).

Of central concern to this study, indeed to our entire lives, is the relationship between sin and our human knowledge of God. Isaiah writes, "Your iniquities have made a separation between you and your God, and your sins have hid his face from you" (Isa. 59:2). Throughout most of the Christian tradition, theologians and laypeople alike have recognized this relationship between spiritual failure and spiritual ignorance. In one of his gentler metaphors, Augustine identifies sin as a mist which blinds him and prevents him from seeing God.[5] Sin disorders our cognitive and spiritual capacities, just as Alzheimer's plaques disorder the brains of its subjects. Fortunately, whereas brain damage is not reversible, sins can be forgiven, the mist can be lifted, and we can be brought back to God.

The disordering effect on the human person and on human nature which sin has is due, in part, to the intricate relationship between sin and memory, a relationship explored in chapter 2. For this chapter's purposes, we need to recall how our sins interact with our memories to become powerful, oppressive forces in our soul. Echoing Isaiah 66:24, Bernard of Clairvaux described the memory of sin as "the worm that does not die."[6] Sin, as with memory, may not disappear with time but it lingers and gnaws until it consumes all or is itself overcome. I suspect that this experience may be familiar to many caregivers, who sit and sip a drink and contemplate the week's labor, the week's failures and accomplishments.

In Bergsonian terms, Bernard is describing the memory of sin in terms of durée—the enduring, impinging past. Each of our sins continues to exist, exerting an influence on habits, our will, our nature, and indeed our hopes. Sadly, as Freudian scholars and therapists might observe, it is sometimes those "events" which we would like to forget or have seemingly forgotten which exert the most profound influence. Bernard's worm eats away, making an emptiness in the soul of which we may remain ignorant for many years. Hence, the Psalmist begs the Lord, "But who can discern his errors? Clear thou me from hidden faults" (Ps. 19:12). As sin is a matter of the endurance of the past, so does each sin build up or empower our sinful nature. The worm grows and its gnawing enervates our capacity to order our lives and to align our will with the will of God.

Sin is not only about disorder and ignorance of God but also about death. We find we must ask not only, Why does someone contract the horror of Alzheimer's? but, more generally, Why must we all die? The traditional understanding of the origins of death was that death entered the world because of sin. In Genesis, God decrees that Adam will return to the dust from which he was made, and Paul writes that "sin came into the world through one man and death through sin" (Rom. 5:12). God created humanity good, capable of not sinning, and destined for living eternally in love and bliss. Rebelling against this purpose has brought into the world the terrors of disease and death, terrors which we have inherited from Adam. God's purpose for us is life eternal, but our sins threaten to thwart God's creative desire. The experience of caregiving is that our fearful weakness when confronting mortality leads to sin and guilt. But while our mortality may incite us to further sins, the sin we inherit is itself the first cause of our mortality. Prior to the eschaton, these teachings about the origins of death will remain mysteries. But I believe that without remembering the link between sin and death, the church's orthodox teachings concerning interrelated doctrines of the creation, human nature, mortality, and the Cross become incoherent.[7]

In this context, the multiple connections between sin and disease can become intelligible. Why do diseases strike us down? Why are we subject to such crippling? Certainly, many Alzheimer's families wonder, Why us? Why must I lose my faculties, and why must my children become my parents? The Bible suggests a great diversity for the etiology of diseases and disabilities. Some afflictions and plagues are the direct result of sin (cf. Miriam's leprosy in Numbers 12). At times, as for Job, illnesses and sores are seen as trials, tests which may even enhance merit. Jesus declares that the blind man has no sight not because of sin but so that "the works of God might be made manifest in him" (John 9:3). His healing becomes an occasion for the revelation of God's mercy.

Because of such diversity, it seems that there is no easy biblical answer for caregivers and for victims as to why they suffer this particular form of death. Our response might be as Elihu's to Job, when he describes the mysterious impartiality of many deaths (Job 34:19). At times, one may ask if one is being punished for something. Is this indeed a trial? Will the glory of God be manifest in this horror? Despite the intensity of its experiences, Alzheimer's disease remains a particular case of the general problem of humanity's subjection to

Death. The disease is not the direct result of particular sins, but it is a particular result of the general condition of our sin-caused mortality. It sounds cruel, but it should not be forgotten, that even if this disease had never come into existence, all Alzheimer's patients would die "anyway." Any given death may assume a savage and perhaps unjust form. But a death in itself is always just. None of us because of his own merits deserves to live forever. Immortality is not an entitlement.

What we cannot allow ourselves to forget is that sin tells us not only why we die but also why Jesus Christ died. If our condition and our transgressions were not so serious, God would not have had to undergo such suffering. One does not have to understand the problem in the rigorous, logical construction of Anselm's *Cur Deus Homo* to suspect that God dying for our sakes suggests something rather grave about the human condition. However the Atonement is understood, he is "the Lamb of God who takes away the sin of the world" (John 1:29). Christ the healer, it seems, had to die for the terminally ill to live. Herein lies the richness of disease as a metaphor for sin. So terrible is disease and so terrible is sin that the former aptly seems to suggest the crippling affects of the latter. And so powerful and merciful is the physician, that he can conquer death and its sting, though at a horrific price.

Sin is thus one of the keys to the power and coherence of the entire Christian narrative—it describes the origin and cause of our deaths, God's terrible Passion, our ignorance, our perpetual weakness, our wavering in faith and virtue. As a reality which governs all the phenomena we experience, it is pervasive. It is the disordering of the soul, which inhibits our will and intellect. Not surprisingly, "sin" describes an enormous range of disobedient works. While some churches' traditions have been more keen on distinguishing between specific sins than others, I believe that preaching the much-needed forgiveness of sins requires that each community understand the particular spiritual dynamics experienced in each person in order to proclaim the Good News most effectively. While we vary considerably in our personalities and traditions, I believe that for caregivers as a group, any one of three different, sometimes interrelated states or dispositions may become dominant. Each of these spiritual states—acedia, guilt, and Alzheimer's apocalyptic—needs serious consideration, because each of them can lead both to graver sins and to a lamentable inability to hear the Word.

The Weariness of Acedia and the Burden of Guilt

Whether it is actually a sin or a state of mind, acedia is a dangerous condition. The term itself is often confused with one of its effects, sloth. But in its classic expositions, in John Cassian's *Institutes* X, Aquinas' *Summa Theologiae* 2a.2ae.35, Dante's *Purgatorio* XVIII, and Chaucer's "Parson's Tale," acedia has a much richer, more subtle meaning. It denotes essentially a weariness in performing good works. Hence, John Cassian studies 2 Thessalonians because Paul, if he is indeed the author, seems to be discussing precisely this problem when he writes, "Brethren, do not weary in well-doing" (2 Thes. 3:13, cf. Gal. 6:9). Cassian and Paul both seem to be concerned primarily with some Christians who were not engaged in productive work, and hence the word Paul uses in the preceding verses, *ataktos*, is translated as "idleness." But this word also means "disorder," and it is not without reason that Cassian could see in this passage a vehicle for discussing acedia, a disposition of disordered love and affections. Writers after Cassian expanded the meaning of acedia so that it applies to all kinds of spiritual torpor (idleness is but one form of spiritual malaise), and because weariness in well-doing engenders further sins, acedia became one of the seven deadly sins.

The earliest contexts for discussing acedia were eremitic and monastic. Spiritual mentors became aware of the devotional problems incurred by their religious who were not fully dedicated to their prayers or other work. These monks became disturbed and their spiritual exercises brought distress not comfort. As the life of a monk brings him into an intimate confrontation with God and with the uncertain adequacy of his own devotional practices, so, too, can the engrossed, often isolated caregiver find herself confronted with questions of her own ability to love a patient fully. (Luther's own profound sense of infirmity even in the midst of a strict monastic regimen might seem familiar to some caregivers who, like Luther, also live under a strict daily routine.) Although many, perhaps most, caregivers' ministries can be examples of love and perhaps holiness to us all, the caregivers themselves recognize that their labor is not always filled with the spirit of love.

Caregivers become painfully aware of their own sinfulness towards their loved ones. Many are aware that their all-too-brief hugs are forced and that "fault may be found with [their] ministry" because they do not always have "genuine love" (2 Cor. 6:3, 6). They

161

experience all too painfully what Dante called "lukewarmness in well-doing." This tepidness is understandable, especially as the disease progresses and the joys of seeing a patient appreciate your efforts diminish. Aquinas opposed acedia to the joy of charity—but where is the joy of caring for someone who does not care? How can acedia not be a feeling welling up inside a caregiver? Caregivers recognize that in some sense it would be meet and right to provide unceasing care and companionship with all of one's soul. But such a total dedication seems impossible even when patients are bathed, conversed with, and fed properly. Acedia exploits this gap which easily emerges between the proprieties of the duties performed and the darkness of the inner disposition.

Acedia, then, is an important category precisely because it is not about ethics or ethical behavior *per se* but about the disposition of the caregiver. The question which acedia focuses upon is not *whether* we fulfill the obligations of caregiving but *how* we do so. Caregivers often become sensitive to how they do things because so much of their work becomes intentional and self-conscious. They must remind themselves to say and do certain things because the relationship with their loved one no longer comes naturally. Preparing a meal for two no longer carries the same anticipation of shared pleasure which once made such labor enjoyable. Do we clean, or exercise, or cook for a person with love in our hearts? With bitterness? With anger? With the "grumbling and questioning" against which Paul warned the Philippians (Phil. 2:14)? Because we are not always aware of the fact that these feelings are affecting our souls, acedia is all the more perilous.

The dangers of this spiritual malaise are so great that it becomes possible to see acedia as a principal cause of many grave sins. Ultimately, because of its enervating, depressing powers, this sin separates the person from the joys of loving, from the pleasures of the creation, and from experiencing the love of God. It is opposed to the rest of the Sabbath—indeed it energizes itself by denying the person respite and joy (caregiving is relentless, physically and emotionally). As acedia enervates confidence in God's love and the pleasures of the Christian life, it contributes to unfaithfulness in a myriad of ways. It leads us to believe that our true happiness lies not in God and God's commandments but in material pleasures, countless diversions, or the forgetfulness of alcohol. It encourages us to entertain dark, angry thoughts, and it leads us to be less faithful caregivers: Why should I care how well I prepare a meal if it doesn't really matter? It also embitters us in worship: Why should we praise a God who has given us this mess and these unrewarding duties? Significantly, Dante's slothful are so destitute of devotional capacities that they alone among those in Purgatory are not able to offer a prayer or a divine office. They have become radically separated from the life of the church. Hence confronting one's acedia may be, in some sense, a prerequisite for hearing church proclamation and participating in the joys of the church.

Because it concerns primarily inner feelings, not actual deeds, acedia can overwhelm even the most dutiful of caregivers. By contrast, the burden of guilt strikes particularly those who are less dutiful, or at least those who feel themselves so. Alzheimer's disease is generous in providing numerous occasions for developing feelings of guilt. Caregivers can get angry at their patient when he refuses to eat, stop squealing, or sit on the toilet properly. We had grown accustomed to communicating rationally with a person, and now we can no longer reason with him. We know that his mind is impaired, and we know not to expect much. Why, then, do we readily grow angry at someone who cannot understand our words? After our anger abates, it is easy to forgive the patient. Quite literally, in the words of Luke 23:34, "they know not what they do." Perhaps, therefore, it is harder to forgive ourselves.

The title of one of the most widely read books of advice for Alzheimer's families, The 36-Hour Day, suggests the dilemma which caregivers face. The bonds of love and the commandments of Jesus require total, self-giving love, more love than can be provided for in a day. Just when a caregiver sets aside some time for her own relaxation, she hears her husband crying out for comfort in the next room. On the one hand, she feels she should go in and aid him, but on the other, she knows that this would provide only a temporary respite from the disorientation. But is this simply a rationalization for wanting to reclaim some of her own life? What should she do? Inevitably, the caregiver is a torn person. She may well feel helpless as she confronts her situation, just as Luther stressed that we are all helpless before the Law. And because we are creatures whose memories often force themselves upon us through their durée, the recollections of leaving the house can become horrible. Even pleasant memories of taking time to ourselves can easily seem as moments of betrayal and abandonment. (It is not surprising that some feminist

163

thinkers have criticized the Christian ideal of love as self-less giving precisely because such a model can lead to a near-complete emptying of the giver.)[8] The memories of sin are durable, and we cannot erase them as we can clean a dirty plate.

We have all felt the need to ask forgiveness of the dead. We stare at their bodies or their coffins, and multitudes of apologies and memories of our failures fill our hearts. We cry not only for the dead, their loss of life, our loss of companionship, but also for our own now-unforgivable mistakes. Compounding the caregivers' feelings of sin and guilt is the fact that there is no human forgiveness by a demented patient on this side of the eschaton. Whereas we can ask forgiveness from most of our friends and family members, we can only hope for forgetfulness from an advanced patient. We speak with them; ask to hear an "It's OK, really"; and desire to see at least a knowing glance telling us that they somehow understand our plight, too. Instead, all too often, we receive an uncomprehending stare. Even if she said, "There's nothing to forgive," it would be hard to accept such a statement since we associate forgiveness with full understanding.

Caregivers may well recognize the disastrous effects of sin on the family as revealed in the story of Cain and Abel. Soon after humans are cast out from the garden for their disobedience, brother kills brother. Families of patients often find themselves in deep conflict over issues of nursing homes, daycare, who should be the caregiver, or types of treatment. But despite the most careful reasoning and the best of intentions, sometimes these disputes can separate family members just as Alzheimer's separates the patient from society. We need to remember that Christ's sacrifice mediates not only between God and humanity but between humans, too, between son and mother, father, brothers, sisters, friends.

Family members themselves who feel they cannot be caregivers may feel deep burdens of guilt and selfishness. Despite the fact that their spouses, children, or jobs quite reasonably make it difficult to assume great daily responsibilities, there is often, perhaps always, a distress of the conscience. Children recognize that their parent is suffering, the man or woman who gave so many years to them needs their unalloyed love. Yet they fail to give it. Youthful memories of being driven to baseball games or friends' houses become juxtaposed with memories of recent failures to commit a few hours to a visit.

What this unatonable situation means is that ultimately no purely human remedy or cure is available to us. Even though some families are fortunate enough to be able to hire full-time at-home care or can afford a first-rate nursing facility, providing well for a patient is not the same as being with the patient, as any family member will tell us. There is something inside us that says that the call to ministering to a person should be answered by family. Although the caregiver cannot cure, she knows that steady, loving attention does make a real difference in the quality of a patient's life. This kind of care, however, becomes increasingly harder to sustain. For caregivers, feelings of failure are almost inevitable. Well-meaning pastors and friends can actually make it more difficult for the caregiver to confront his guilt. A caregiver may be told, "You are doing such a good job," and he may get affirmed so many times that he may not get the opportunity to let his guilt emerge. Talking with a caregiver who is burdened by his sin is not easy, and it requires the particular discernment of friendship.

One of the central dangers of the powerful remorse and guilt which accompanies caregiving is that these feelings can so overwhelm us that we can no longer perceive the merciful mediation of God. In their own ways, Dante's *Purgatorio*, Augustine's *Confessions*, and Luther's spiritual struggles each bear witness to the obfuscation of God's love by human sin. An agonizing heart, after all, may choose to harden. (A hardened heart can be useful in caregiving.) And a heart that asks why a loved one suffers such deterioration may turn bitter in its hardness. Although caregivers do not wander the earth like Cain, they may well share his terrible feeling of separation from God. The church must recognize their special need to hear the promise of forgiveness given in Jesus Christ. That God can forgive us means that we may hope that we can, as the Lord's Prayer suggests, forgive and be forgiven too.

Thus far I have been considering only the sins of the caregivers. Is sin an appropriate category for advanced Alzheimer's patients? Can a person sin if they can no longer reason or will in any recognizable sense? My father has stressed the importance of remembering my mother is still a moral agent and deserves to be treated so. It is significant that sometimes she still says "I'm sorry." My mother seems to have retained a sense of her own sinfulness even into the middle stages of the disease. I had planned on reading some of the psalms to her one afternoon, but when I began with the first lines of Psalm 8, she burst into tears, crying out her awareness of her faults before

165

the majesty of the Lord's name. Oddly, perhaps, while this caused her great distress, I was comforted by this event as it demonstrated her continued connectedness with herself and with her God.

A diminished capacity for sin does not guarantee the presence of good, or, to use more theologically suggestive terms, the presence of merit. It is not enough for us to be able to say that we have done nothing to anger the Lord. The central issue, for patients as well as for those of us who retain our subjecthood, remains: How can we live a life pleasing to God? How can we do as we should, to fulfill the Law and to love God and neighbor? How a de-subjected patient can do this remains mysterious, but to deny him this dilemma would seem, in a way, more cruel than to argue that the rest of his life is soteriologically insignificant.

Whether or not a patient can still sin, Alzheimer's caregivers do behold the loss of rational self-control that is a mark of sinfulness. The patient's behavior seems to be an icon of sin and rebellion. As an Orthodox icon's startling non-natural features leads the viewer from the natural into the supernatural world of grace, so does the patient's distorted image lead us from our own work-a-day world to our own sinfulness. In the patient's disordered behavior, we can recognize our own uncontrolled sins, our own stammering, our own ragings. Perhaps if we can have the courage to be with these families, we can see that we all have Alzheimer's *coram Deo*. And if we can empathize with their feelings, we may also become more sympathetic to Alzheimer's apocalyptic.

Alzheimer's Apocalyptic and Church Proclamation

An apocalyptic mindset is the third of the different ways of cognitively, emotionally, and morally responding to the crises of caregiving. It, too, may or may not be sinful in itself. But apocalypticism, while it has valuable reminders concerning the Kingdom of God for us all, can also encourage anger, impatience, and bitterness. Like acedia, it can give birth to many sins. Moreover, in contrast to acedia, apocalypticism may also lead to the forgetting of one's own sins. It may be in this sense that it is most dangerous, as it may lead us down the paths of self-righteousness. In order for the church to address those Alzheimer's caregivers inclined towards these feelings as well as those more captivated by acedia or guilt, we need to consider the relationship between apocalyptic thinking and the church as a whole. An apocalyptic mindset likes to see in apocalyptic texts the hermeneutic keys to Scripture. The Cross is read in light of the Apocalypse. We shall see, however, that we would do well to follow Paul and do the reverse; we will need to consider how the Cross reconfigures Jewish and Christian apocalyptic traditions. Then, it will be possible to see how the church's proclamation of the forgiveness of sins can address the acedia, guilt, and/or apocalypticism which may come to seize caregivers.

While "apocalypticism" is a difficult term to define and employ theologically, the word's descriptive powers seem useful for characterizing a disposition which could be called Alzheimer's apocalyptic.[9] Such an apocalyptic is more of a sensibility or attitude engendered than a theology formally developed, and it is precisely such dispositions which are crucial to our devotional lives. The experiences of caregiving—the enervating process of planning for long-term care, the witnessing of irrevocable deterioration in a spouse, the constant cries of agony or disorientation, the God who seems unvindicated by history—all of these contribute to a state of mind which resembles apocalyptic traditions. The harsh realities of Alzheimer's caregiving destroy all of a family's hopes for the future. My father and mother had imagined any number of retirements, any number of gardens to be enjoyed, any number of things they had always wanted to do. "All that's gone now," my father has sighed many times. Because the future seems so veiled by the unknown—who knows how long this process will last?—there may be a desire for a radical "apocalypse" (literally, an "unveiling"). As with Daniel and the Apocalypse, the historical future is bleak, and something beyond the old heavens and earth is sought. At times, understandably, and not all selfishly, some caregivers privately hope for the complete and sudden end, not of themselves but of the patient.

It may be difficult for the church to engage such families, because so much of modern theological reflection is predicated on a confidence in the historical future. Either we have a general trust in the future (Who knows what delights new technologies will bring?) or we believe that active Christian praxis will lead to a better, more just world. Hence, in order for non-caregivers to understand this mindset—its fears and hopes and its way of thinking—and in order for the church to formulate its Good News to Alzheimer's families, it may be helpful to consider an apocalyptic (or proto-apocalyptic) text, Isaiah 24–27, sometimes called the Isaiah Apocalypse.

My choice of a problematic, interpolated biblical text is intentional.[10] As seen in previous chapters, the process of interpolation and canonical acceptance itself mirrors the workings of human memory. In our own minds, we interpolate others' thoughts and experiences which reshape our lived experiences, and we constantly add and synthesize our memories of the past into a whole, a whole which we accept as being constitutive of who we are. Our memory is canonical. Similarly, the Isaiah Apocalypse is canonical, for we recognize that it, too, is part of God's revelation. As with any portion of the church's memory, the central question becomes how this text fits into the total understanding of Christ, the church, and human salvation. Because of its powerful imagery, an apocalyptic text has the danger of assuming greater importance than perhaps should be granted.

The evocative language of the Isaiah Apocalypse could be applied to Alzheimer's patient's and their minds. Desolation, twisted surfaces (as in brain plaques), pollution, chaos, the pit and the snare, and the crying out—all of this resonates with caregivers. "All the merry-hearted sigh, . . . the mirth of the lyre is stilled." Decay and death impinge on the totality of existence. The language is biblical, the reality is contemporary. As with other readings throughout the Jewish and Christian traditions, Alzheimer's families reading Old Testament passages in light of contemporary problems produces both an identification with the past and a fresh interpretation of the text's applicative meaning. Because these images are so familiar to us, this "reading" need not be done only through printed words, but also through the evocation—or eruption (*durée*)—of images and ideas from the memory.

Personal identification with people who lived over two thousand years is possible because of the similarity of human experiences. The contexts of most apocalyptic texts, the persecutions of Jews and Christians by the powers of this world, suggests that believing in the traditional covenant promise of earthly prosperity for the faithful had become an impossibility. For Alzheimer's families, too, earthly prosperity may be completely unimaginable. Not only are family resources committed to long-term terminal care, but, more importantly, a person is dying. Human dissolution is not so much an event which strikes a family once every so often but rather a process which comes to dominate everyone's life for many years. As with exiled Jews, the memories of rejoicing in a blessed home seem far, far away, and hoping for a better tomorrow seems foolish. It is important to remember Ernst Käsemann's observation that for apocalyptic literature, it is often the Lordship of God over the entire creation, not just his rule over human history, which is at stake. Although Isaiah laments primarily social and political disasters and Alzheimer's families cry over biological processes, the experience is similar: the Lordship of God over this earth is in question.

Hence, one of the major concerns of apocalyptic, the problem of theodicy, is also a question which Alzheimer's families may ask. Isaiah declares that the origins of his world's catastrophe lie in human sin; men and women have "broken the everlasting covenant." Despite human and cosmic entropy, God's justice is not doubted, and human responsibility is affirmed. Still, the righteous do suffer. With Alzheimer's, there is the same problem of why a good God would allow such horrors to befall a family. Regardless of a person's understanding of the mysterious theological and biological causes of the disease (people will view these differently), family members may come to develop apocalyptic feelings as they confront the realities of the disease, the dissolution it brings, and the suffering it causes.

Paradoxically, we might think, Isaiah also declares, "From the ends of the earth we hear songs of praise, of glory to the Righteous One." Although this rejoicing and triumph of the righteous seems located in future time, it is possible to express this joy now. Hence the use of the present tense for future bliss. And in words resonant with our discussions of other topics, the prophet describes ecstatic hopes of the faithful, "Thy memorial name is the desire of our soul. My soul yearns for thee in the night, my spirit within me earnestly seeks thee." The anxiety underlying present joy is underscored by the decisive gap between current sorrows and future fulfillment.

How is Isaiah able to present such joy amid the ruthlessness of the present? The prophet affirms the triumph of the Creator over humanity's self-destruction, "He will swallow up death forever." Moreover, in what becomes one of the hallmarks of apocalypticism, Isaiah proclaims the resurrection: "The dead shall live, their bodies shall rise. O dwellers in the dust, awake and sing for joy!" The impossibility of historical or political relief leads Isaiah to recognize that the resurrection (however understood) is the vindication both of the righteous sufferers and of God. Ultimately, for Alzheimer's families as well as those millions who have found themselves in horrific periods in history, there can be little confidence in the world

169

as it is constituted. For apocalyptic writers, Alzheimer's families, and history's victims, "salvation" may well appear to be radically discontinuous with history. So drastic are the crises, so profound are their origins, that only divine intervention in resurrection and cosmological transformation can seem to be "an account of the hope" of Biblical witnesses (1 Pet. 3:15).

Even the prophecies of torment for the wicked which are often part of apocalyptic are not strangers to the Alzheimer's family. Bitterness and anger regarding other people are not uncommon, especially if the caregiver feels that her suffering is not appreciated by another family member. In order for others to know what they go through, caregivers sometimes desire for others to live in the house, for others to hear the screams, for others to have to change the patient's soiled clothes. Indeed, there is a mindset which desires to place others in the Inferno of the caregiving home, just so that the agony of the caregiver can be appreciated. Presuming to think for God, we sometimes desire wrath to be visited on those whom we perceive as unrighteous. Then shall the caregiver's suffering be publicly vindicated. Because the experience of Alzheimer's can be so fundamental, the sense of total judgment and near-complete annihilation found in the Isaiah Apocalypse may well be something that caregivers sometimes expect. As the "kings of the earth" are to be laid low, so has this disease already struck even a former president of the United States.

While apocalypticism can encourage a deep moral and spiritual life, apocalyptic intimations can also entail devotional and ethical dangers. They may lead to a desire for the hastening of all things, not just the cosmological end. Because time becomes so important, impatience asserts itself more easily. Self-destructive, nihilistic behavior seems not out of place—all is lost, after all. There may well be a hardening of the heart and a refusal to experience joys (much like acedia's opposition to spiritual pleasures, only this refusal may be of all forms of joy). Why should I enjoy myself while my husband suffers? In contrast to those who feel overwhelmed by guilt, there may be created a sense of self-righteousness. God is no longer needed as the caregiver has atoned for her own sins. The caregiver may feel justified in dividing the entire world into the good and the bad, the saved and the damned. Together, all of these feelings can inhibit the caregiver from offering the loving care she would want to provide, and they can lead to any number of different sins. I have no doubt that God looks at caregivers in the special context of their calling, but I also have no doubt that even the most faithful caregiving is not a license for antinomianism.

As apocalyptic writers and the sufferers of the past and present might suggest, the issue raised by earthly calamities is indeed the righteousness of God. How do we interpret this problem in the context of the entire Biblical witness and the history of salvation? If we follow Paul's lead, we see through his use of apocalyptic themes that motifs and teachings which emerge from their particular historical contexts are indeed important for the church as a whole. We also gain a better purchase on why seeing apocalyptic at the heart of Scripture is potentially dangerous. Most importantly, we are reminded that the real point of departure for understanding how the holy, just, and merciful God works in a world trampled by the Four Horsemen of the Apocalypse requires a different starting point, namely, the Cross.

As my father has observed, Paul both draws on apocalyptic themes and radically transforms them in light of the Cross and the resurrection. By beginning with these events, Paul "dissolves" the issue of theodicy. Because God does not allow afflictions which he himself has not experienced, we cannot demand from God that he prove himself to us. God already has acted on behalf of the world— the transcendant God of apocalyptic texts is now quite immanent, immanent even unto death. Moreover, that God suffers for the sake of sinners means that this-worldly notions of "distributive justice" are hardly reliable. The logic of justification—that God justifies the sinful because of Christ—means that no one gets "what they deserve" since not even the righteous are righteous without Christ. For Paul, "before faith came" (Gal. 3:23) even humans living according to the law were slaves to sin. By seeing human experience from this perspective, the "Why me?" asked by Alzheimer's sufferers becomes logically the same as the "Why me?" asked by those whom Christ draws to himself. In part because of God's own suffering and in part because of his deep understanding of the radical servitude of sin, "unjust suffering never appears as an issue" for Paul.[11] Paul was hardly a stranger to suffering, but he understood human misery as a sharing of the divine mastering of the cosmos' hostile powers. Paul retains many apocalyptic themes or categories (salvation is discontinuous with worldly history; the creation, too, awaits redemptive transformation), but these are transfigured through a recognition of God's own suffering.

Is Paul's reading faithful to the Jesus Christ of the Gospels and his own relationship to apocalypticism? Bultmann argued that the apocalyptic elements in the Gospels did not originate with Jesus. But it seems that the Jesus with whom we are familiar—the Apostolic Jesus, the One in whom we can trust without being naïve—does present apocalyptic themes and topics (e.g., the resurrection, the vindication of the just, and the punishment of the wicked at the end of time; cf. Mark 13 and Matt. 24). Curiously, whereas Bultmann argued that even Jesus' apocalyptic tendencies could not be adopted or appropriated readily by moderns, it may be the case that the experience of Alzheimer's disease shows us not only why we can, but also why we must not forget apocalyptic themes and thinking. Jesus' own emergence from the context of apocalyptic Judaism and his use of these themes suggest that he was born into the same world as Alzheimer's families, indeed the same world as us all. He, too, was born in a time and a place where there was little certainty about the future of worldly hopes.

The abject brokenness of the earth and people in Isaiah is transfigured through the brokenness of God on Calvary. In *The Disabled God*, Nancy L. Eiesland develops a liberatory theology of disability through a recognition of the fact that God has chosen to work through lacerations, a broken body, and spilt blood. While Eiesland, does not do justice to the gravity of human sinfulness (I believe she misreads Luke 5), she does illuminate the importance of seeing God not only as Pantocrator but also as fellow caregiver, fellow sufferer.[12] The church can presume to speak to Alzheimer's families because the church is called into existence through the desolation, despoiling, and twisting of God's own body. The tangles and plaques on the brain of the Alzheimer's patient can be seen in the matted hair and blood-stained garments of Christ. Both this disease and the Cross are prolonged experiences of death. The cry of Alzheimer's and apocalyptic desire is "Let it be over." Not without significance did Christ declare, "It is finished."

Caregivers seek the peace that apocalyptic foretells, and in the context of their daily labors, the peace which Christ's work provides is a great joy. But that peace may come most swiftly, I believe, when we realize that what we now experience as present suffering is a vehicle for being glorified with Christ (cf. Rom. 8:17). Paul declares

(2 Cor. 1:5), "For as we share abundantly in Christ's sufferings, so through Christ we share in comfort too." As he observes in his criticisms of early Christian practices in 1 and 2 Thessalonians, preparing for the Parousia (whether understood apocalyptically or not), requires patience amid afflictions, not acedia, anger, or antinomianism. We are heirs of salvation, but we have not deserved this great gift. How can creatures as sinful as deicides aspire to such a glorious hope?

As Brevard Childs underscores, the Biblical understanding of sin is never separated from the real possibility of atonement and reconciliation. The sinner is "not . . . an individual suffering alone with a tortured conscience."[13] In Luther's phrasing, those persons "whose conscience is troubled, uneasy, erring, and terrified, who would gladly be loosed from their sin and be righteous" may examine themselves and their souls with the confidence that their sins are forgiven. As a consequence, they will discover what many a Gospel singer knows, "a joyful conscience and a glad heart toward God."[14] Without sin and evil, we would still desire God, but we would not need him so desperately. Our hope amid despair is real because of the life and work of Christ.

Jesus' own ministry, while set in an apocalyptic context, seems to have been concerned most profoundly with the forgiveness of sins. The Alzheimer family's despair originates from the impossibility of cure. From this lack of healing, their particular anger, weariness, and guilty conscience, all arise. Yet, for Jesus, healing and the forgiveness of sins are linked. In Luke 5:17-26, the man who was paralyzed was, like all of us, also the man who was in need of forgiveness. Moreover, Jesus relativizes the impairment of disease and disability by declaring that forgiveness exceeds healing. Especially for Alzheimer's families who might prefer healing to forgiveness, such a strange pronouncement makes sense perhaps only within an eschatological framework, only when we realize that the stakes involved with forgiveness are nothing less than eternal life. Fortunately, through Baptism, the Lord's Prayer, and confessions of sins, the church is well prepared to preach forgiveness. Not surprisingly, Luther is able to declare "that the whole church is full of the forgiveness of sins."[15]

Regardless of the literal or metaphorical meaning of Isaiah's or Ezekiel's resurrections, the resurrection of Christ confirms the apocalyptic hope of transhistorical vindication and rejoicing. Further, through the joy and sorrow with which we contemplate the Cross and the resurrection we see simultaneously our sinfulness and our redemption, and we know not whether to cry or to sing. David, Augustine, Bunyan, Luther, Francis, Gospel hymns—each of these exhibits the commingling of sorrow and joy. The familiar song "Put Your Hand in the Hand of the Man from Galilee" embodies this transformation in our disposition quite well. The melody is up-beat and optimistic, but the singer is confessing his own sinfulness— "Everytime I look into the Holy Book I want to tremble. . . . And it causes me shame to know that I'm not the guy I should be. . . . Take a look at yourself and you can look at others differently / by putting your hand in the hand of the man from Galilee." God's hanging from a tree challenges our own miseries and evokes joy and renewed life. Because our sins have been forgiven by the Lord who extends his wounded hand to us, we can receive our place in the Kingdom of God and live new lives accordingly.

As with the early church's unfulfilled expectations of an imminent apocalypse or Parousia, so too must the churches prepare families for a much longer period of patience and labor. Although the eschaton does not seem to be at hand, its mysteries can be experienced now. Thus the fourth Evangelist, Paul, Luther, and many others stress the possibility of enjoying salvation even in the present. We can know the freedom of a Christian. The Kingdom of God can be experienced even before the eschaton. As the previous chapters have suggested, the church has a responsibility to strengthen memories, for the fortification of memory is preparation for each day's grasp of the Kingdom.

With the church's aid, we can allow the words of John 3:16 to impinge upon our suffering; we can allow them to well up inside us whenever our consciences are oppressed by guilt. Indeed, in our confessions, we do weaken the resistance to the memories of grace which sin generates. Grace, like sin, has *durée*. The grace of Christ, of Baptism, and of the Holy Spirit endures, and such mysteries can, if we let them, burst in upon our sinfulness, in our weariness, guilt, anger or impatience. We must remember the suffering of God as if it were our own. For when we attempt this, we are humbled and grateful. (In the *Imitation of Christ*, we learn that humility is one of the best treatments for acedia.) Literally and etymologically, Christ's *passion* enables our *patience*. The apocalyptic longings can be endured and eventually relieved. It becomes possible to strive to love God and others freely again.

What the Church Can Learn

As the church can strengthen the memories of Alzheimer's families, so too can these families fortify the church's own memories through their example and experiences. In contemplating the psychology of these families we remember the power and need for apocalyptic witness in history. When we watch genocide in [choose a country], or people struggling to survive in a [choose a natural disaster], or humans languishing from [choose a disease], our impulse may be to wish for aid, relief, liberation, or some such temporal amelioration. Because we are humans capable of sympathy, part of us longs to save sufferers any way we can, but this is not always possible. Ultimately, anytime one of the Four Horsemen visits a person or an entire land, there is need to recall the insights of apocalyptic—the ultimate triumph beyond time, the promise of the resurrection, the vindication and justification of Creator and creature. Consequently, in apocalyptic imaginative horrors and the realities of Alzheimer's we can discern a "dark background for a profound hope."[16]

Both apocalyptic writings and the realities of disease remind us of the dangers of clinging too tightly to the pleasures of this world. It is hardly surprising that many, such as St. Francis, have experienced conversions because of an illness. Such confrontations with disease and death often produce the most profound theological experiences. As time becomes more precious, we are forced to choose between competing goods, and as we are compelled to make tough decisions, we are led to consider why we should prefer caregiving to fame or wealth. The double meaning of Ignatius' remarkable statement that "My Eros has been crucified" underscores how we can learn from Alzheimer's families.[17] His previous worldly desires have been transfixed to the Cross and now have become dead to him. At the same time, he also confesses that the God he loves and desires has been slain for our sakes. Similarly, in the dutiful love of caregivers who sacrifice their lives for their beloved, so, too, do we see our temporal aspirations challenged. So, too, may we see our God before us. As we realize how our loved ones suffer and die, we begin to see the suffering of God more clearly. As our misery became his on the Cross, so may his become ours. As Nicholas Wolterstorff writes remembering his deceased son, God's suffering "I never saw before" but "through the prism of my tears I have seen a suffering God."[18]

Although the emphasis of this chapter has been on the sinfulness

175

evoked by Alzheimer's caregiving, it would be a grave mistake not to recognize how we can be humbled by the love and the giving of families. When seeing love manifested by such deeds, we may echo what the Disciple says to the Lord in *The Imitation of Christ*, "When I think of some devout Christians who frequent your Sacrament with the greatest devotion and love, I feel ashamed and confounded that I approach your Altar . . . with so tepid and cold a heart; that I remain so dry and lacking in love; that my heart remains unkindled in your presence, O God."[19] As we behold the diseased body and the devotion of caregiving, so too can we see the broken body of Christ and the need to approach with ardor and gratitude. As caregivers struggle to do things right, so too do we need to struggle to make our own hearts right. We all may suffer from acedia, and we may all need inspiration from dedicated caregiving.

Above all, we perhaps can remember how to love God. Caregiving at times seems analogous to the worship of the transcendant Almighty. The love for an advanced patient often seems unrequited. The lover seems alienated from her presence even when she is in the room. The caregiver confronts an unresponsive object of devotion and rarely receives a thank you. We can see in this love, perhaps, a model for loving a God who sometimes seems remote. We love and worship because these things are right, not because they bring rewards. At the same time, we must recall that the experiences of a dissolving person and a transcendant Deity are temporary and, to some extent, illusory. At the resurrection, we will share the love of this person once again—indeed we may expect it to be magnified in the presence of our Lord.

Appreciating any love requires a knowledge of the object of that love and, in our case, fathoming God's love for us requires us to know about how sin makes us less lovable. As the American Lutheran Church's *Disability Within the Family of God* declares, "Each of us is disabled by the Fall. . . . Every Christian, therefore, is a 'dis-enabled' person."[20] Hence, in seeing the mental chaos of the Alzheimer's patient, we can readily see ourselves and our own inability to order our lives properly. In recognizing the angry, fearful sinfulness of the caregivers, we remember our forgotten transgressions and find our own existential comfort challenged. And by seeing his broken body on the Cross, we come to recall the magnitude of our sins and the even greater magnitude of God's love. The mnemonic lessons of Alzheimer's families are painful for all initially, but they are not without purpose, redemption, or, ultimately, joy.

Chapter 7

Beauty, the Church, and Christology

What happens when we smell a rose?
— Josef Pieper, *Leisure, the Basis of Culture*

According to most of the theologians and philosophers who have meditated on the experience of the beautiful, beholding a rose is an affirmation of the world's goodness and of humanity's place in it. Losing this feeling is precisely one of the great dangers Alzheimer's families face. It is by no means clear how a person can maintain his or her confidence in the goodness of creation when confronted with chaos and disease. Stoic apathy and detachment, at once so secure and so limiting, may appear to be our best defense. Even with such stiff-minded protection, the cosmos may still come to seem an ugly place. The patient who loses control of limbs, who blabbers incessantly, who dribbles liquids, can seem an embodiment of disproportion and the very opposite of the beautiful. When caring for this person full-time over the course of many, many years, it is easy for that reality to color the rest of the world. We may be more likely to see disorder and decay everywhere. We might notice the trash along the highway, not the leaves of a New England fall. The earth may appear as it did to Jeremiah (4:23), "waste and void."

At the same time, it is possible for a caregiver to have the opposite experience, as her soul longs to be reunited with the goodness of nature. When looking out of a window with a patient, the caregiver may ask the patient if he also notices the chirping of baby chicks or the simple sound of leaves blowing across the grasses. But what she really means to ask is: "Can you please let me know that you, too, can still see what I am thrilled to see?" The patient says "Yes, yes," but the caregiver may wonder if this is simply a socially conditioned response. There is perhaps no greater joy for a caregiver than to hear a patient singing a song or humming a remembered tune. In this moment, we behold him defying the disease, and we can sense the presence of peace. We become quite saddened when we suspect that he can no longer experience these joys. And when we recall moments of the beautiful which we shared with the patient—moments he has forgotten—our lament grows. We become more grateful for our own capacity to be overcome by beauty. We may accept the responsibility of seeing—and remembering—the beautiful for him.

I must rely on the reader's own memories here. Those who have yet to experience the beautiful and those who have managed to put such experiences out of their minds will not read this chapter the same way as will a person whose memories are resplendent with the beautiful. But if we can recall some of our own experiences of the beautiful, we may remember a sudden sense of intense joy, a halting of our activity, a suspension of time, a sense of peace, a sudden welling-up of praise. Whatever it was, we liked it, and I would be willing to guess that we also had an urge to share the experience, whether by tapping someone's shoulder or writing a letter. Indeed, it is our shoulder which has been tapped by something else. For we have not summoned beauty, beauty has summoned us beyond ourselves.

It is this experience of joy, peace, and gratitude which caregivers need. The church should help provide this ministry of beauty in the face of ugliness. As a slow, solitary sustained note or melody sometimes unites and maintains an entire symphony for a few moments, so too do experiences of the beautiful sustain the human person and prepare her for the *allegro vivace*s required of a caregiver. Or, to choose another image, the beautiful may undergird our lives just as in Handel's "Hallelujah Chorus" the bass singers' weighty "Lord of Lords" underlies the sopranos' many vibrant "Hallelujahs." Because of its intensity, beauty can refresh our souls and energize us in our pursuit of goodness, truth, and holiness. It confirms that we are all part of a larger, inspiring world that is more real and "true" than a patient's nursing home room. We need to discover how a person can be reattached to the world through the beautiful. If we recall our previous experiences again, we may remember that at least for a brief moment, we felt secure in the bosom of nature. As Alzheimer's disease offers a cruel, savage nature—or worse, an indifferent nature— so does the beautiful promise a providentially ordered cosmos.

The subject of beauty is not without its perils. The prophets Amos and Isaiah both criticize their contemporaries for being overly engaged with material and aesthetic concerns. The near-worship of beautiful things obscures personal and social iniquity. The "fair words" of Jeremiah 12:6 and the "fair and flattering words" of Romans 16:18 suggest that the beautiful is as subject to human perversion as most things are. In Ezekiel 28:17 we are reminded that human beauty may stir us to pride and rebellion. Indeed, because the beautiful is so alluring and compelling, the danger for abuse and idolatry is all the greater, as Moses well knew as he shaped Israel's remembering in Deuteronomy 4. Even when we are well-intentioned, we ought to be wary. Jaroslav Pelikan's *Fools for Christ: Essays on the True, the Good, and the Beautiful* examines the potential for our mistaking the beautiful, the good, or the true for the holiness of God. He reminds us that ultimately, the central Christian category must remain holiness. In this light, I want to examine how the experience of the beautiful can help us to perceive the holiness of God and to aspire to his righteousness.

The first section of the chapter provides a descriptive statement of the phenomena of beauty and the sublime. Although I will use the term "aesthetic" loosely, applying it to both human and divine creations, I will focus on the question of natural beauty as a theological decision. As Genesis, Milton's *Paradise Lost*, and Barth would attest, the real action, and hence the artistry, all begins in heaven, not with humanity. Nature, as God's creation, has chronological, ontological, and aesthetic priority over human art (cf. Jesus' comparison of the lilies of the field to Solomon's regal glory in Matt. 6:28-9). The second section discusses the church's cultivation of the capacity for beauty, particularly for caregivers. Finally, the last section considers once again how the church as a whole can learn from the experiences of caregivers. As William James observed, those with a profound sense of suffering are often those most capable of deep raptures and joys.[1] Perhaps all of us can strengthen our own ability for being overcome by the beautiful through a meditation on caregivers as Christian artists.

Josef Pieper's study of leisure, a term which as he develops it resembles our discussion of beauty, suggests that we are all in desperate need of leisure for the experience of the beautiful. This experience, to the extent that it requires some cultivation or preparation on our part, seems to require the leisure to cultivate ourselves. We may not recognize it as clearly as we can see it in caregivers, but our work, our responsibilities, duties, and chores perpetually threaten to dull and desensitize us to the mysteries and beauties of creation. Hence, we will need to see how the church can prepare us all for the Sabbath moments of rest needed for the cultivation of the sense of beauty. To reformulate the quotation with which this introduction began, What happens if we stop smelling roses?

This chapter is all too brief and limited study of this subject, but I hope that it can be, like the beautiful itself, suggestive of a greater, more glorious and holy reality. I doubt that I will be able to put my finger on the beautiful, but perhaps like a violin's vibrato, rocking back and forth over the precise note may enhance a sweet sound.

Descriptions of the Beautiful

That God's creation is beautiful is declared in the creation accounts, the Psalms, and many a Gospel song. The "Praise" and "Works in Creation" sections of hymnals contain countless paeans to the splendors of God's cosmos. The great cathedrals are beautiful human responses to the creation and God's work in history. Even those churches that look askance at ornamentation have flowers on the altar or communion table. These bouquets are often donated in memory of someone (we associate remembering with beauty). The church is a repository for beauty—for proclaiming the beauty of God and his creation and for preparing us for experiencing the joys evoked by his work. Beauty does inhere in the creation, but are we capable of perceiving it? We are not wrong when we sing "For the Beauty of the Earth." But what about our perception of its splendor? Moreover, what is the theological significance of these feelings and passions which arise in us? Are they, as Barth maintained, part of the way in which God draws us toward himself?

This experience of beauty is something that cannot be taken for granted, just as our ability to know and do the good cannot be assumed. Hence, to cultivate our appreciation for the beautiful, we need to seek assistance from others who have contemplated the subject at great length, others who have expressed verbally what we may experience in our souls through visual, aural, and olfactory stimuli. While we cannot agree with those who argue for the sufficiency of a moral aesthetics (Jonathan Edwards and Kierkegaard, in their own ways, critiqued such sentiments), we can learn from secular descriptive insights concerning human phenomena.

Philosophers, theologians, poets, and artists of all sorts have attempted various, often contradictory, definitions of beauty and related concepts such as the sublime and the aesthetic. There are, to be sure, great differences in their theories. Terms which seem to give us some clue about the nature of beauty have a tendency to break down upon sustained analysis. What seems to be pleasing symmetry is not necessarily a source of beauty, as the humorous title of one of Edmund Burke's chapters from his *Philosophical Inquiry* on beauty suggests: "Proportion not the Cause of Beauty in Vegetables." Similarly, as any tour of churches of different confessions will reveal, the church catholic itself has disparate traditions concerning beauty and religious art. (We will need to remember that while churches may share a common affirmation of the beauty of the creation, they may well experience this beauty differently and incarnate it in church art according to varying cultural tastes.)

Although we can doubt the ultimate success of our individual predecessors as they considered this subject, we should not doubt that the experience of the beautiful as a human phenomenon is a powerful one. Hence, George Santayana profitably examined our experience of beauty as "phenomena of mind."[2] Whether it describes our proclivity towards creating art and adorning objects or our experiences of nature, this subject remains central to humanity's self-understanding. Whatever it is, beauty is captivating, awe-inspiring, capable of transforming a simple act of seeing into a profound vision which can shake our bodies or syncopate our breathing. How can we approach the mystery of beauty and how can we prepare ourselves for it?

The following discussions may help remind us of what beauty intimates and how we can better sense it. In a passage from the *Symposium* which illustrates why many Christians have often found Plato to be the most penetrating of the philosophers, Plato describes how a person may be led from beautiful youths and sexual attraction, to spiritual beauty, dedication to a virtuous life, and to love itself. Whatever beauty is, it opens us up to new, unexpected possibilities. It represents a beginning to the intellectual and spiritual pilgrimage towards love, love both human and divine. In his *Critique of Judgment*, Kant tries to identify what curious things were at work in the human person when he experiences the beautiful (or the sublime). He identified a strange mix of freedom, delight, universality, and disinterest, topics that others—but not all—have woven into their discussions of this subject. Jacques Maritain and the neo-Scholastic tradition seek to define the metaphysical characteristics of beauty. Following Aquinas and Bonaventure, they consider beauty as a transcendental property of being (along with unity, goodness, and truth). Although these Christians differ as to how beauty might be related to the other transcendentals, they all agree that it remains a significant question. As with Plato's description, the experience of beauty takes us out of ourselves and enables us to contemplate the original splendor of prelapsarian creation. The beautiful "has the savor of the terrestrial paradise, because it restores, for the moment, the peace and simultaneous delight of the intellect and the senses."[3]

Emerson, who shared "the incessant drive of the Puritan to learn how, and how most ecstatically, he can hold any sort of communion with the environing wilderness," provides a sustained description of the beautiful and its effect on us.[4] For him, beauty needs to be seen in the context of the effects of modern science on our perception of "objects." Natural science dissects objects from the whole of creation, indeed separates the observer's soul from the cosmos. "The want of sympathy makes his [the scientist's] record a dull dictionary." Hence, Emerson speaks of beauty and the "soul's avowal of its large relations." Echoing Plato's imagery in the *Phaedrus*, Emerson states that beauty "plants wings at our shoulders." Yet, beauty is not purely sensory, for "We love any forms, however ugly, from which great qualities shine. . . . All high beauty has a moral element in it." Despite his descriptive powers, he states, "beauty is still escaping out of all analysis." In contrast to laboratory specimens, "It is not yet possessed, it cannot be handled."

Santayana's description of our experience of beauty shares Emerson's elusiveness: "Beauty as we feel it is something indescribable . . . It is an affection of the soul, a consciousness of joy and security, a pang, a dream, a pure pleasure. It suffuses an object without telling why; nor has it any need to ask the question. It justifies itself and the vision it gilds. . . . Indeed, if we look at things teleologically, and as they ultimately justify themselves to the heart, beauty is of all things what least calls for an explanation. . . . Beauty is a pledge of the possible conformity between the soul and nature, and consequently a ground of faith in the supremacy of good."[5]

The description of powerful experiences of the senses includes not only moments of the beautiful, but also moments of the related but distinct concept of the sublime. Again, specific analyses and definitions differ considerably, but in Burke, Kant, Santayana, and others we can glimpse articulations of moments which may have made us shudder in awe. Whereas beauty tends towards pure delight, the sublime tends towards the disquieting, the terrifying, and the humbling. We sense a confrontation with a world which we cannot control and which may not care about our own existence. This vision does appear, in some sense, to be beautiful, but we feel less certain about our own place in the cosmos. The sympathy between fellow creatures dissolves into anxieties about the human condition. As we read in Psalm 8, accustomed to human self-exaltation, we gaze upon the innumerable, magnificent, distant stars and feel very insignificant indeed. Psalm 19 juxtaposes the proclamation of the heavens praising the "glory of God" with the unfathomable depths of human sinfulness. The vastness of the skies and the darkness of the human heart are twin aspects of the sublime (and perhaps of the holy as well).

We may sense that if we follow Burke's terminology, beholding an Alzheimer's patient is sublime. We feel terror; we become lost in the disease's obscurity; we dread the presence of such a powerful disease; we see in the vacant eyes darkness, solitude, and silence as well as the vastness of a disappearing mind; in that vastness, we see the infinity of seemingly lost memories; we sense unfathomable pain as a patient screams; and when she articulates sounds, we hear what may seem to be "the cries of animals."[6] At the same time, if we borrow from Santayana's interpretation, we may see that Christ is, in some sense, sublime. Through him we can aspire to an "immunity " from evil and a "universal standpoint"; we can experience "liberation" and "ultimate peace."[7] And thanks to the Psalms, the experience of sublime terror can be transformed into the experience of sublime, joyful praise.

If the beautiful and the sublime remain definite but elusive experiences, we can, however, describe how these experiences relate to some of our other central subjects, particularly memory, the soul, and immortality. The central issue of Alzheimer's disease, human memory, is also a central element in the human experience of the beautiful. We bring to a vision our vast range of memories, and whether or not we are overcome by a sight is due, in part, to a combination of the sight's familiarity and its strangeness.[8] Because the current experience so greatly overpowers lesser ones which we retain in our memory, we can hail this vision as something spectacular, something excellent and beautiful. As we cultivate our facility with memory mobilization so we improve our capacity to recognize distinctly beautiful objects or events. Moments cease to be isolated or discrete, and the sunset we behold recapitulates previous joys and events. The current oranges, reds, scarlets, and purples recall to mind earlier sunsets, earlier moments which we may wish to share with those with us in the present. If we find ourselves alone at such reveries, we may feel all the more solitary, and a bit wistful at our frustrated desire to communicate joy.

As the experience of the beautiful often generates a refreshing sympathy between the human person and the cosmos, it should not be surprising that those theologians and philosophers who take beauty seriously also take the soul seriously (e.g. Plato, Aquinas, Kant). Beauty seems so wondrous that understanding its effects in terms of brains and neurons seems totally inadequate. The cerebellum hardly strikes us as beautiful, but the soul as the *imago Dei* certainly seems to be capable of being beautiful (and also, through sin, quite ugly). In chapter 4, I suggested that the issue of "quality" was a strong argument in favor of the soul's reality. That we experience sensory input not as raw data but as different qualities admitting of a great number of stirring resonances suggested that a mechanical or physiological explanation of consciousness would be inadequate. Similarly, when we consider our experiences of beauty and of its related experiences—above all peace and love—we sense the need to acknowledge the workings of the soul.

Whenever we try to describe these marvelous relationships, we must have recourse to metaphors, such as Plato's wings of the soul. The workings are so mysterious and so open-ended that only metaphors have the suggestive power to move our understanding in the appropriate direction. We may describe the effect of beauty on the soul in the following manner. As the D string of the violin will vibrate sympathetically when a D an octave higher is played on the A string, so too does the soul resonate in sympathy with its fellow creatures when it beholds their beauty. As the D string moves, so does the soul stir.

Because beauty sometimes seems to have the capacity to stand on its own, reflections on the beautiful often form a part of natural theology, a natural theology devoid of any serious consideration of the central anthropological dilemma, sin. How different in its message is Psalm 19. In verses 1-6, the psalmist beholds the skies and hears the "heavens telling the glory of God." In verses 7-14, God's magnificence extends from the material creation to the perfect "law of the Lord" which revives the soul. Indeed, these righteous ordinances surpass the beautiful and sweet works of nature, gold and honey. Precisely because the psalmist recognizes the righteousness of God, he is led to examining his own sinful conscience and to acknowledging its "errors" and "hidden faults." Then, he addresses God and prays that his response be acceptable to the "Lord, my rock and my redeemer." Like an icon that points through its material reality to a heavenly or spiritual reality, so can our experience of beauty, when properly shepherded, point through itself to human sinfulness, to God, and to our reconciliation.

Beauty and Belief; or, A Christian Rhetoric

In his consideration of the eternity and glory of God, Barth observes the frequent Biblical references to the human enjoyment of God and asks, "Why also joy, why specifically joy, according to the witnesses of Holy Scripture?" He argues that God "acts as the One who gives pleasure, creates desire, and rewards with enjoyment." In exploring these divine attributes and activities, Barth employs the idea of beauty. To say that God is beautiful "is to say how he enlightens and convinces and persuades us."[9] In other words, to examine beauty theologically, we enter into the realm of one mode of Christian rhetoric. Our concern with beauty is, after all, not with beauty for its own sake, rather it is a concern with how the beauties of God, his creation, and the church persuade us of God's glorious governance of the cosmos and his redemptive mercy. As Barth sensed, by overlooking beauty, we may be missing part of the experience of God's presence in the world.

In exploring the beauty of God, Barth was well aware of Protestantism's reluctance to explore this subject. Nevertheless, he persevered, and did explicate the ways in which even Protestants can, or should, speak of this topic. There is no need to rehearse the specifically Protestant obstacles to a theological consideration of beauty. I am convinced that Protestant, especially Gospel, hymnody is a testament to the interest which Protestants have in the religious experience of the beautiful. Confessional differences will separate the churches in their explorations of the beautiful. A strong doctrine of

185

sanctification leads more easily to a theological aesthetics. An emphasis on justification tends in the opposite direction, though William M. Thompson suggests how an understanding of justification that respects how we are transformed in Christ creates possibilities for a Protestant aesthetics.[10] Our treatment of beauty as a type of Christian rhetoric, then, will have to remain but a discussion of the basic doctrinal points and theological contours needed to delineate a Christian aesthetics in the context of the realities of Alzheimer's. With the disorientation caused by this disease, nothing less than the relationship of humanity to the rest of God's creation is at stake.

Fortunately, good resources are available. Hans Urs von Balthasar's *The Glory of the Lord* represents one of most sustained treatments of the historical and theological aspects of Christian aesthetics. Following Heidegger, he asserts the centrality of Being itself, and following Hoelderlin, he asserts that God's glory is to be understood as the union of holiness and beauty.[11] Another work which deserves mention is Patrick Sherry's *Spirit and Beauty: An Introduction to Theological Aesthetics*.[12] This work takes more Protestant contributions into consideration (especially Jonathan Edwards' Trinitarian approach to beauty) as it explores the roles of the Holy Spirit in natural beauty and art. While my own focus has been more Christological than Pneumatological, I remain indebted to this work. Readers seeking a good introduction to the problems of theology and beauty will be well-served by Sherry's study.

I would like to unfold this discussion in two stages. The first treats of specific doctrines which seem central to a Christian consideration of beauty. Here we speak of what is traditionally called the objective aspect of beauty. The second stage examines more of what we might call the subjective (or self-involving) side of beauty; this stage considers how the church through its liturgy, preaching, and art guides our personal experiences of the beautiful. If it is true that all sensory perception involves interpretation (if there is no "pure" sensation), then our understanding of the powerful human experience of the beautiful becomes a central ecclesiological issue. In this light, we can understand one aspect of what Pope John Paul II means when he states in the recently published *Catechism of the Catholic Church* that doctrine itself is beautiful.[13] Since our doctrine can be beautiful, we should not be surprised if it can help us to appreciate beauty. Together in these two approaches, we might say, we will have both what Christians should affirm propositionally about beauty and how

Christians through the church can come to experience the beautiful as faithful raptures or reposes.

The most obvious starting point for a consideration of the objective beauty of the world is the doctrine of the creation. The refrain-like, nearly hymnic "And God saw that it was good . . . And there was evening and there was morning" suggests that God was satisfied with the work of the creation. St. Francis' intimate perception of our creatureliness allowed him to hail Brother Sun and Sister Moon and to see beauty throughout the creation. (Through Francis we have the hymn "All Creatures of Our God and King.") In his embrace of poverty, we see the non-possessiveness of Christian beauty. We may covet and own many beautiful things, but ultimately everything is God's.

The separation of the natural sciences from theology in recent centuries has hampered considerations of the beauty of the creation. In the doctrine of evolution, for example, the natural world's mysterious workings are seen to be the result of savage forces of natural selection, not benevolent Providence. Moreover, Alzheimer's disease, the Lisbon earthquake, and countless other "natural" disasters make it very difficult to perceive any form of immanent kindness, let alone beauty, in the cosmos. Still, God created the world, and at times it is experienced as beautiful, as something enrapturing. Like it or not, in a hurricane-ridden world, the water of Baptism reminds us that God gives us new life through the natural order. God works through the creation, not in opposition to it. As ordained in Genesis 9:13-17, the splendid rainbow is a mnemonic aid for God and Noah of the "everlasting covenant between God and every living creature of all flesh that is upon the earth." God's works of created beauty can become a sign of his promise for everyone.

Both Barth and von Balthasar wisely speak of Christ as the center of a Christian doctrine of beauty. As the *eikon* of both humanity and God, the perfection of created humanity, the God-man who makes praise of God and his work possible, the One through whom all things were made, he stands at the heart of our aesthetics. We stylize our images of Jesus. It is hard for us not to imagine the Jesus of the Sermon on the Mount as an upright, beautiful speaker. Artists and those who seek these images sense what Barth declares—the "self-representation of God" in Jesus Christ "arouses joy."[14]

At the same time, Christ also challenges all human conceptions of beauty. Barth accurately reads Isaiah 53:1-2 ("Who has believed what we have heard? . . . He had no form or comeliness that we should look at him, and no beauty that we should desire him."): "If the beauty of Christ is sought in a glorious Christ who is not the crucified, the search will always be in vain."[15] Santayana expresses the beautiful in terms of a peace brought about by a certain harmonizing of experiences. Because the "various impulses of the self" are suspended into a single image "a great peace falls upon that perturbed kingdom."[16] The beautiful draws us in our entireties toward itself. Christ is supremely beautiful to us because he arouses not only the divine image which we bear gladly, but also because he calls forth the sinner which we hide. Only when beholding the fullness of Christ's life, passion, death, and resurrection are we able to behold ourselves in our totality.

A Christological consideration of beauty, then, is a terrible thing to imagine. Yet it describes a way of contemplating human experiences which Christians are called to do. We are not allowed to enjoy a sunset apart from the Cross. We are not allowed to take delight in a rose without recognizing the crown of thorns. It is not that such beautiful pleasures are denied to us. We are not Manichaeians or dualists. Rather, to be faithful to God's work we must recognize that the Person through whom beautiful gifts were made was also the Person nailed to a tree for our sakes. Our delight yields to sorrow and shame, and these in turn, yield to gratitude, praise, and joy. Indeed, when we recognize just what has been wrought upon our sinfulness, we can share the peace that passeth understanding. This is the central movement of Christian aesthetics.

It is impossible to understand this transfiguration of experience without considering briefly the relationships between beauty and the Trinity. Barth's discussion of the Trinity's radiation of joy is insightful. We acknowledge that the Trinity is self-communicating love, and hence we should recognize that, as a consequence, the Trinity's fullness of love overflows with a splendor of its joy. Barth, again exploring how it is that God draws us to himself, summarizes: the Trinity "attracts and therefore it conquers. It is, therefore, beautiful."[17] Our experience of the beautiful, then, is grounded in the compelling power of the Triune God who, is above all, love. As two lovers attract us to their delights and their love, so are we attracted to God through recognizing the Trinity as lover, as source of beauty.

Because our consideration of beauty is Christological, we cannot, no matter how much we may be tempted, separate sin from beauty. Barth, indeed, argues that our sinfulness impedes our ability to perceive how the creation itself forms a chorus of praise to God's glory.[18] Part of our punishment, then, is knowing that we are surrounded perpetually by beauty while being able to perceive its glories only irregularly. We are, once again, as Alzheimer's patients—surrounded by a world much greater, more coherent, and more beautiful than we have the cognitive capacity to experience. We catch glimpses, but we recognize them as fleeting. Because we acknowledge the deep affect of sin on our experiences of beauty we are able to avoid the trap of treating beauty as some form of revelation or epiphany. We recognize, instead, that sinfulness sometimes blurs our categories. Sin often seems to be attractive, whereas it is quite ugly. And virtue is indeed beautiful, but it seems rather "drab at first sight."[19] In recognizing the link between sinfulness and beauty, we cannot separate death from beauty. Our subjection to death makes us cherish the beautiful all the more, for mortal creatures value perfection, with its intimations of immortality all the more. Similarly, part of the beauty of flowers lies in their fragility, and part of the reason we are attracted to them may be that we can see ourselves in their withering.

Because of our sinfulness, our present experiences of the beautiful can be but anticipations or foretastes of eschatological beauty. Von Balthasar writes, "This presence of what belongs to the future is the true source of beauty in the New Testament."[20] Because the eternally beautiful God has become a human, because the full glory beyond time has come into time, we can sense the beautiful throughout time. The Incarnation makes it possible for Christians to perceive beauty even before our resurrection. As the resurrected body is the ultimate body, so too will the experience of beauty at the eschaton be ultimate. The new Jerusalem will be filled with beauty as Old Testament prophetic utterances and the rich description of the Apocalypse suggest. Until the end of time, our souls contemplate the fulfillment of the promised glory of the Lord, and we sing the hymn, "For the Beauty of the Earth" with, as the hymn puts it, our "Friends on earth, and friends above."

How the church prepares us actually to experience and recognize these moments, events, and realities is the subject of the rest of this section. Barth concludes his discussion of the beauty of God by stating that although the church is the place where the "secret reality" of God's creation is known "more and more . . . in faith . . . we shall be both comforted and shamed by the fact that there is no sphere in heaven or on earth which even here and now is not secretly full of the glory of God."[21] The church does have a heavy responsibility for teaching us how to perceive such plenitude.

Each person needs the church's help to perceive the beauty and the glory of God. Just as we love only a few but should love all, so can we sense beauty intermittently when we should see God's mysterious presence throughout the creation. We need help not only because of our sinfulness but also because of our own deficiencies in habits. Whereas we should understand aesthetics to mean the study of beauty primarily in nature and secondarily in human works, we have sometimes restricted ourselves, following Hegel's focus on human productions, to a purely anthropological aesthetics. At times, we may have fallen into Roland Barthes' and the Structuralists' trap—assuming that the world is chaotic and incoherent and that only art brings structure and order.

Consequently, we are not always skilled in understanding how beauty relates to the divine economy as a whole. The word the medieval scholastics used for beauty—*pulchritudo*—suggests also excellence, propriety, and purposefulness; can we recover this sense faithfully? I believe we can be confident that Christ has made it possible for us to rejoice in the creation and its glories. Our sins are forgiven; our hearts can melt; and our eyes can learn to see God's workings all around us. As we are reconciled with the Creator, so can we become closer to the creation.

We have seen the centrality of memory to both Christianity and to the experience of the beautiful. Although "the imagination of man's heart is evil from [our] youth" (Gen. 8:21), the memory and imagination may be rendered faithful with proper shepherding. The church should help guide our remembering through its liturgy, its art, and, ultimately, its contemplative or even mystical traditions. The Holy Spirit and memory's *durée* can help lead us to perceive the presence of the Lord. The purple of sunset suggests imperial purple— we suddenly remember the Lordship of Christ. A tree's branches are delicately fashioned—so should we recall the tree which we all planted on Golgotha. Following the medieval four-fold tradition of exegesis, we might see this tree according to each of the four senses: the beauty of the created tree itself (literal); the Crucifixion (allegorical); our need to bear our crosses and suffer with Christ (tropological); and the tree of life of the new heaven and earth described in Revelation (anagogical). Beauty guided by the church's memory is both a reality in the creation as well as a rich, symbolic text. When an experience of beauty leads us to remember Christ and his work then we can discern the Spirit liberating us to praise God.

In the previous section, we saw how Psalm 19 juxtaposed the "heavens telling the glory of God" (vs. 1-6) with the "law of the Lord" (vs. 7-14). That verses 7-14, the passages which explore God's right-eousness and human sinfulness, may have been added by a later author is suggestive of how the church may shepherd our experience of beauty. The church accepts such "interpolations" as canonical, as part of the essential text, because it recognizes that the Psalm in its current plenitude is a faithful testament to God and a proper human response. So, too, may we want to interpolate confessions of God's righteousness into our memories of experiencing beauty (if we were not so spiritually moved at the time we had such an experience). As we remember that halcyon sunset and the exquisite way its colors descended behind a thin row of pine trees cresting a hillside, let us now remember to add our praise of God's glory and Christ's redeem-ing work. Our subsequent remembering of this sunset, will thus, like Psalm 19, contain a proper fullness. We may call such a devotional operation a "Christological redaction" of beauty.

The most significant opportunity for guiding our memories is the liturgy. The pleasure we take from a service varies depending on the quality of the service and the quality of our hearts. A skillful organist, through pauses and changes of pace, can enhance the passion aroused by a hymn just as taking "Joy to the World" at too slow a pace can suggest that there is no joy in the world whatsoever. Indeed, when there is a good choir and beautiful voices in the congregation we feel like we are truly a part of a loving community. At such moments, we love to sing "Amen" together because our voices are communing beautifully. On the other hand, when we sing at differ-ent tempos or out of tune, we feel the exact opposite. We feel like withdrawing from a congregation and separating ourselves from the cacophony (not unlike the way an Alzheimer's caregiver may with-draw from society or a patient from the world). Music itself depends on our ability to remember the preceding notes, tunes, keys, and tempos, and not only do we remember these but we also come to anticipate recapitulations or returns to themes or keys. In particular, we come to anticipate the "Amen" of a hymn. Hence, if we learn about beauty through hymnody, we may develop the habit of saying "Amen" when we experience beauty outside of the sanctuary.

191

As the doctrine of the Trinity suggests, the experiences of joy, love, and beauty are, properly speaking, communal rater than private or subjective. The emphasis on the ecclesial apprehension of icons in the Orthodox tradition helps make this clear:

> [The icon's] function consists not in aesthetic contemplation but in participation in the act of worship, in bearing witness to 'sobornost' (communitariness) not through subjective but rather 'sobornyi' (communitarian) experience, through the experience of the saints about the highest religious truths. . . . In joining with the 'sobornyi,' collective experience that exceeds the capacities of the individual, in bringing oneself into harmony with this communitarian experience, a human being finds himself raised upon the shoulders of giants and attains the capacity to 'jump higher than his own head.' The individual does not disappear but ceases to dominate; he becomes a voice in the choir. But after all, the choir itself is composed of voices; and it is through these individual traits that are now dissolved in the whole that the variety of the iconography we know is achieved.[22]

Josef Pieper's discussion of worship illuminates why it is possible to learn to see beauty through the liturgy. Worship, he observes, "creates a sphere of real wealth and superfluity, even in the midst of the direst material want—because sacrifice is the living heart of worship." Such sacrifice, because it is non-utilitarian, creates an atmosphere where "generosity reigns."[23] When the Spirit gives us the strength, we give freely without consideration to our own ends, and we communicate with God and with each other. Similarly, beauty is all about the real wealth and superfluity of the creation. The glories of nature are available to those whose hearts and eyes are prepared. And we must train ourselves to share this wealth generously in communal praise and shared experiences. As the liturgy expands our perceptions of the cosmos, so does it prepare us to see beyond sensory data and perceive God's work. Indeed, we see not data but *data* in its Latin meaning—"gifts," gifts of God. Such gifts entail great responsibilities, as environmentalists quite appropriately remind us.

It may be that, too, Gerhard Nebel's emphasis on beauty as an event, rather than a substance or an inhering quality, will be helpful to Protestant aesthetics.[24] The liturgy, as an event, is beautiful in that it points to God's forgiveness and love. The beauty does not reside in the ornamentation of the church but in the fact that we experience new possibilities for our lives, we anticipate the fulfillment of the

Kingdom of God, and we begin to live anew in its present gifts. There are many different ways of construing the beauty we sometimes experience, and, again, each church will need to guide its people according to its own understanding of Christ, the sacraments, and the church. As a Choral Call to Prayer during the liturgy suggests that beautiful music leads to prayer, so too does the church teach us that an experience of beauty is to usher in praise.

It is also through the liturgy that we participate in Sabbath rest and delight. Speaking from a Catholic perspective, Pieper observes that the "liturgy knows only feast days."[25] The superabundance of the Sabbath is a sign that we can rest from our fields for a bit, and this superabundance appears in liturgical celebrations perhaps most clearly in our songs. To miss the pleasure God ordains for us in the creation and Sabbath is to miss God's love—indeed in the light of the loving nature of the Trinity, it is to miss God's nature itself. Many caregivers are not able to attend the liberating services of the church because of their commitments to their wards. Like Martha of Luke 10:38-42, they are "anxious and troubled about many things," and are unable to take the time to hear the Word. Here churches and friends are capable of demonstrating their love. Coming by to stay with the patient in order to allow the caregiver to worship is a greatly needed act of service.

In addition to the liturgy, church art is rich in resources. The second chapter of this study observed that pre-modern mnemonic systems utilized beautiful images (as well as ugly ones) because of their greater power over the mind, because of their greater *durée*. Depictions of Jesus are both a sign of presence and an aid to memory, and as part of that aid, the images are often stylized to express the peace, the glory, or suffering of Jesus. The artists seek to depict the God-man beautifully (or in the ugliness of suffering greater pain) so that the image will remain in the mind more powerfully. If we presented pictures of different churches, icons, and religious images from different centuries, continents, and sides of the railroad tracks, it would be clear that Christian art is diverse, woven into the social fabric wherein it was created, and by no means appears universally beautiful. That diverse Christians find different artworks beautiful suggests that the beauty of Christian art is found in particulars as well as universals.

Because of this variety in Christian art we arrive at an experience of the interplay between intellect, soul, and sin—or to reformulate it, the interplay between doctrine and personal apprehension. The mind may know that the subject of the painting is beautiful—for example, the woman's anointing of Jesus in Matthew 26:10—but the artwork itself fails to stir the soul. The intellect and will have to exert themselves to appreciate the glory of the subject. The mind tells the soul to be excited by the depiction of a beautiful event, but the soul remains sluggish. Perhaps the painting seems to be nothing more than kitsch or the work of an amateurish hand. How much better we would be if we opened ourselves up to the subjects of sacred art and admitted to ourselves that the depictions of the great, merciful stories of Scripture—no matter how tacky, cheap, culturally strange, or scandalous—should cause us to shudder. (It is curious that while many find Andres Serrano's *Piss Christ* offensive, the Crucifixion itself often seems less shocking.) Such an encounter with "distasteful" Christian art underscores the importance of doctrine. As Paul Holmer observes, Christian teachings are not only objective they are "also adverbial. That is, they are only appreciated and understood when they begin to modify all of us, and in deep ways."[26] Doctrine shapes our ability to perceive, experience, and worship, and it humbles us into acknowledging that our own artistic tastes are not universal. It spurs our imaginative meditation on art, chiding us for spiritual sluggishness. Doctrine is a charioteer to the great passions of the soul, driving us on or reining us in as necessary.

A devotional experience of beauty sometimes exploits the gap between aesthetic feeling (or its lack) and doctrinal knowledge. Handel's *Messiah* and the Bach *Passions* are beautiful, and if we lose ourselves in the music we forget that some of the events celebrated with such exquisite sounds are ugly. When we acknowledge that beauty expresses a profound ugliness, we begin to see that it also expresses an unfathomable love. There exists a perpetual dynamism in these movements from aesthetic joy to shame to gratitude to forgiveness to ignorance to faith. Similarly, beauty plays upon the contradictions in our emotions when we remember Alzheimer's patients during an experience of the beautiful. The ugliness of the disease and the inability of the advanced patient to perceive the beautiful causes us to cry when we experience so gloriously what they cannot.

Because our doctrine of creation recognizes its beauty, and because we are not always capable of perceiving this glory, Christians have recourse to the great artists and poets, both Christian and non-Christian. The great English poets of the seventeenth century—for me, especially Donne and Herbert—produced a great number of poems which expand our vision. They have taken ordinary objects, themes, events, and transformed them into extraordinary experiences. In Donne's "Good Friday, 1613. Riding Westward," a simple ride becomes an orientation into a Christological geography. Although he hides in shame from the rising of the sun behind him, he is overcome by the work wrought in Jerusalem. How can this happen? Speaking of Christ's death, "That spectacle of too much weight for me," he states, "Though these things, as I ride, be from mine eye / They are present yet unto my memory." It is as if Donne is riding away from Christ as he hangs upon the Cross. Donne has trained his soul through his memories to be able to render the past event present.

Poets deepen our perception of the beauty of creation by changing our habits of thinking. Despite our predilection for pure or unstained objects, Gerard Manley Hopkins' "Pied Beauty" teaches us to cry, "Glory be to God for dappled things— / . . . All things counter, original, spare, strange; / Whatever is fickle, freckled . . . / . . . He fathers-forth whose beauty is past change: / Praise him." Similarly provocative is George Herbert's "Ev'n poysons praise thee" in his "Providence." A good friend of mine, Roy Nanjo, a photographer, suggests to me that a good photographer can make any object the subject of a great photograph. By paying attention to details and by manipulating familiar images which resonate with viewers' memories, he can transform a simple object into a piece of art. Christians can accept this possibility not only as a statement of human potential but also a statement of God's beautiful workings in the creation.

Christians can find delight and guidance also in Christologically appropriating non-Christian poets. We read on multiple levels, seeking to understand not only the author's distinct point of view but also the truth in the poem which we appropriate within the context of church teachings. As the Psalms incorporated language from the practices of ancient Near Eastern monarchs, so can Christians adumbrate non-Christian insights into the Christian world. The world of any poet, our world, is not neutral space to be reconfigured by a poet, but space created by the Creator whom we worship. Different poets train their—and our—eyes on different aspects of the beauty of the entire creation, and we have need of them. With their help, we can deepen our singing of "All Creatures of Our God and King." ·

Can caregivers listen to a sermon on beauty or join a discussion with a friend on poetry? Yes, they can, because Alzheimer's families no longer look at the world with prosaic assumptions; they take nothing for granted; they all recognize they have the need. Indeed, I suspect that if we were to have the courage to converse with those in despair, those who suffer, and those in need about impractical subjects like beauty, that we would learn quite a bit about the Good, the True, the Beautiful, and the Holy. We often remember the details of our surroundings at our saddest moments, at funerals, at separations—at these moments we are attuned, it seems, to the creation, because we sense that our place in it is disturbed.

The themes of the joy given by God, of the attractive powers of God's nature, and of the longing we feel for God's love and holiness were important for Barth's and Balthasar's theological discussions of beauty because they recognized that in considering beauty and the manifold pleasures it provides, they were examining a central aspect of how God arouses joy in human beings.[27] This deep longing for God does not always have much of a role in socially-oriented theologies. Yet it is precisely this which needs to be preached and born witness to in churched circles if the church is to minister to caregivers. Many caregivers long for feelings and intimations of the beautiful. Their task often leads them to desiring unification with God and his cosmos. Because of their heightened awareness of the real ugliness which does exist, they appreciate and desire the opposite all the more. By shepherding our perceptions of the creation, of beauty, and ultimately of the Creator, the church can help all of us to share God's love. It is not only through the kerygma but also through a Christian rhetoric of beauty that we can come to this love.

The Caregiver as Christian Poet

The chorus of this book, which echoes Barth in some respects, has been proclaiming that all of us, in some degree or another, are afflicted with the trials of Alzheimer's disease. As sinners, we are patients, cognitively impaired and needing help. And as the experience of any two-income family or anyone working multiple jobs will confirm, we are all in danger of becoming, like full-time caregivers, people without the leisure to feel at home in the gifts of the creation. Consequently, our souls may not be properly tuned to resonate with notes of beauty. To switch imagery, in our hurry to wolf down our food, we gulp away without appreciating the sweetness of a red bell pepper or the distinctive flavor of cardamom. Fortunately, we are in a position to learn about experiencing beauty and the creation from those who are actual patients and caregivers.

Fergus Kerr, whose critique of modern subject-based theology is cited in an earlier chapter, suggests why considering beauty from the perspective of the Alzheimer's patient is crucial. The modern, scientific (Cartesian) paradigm, he shows, strives to observe nature "as it is" and such an endeavor requires that the observer be dissolved and be separated from the world.[28] Only when we realize that this is exactly what happens with an Alzheimer's patient—the eliminated and separated observer—do we realize how horrible this way of looking at nature really is. By trying to see the creation through the perspective of a patient, we see that what we need to do is exactly the opposite. We need to see how the observer is really a part of the entire creation and is properly at home in the beauty of the cosmos.

For all our preference for rational denomination and deliberation, this feeling at home in the creation is not dependent on cognizance or intellectual propositions. Significantly, Kerr concludes his examination of Wittgenstein's theological considerations with a quotation from Augustine's sermon on Psalm 32, a Psalm which moves from forgiveness to shouts of joy:

> Wherever men must labor hard, they begin with songs whose words express their joy. But when the joy brims over and words are not enough, they abandon even this coherence and give themselves up to the sheer sound of singing. What is this jubilation, this exultant song? It is the melody that means our hearts are bursting with feelings words cannot express. And to whom does this jubilation most belong? Surely to God, who is unutterable. . . . If words will not come and you may not remain silent, what else can you do but let the melody soar?[29]

When confronted by the dissolution and suffering of Alzheimer's disease, it is forgiveness and, ultimately, the promise of the resurrection which allow us to rejoice.

Alzheimer's patients can still respond to beauty, and those who were regular members of churches retain the capacity to participate in musical or rhythmic aspects of worship.[30] That people in advanced stages of this disease can still experience beauty—indeed can still hum and still, in Hopkins' phrase, "Give beauty back"—suggests that the joys of beauty and the peace of being in God's creation do not depend on a fully conscious, rational subject. Beauty is, ultimately, an experience which relativizes the Cartesian intellect and our notion of subjecthood. The Cartesian self seems stuck in its own world; it cannot decide to summon or to create the experience of the beautiful on demand. We can make ourselves drunk, but we cannot stun ourselves with a sunset. The reality of beauty tells us that the soul, the whole person, is not isolated. Through our senses, the mind receives not only sensory input but evocative calls to passion, to joy, and to love. We live in a world of quality not just quantity, not just quantifiable patterns of wavelength and neural stimulation. We dwell in a land of grace and the Holy Spirit, and our deepest, most wondrous experiences are far from autonomous. Like memory's *durée*, beauty strikes, grabs, and pulls us out of ourselves.

That a cognitively impaired person can give beauty back may lend support to Kant's stress on the disinterestedness of a free aesthetic experience. For him, we can delight in apprehending the beauty of something for its own sake, not for what the beauty does for us. In a Christian context, we may interpret this in terms of apprehending the glory of God for his own sake. In contrast to such an understanding of the beautiful, however, many of our century have stressed precisely the interestedness of all human experience. We may take for granted that all aspects of life are driven by our political, economic, social, etc. concerns. To the extent that beauty helps our souls to sense our parts in the economy of God, and to the extent that such intimations lead us to love others, beauty can have important social dimensions. Caregivers especially teach us this. When their sacrifices and work are offered in the spirit of love and devotion, they teach us that we are most human when we are not so selfishly interested in our own activities. Hence, we learn about a free experience of beauty, and the praise it evokes, from them, too. As the eyes of the saints in paintings are looking heavenwards, as these eyes lead our own eyes to contemplate God, so too can we follow the eyes of caregivers and learn from them. Caregivers do not always meet our gaze—they are too busy or simply weary—but we should follow their lead if we can.

Let us return to one of the most frequent acts of caregiving, the act of seeing for the patient. In contemplating this act of pointing out details so that they may be perceived by a diminished mind, we can see how the perception and stimulation of beauty is one of our most wonderful opportunities as human beings. As poets teach us to see what we otherwise would not, so caregivers serve as poets to patients, and by extension they become poets to us as well. They remind us of the privilege of experiencing the beautiful and of the importance of asking if others see what we behold. Indeed, they remind us that in our simple, quotidian acts of perception, we may not be seeing all there is to glorify. (May I ask you to pause, gaze out the window, and wonder?)

The caregiver-poet, then has something to tell us about Christian or sacred art. Despite the nigh-impossibility of the task, artists and theologians have sought to formulate guidelines or principles for Christian art. Von Balthasar observes that "there is no simple recipe" for creating such works.[31] Good art, of any kind, defies absolute formulation. But Jaroslav Pelikan's study of Bach illustrates the importance of a guided aesthetics for churched people.[32] Bach, like his contemporary, Jonathan Edwards, struggled against contemporary claims about the morality or potentially salvific capacity of beauty and art. Many today still claim a special liberating status for art, as Frederick Turner's *The Culture of Hope* and Robert Hughes' *The Culture of Complaint* (both written in the wake of the Serrano and Mapplethorpe controversies) illustrate. For both Bach and Edwards, human sinfulness clearly precluded naive sentiments about paintings and cantatas. The dangers of an unfaithful, idolatrous aestheticism remain great, and Bach, in particular, was concerned about the proper work of the Christian artist.

Pelikan stresses four insights from Bach. First, the highest activity of human beings is the praise of God encompassing the whole person. Second, Christian art is indeed praise as it is undertaken in a freedom which accepts that this freedom is itself bound to the form of Christ, the form which makes all freedom possible. Third, this type of art is at once historical and contemporary, drawing on the work of God in the past but manifesting it in images and forms evocative in the present. Finally, Christian art can illuminate and transcend the words and media it employs, but it does not compete with the Word itself. (Orthodox iconography's respect for the material creation— the egg yolk, wood, fish glue, minerals used for colors, etc., represent the creation itself—would suggest an even greater theological respect for the material components of a physical artwork.) It is in these contexts that Pelikan can describe Bach's thought with a phrase echoing Psalms 29:2 and 96:9, "the Beauty of Holiness." It is our refusal to separate God's glory and beauty from his holiness and mercy that describes Christian aesthetics.

The caregiver who accepts his task with love and faith supplements this description of Christian art. Because caregivers love the recipient of their labor, indeed because as sinners they forgive and seek to be forgiven by their patients, they exhibit a different relationship in their "performance art." Art in this sense becomes a beautiful work manifest in the world through human effort and craft. In our own ways, we all have the capacity to be sacred "artists." Whereas a musician knows that a performance will "exist" only in memories of the musicians and audience, the caregiver is fully aware of the fact that her own subject of attention is subject to dissolution and death. The most intimate member of the audience, the patient in the front row seat, eventually will appear to remember nothing of what has been done. And as caregiving entails a difficult emotional and existential strain, the caregiver, too, may not want to remember all of the details of what transpires during the shouting or the wiping of a fanny. Such art, such labor as exemplifies beautiful devotion, is not brought forth for the pleasure of all eternity but simply because it, too, discloses the beauty of holiness.

One of the things which makes a Gothic cathedral, an icon, or caregiving so beautiful is precisely the interplay between the human creative will and the devotion to sacred traditions of composition (the binding to form on which Bach insisted). The artist yields the possibility of infinite self-indulgence and accepts the responsibility of transmitting a composition which is based on reverence for proper representation. There is a careful purposiveness in all details. The work is not a revelation of the mind or peculiar inner vision of the individual artist but rather an attempt to be faithful to God's initiatives as transmitted through the church. Instead of the "free play of signifiers" indulged in by deconstructionist theories, there is a devotional semiotics which might be called a "canonical play of signifiers." Personalities do emerge in the art, but these are signs of persons who respect their communities' liturgical and devotional needs.

Similarly, the caregiver, while being able to dominate the patient as a sculptor can hammer at marble, refuses to treat the person as a lump of stone to be dealt with for the sake of convenience or self-expression. Great attention is paid to dressing, bathing, and feeding. Gerontologists have underscored the importance of preserving an elderly person's own aesthetic sense; they recognize that his particular style, as manifest in clothes, decorations, food, and floral arrangements, is an integral part of who he is.[33] The caregiver respects the patient and his style as someone who is sacred just as Christian art should respect the sacred subject and its inherent integrity. The caregiver asks not "How shall I make up this person today?" but "How would he want to be dressed today?" The importance of continuity with the past is clear precisely because the sense of the past's fragility is so strong.

The caregiver's respect for the patient is reminiscent of icons. We need to see their work as "non-realistic." Just as icons differ from realistic art in that they admit of no external light source (so that the saints themselves radiate their splendor from within), so too do Alzheimer's disease patients need to be seen as caregivers see them, "non-realistically," as still radiating the *imago Dei*. In the caregiver's work, we see loving devotion which sustains a person in the continuity of living, splendid personhood, just as God's providence preserves the creation through tempests, blights, and earthquakes. Such precious labor and caring deserves to be remembered, and as we shall see in the next chapter, we need to see how caregiving, like providence, is central to human history itself.

We all can benefit from caregivers as Christian artists, because we all need help. How we decide to respond to the beautiful—whether to accept it as a self-sufficient god or to pass into praise of the Creator—is ultimately woven with existential, intellectual, moral, and spiritual aspects of our full person. Our sinfulness threatens the integrity of our responses, and we need at all times to recall the Christological foundation of the beautiful. As an icon points beyond itself, as the Psalms point beyond despair, so too do we need to see how beauty points to Christ, the One through whom all things are made and who himself was made man. Beauty offers a temporary respite from caregiving and from the anxieties of our mortality; Christ offers a true victory, and through our experience of the beautiful, we may pass from brief relief to enduring, grateful triumph.

Chapter 8

Caregiving and the Freedom of Churched History

Wherever this gospel is preached in the whole world,
what she has done will be told in memory of her.
— Matthew 26:13

The act of prayer entails thinking about God in history. Because we pray to God for a cure for this disease or to comfort patients and caregivers, because we ask God to "do something" in our world, we ask God to work in human, historical time. Yet even the most devout person at prayer is confronted with contrary feelings. The sufferings of Alzheimer's disease frequently lead people to ask "What's God doing in all this?" The attributes and qualities usually ascribed to God—goodness, mercy, omnipotence—seem to be unusually absent. God's providence, his rule over history, seems meaningless. The issue of theodicy, the role of God in the history of human affairs, particularly human suffering, easily comes to the forefront. Hence, a discussion of history considered both as a field for God's work and as a way of thinking about human existence is very much needed.

Such a discussion is needed also because of the very nature of the disease. Because contracting the illness is related to genetics, family members find themselves very much concerned with what is perhaps the oldest form of history, genealogy. I find myself wondering about previous generations in my mother's family, especially about their susceptibility to this disease or others, and so I try to learn about who people were, how they died, and what they were like, particularly in old age. Secondly, those who know a caregiver who performs her duties with love and devotion will agree that this love deserves to be remembered. As the ancient historians well sensed, noble deeds are to be preserved not only for their own sakes but also so that future generations may emulate them. Caregiving certainly could be a central component of Christian remembering, but we want to consider how it might be proper to say that caregiving should also be "history." Finally, Alzheimer's evokes a theological consideration of history because it challenges our ability to remember the past. In chapter 1, I suggested that Alzheimer's is a disease which is about the breakdown of narratives. With a theological consideration of history, we may be able to help recover and sustain the narratives which are being lost.

This final chapter, then, explores a number of aspects of the relationships between God, caregiving, and history. In particular it focuses on how thinking about historical issues within the context of the church's teachings can help caregivers. Doctrines do make a difference: they remind us to ask certain historical questions; they challenge us to be honest in our thinking about the past; and they even help create the preconditions for such activity. This chapter also considers how thinking about caregiving as history, or more broadly, thinking about agapic love as history, helps the church to understand better God's own work in history. This consideration of history from within the rich perspectives of the church's traditions and mission can be called "churched history." Such a phrasing emphasizes the particular confessional biases and concerns which Christians may need to bring to their ideas about history. Moreover, this phrase hopes to suggest how the amateur and professional work of history can be of great service not just to families and to the academy but also to the church.

The first section of this chapter, "The Caregiver as Historian," explores how caregiving at times requires or evokes history from caregivers and offers some suggestions about how the church's teachings and practices can aid these people. The second section, "Jesus as Historian," considers Jesus as a paradigm for historical reflection both for caregivers and the church as a whole. If we are looking for a model of how a caregiver might think about history, certainly we will find no better exemplar than the divine caregiver. As we shall see, for Jesus caregiving lies at the heart of history, because agapic love lies at the heart of proper human relationships. The final section, "The Freedom of Churched History," draws together several themes from this chapter and asks us to consider how thinking about caregiving as history may help free us to become better Christians. Here, it will become possible to return to the problem of God's providence, not from the perspective of an omnipotent God, but from the perspective of the Lordship of a crucified God of love and caregiving.

This chapter's use of the word "history" might strike some as inaccurate. History, after all, suggests an objective past, the result of self-critical scrutinization of all available source materials. The historical-critical method is often intended to correct the theological biases which such a notion of "churched history" freely accepts. History respects the distance in time and space from its objects of inquiry and is wary of identifying too closely with its material. Are caregivers to become professional historians? Is not "remembering" simply a better term for the reflections on personal relationships with patients? Is not the Hebrew root *zkr* with all of its rich religious and existential connotations a better way of thinking about God in history?

By the standards of the academy (even at a time when historians seem rather uncertain about their discipline), I do use the term "history" quite loosely.[1] In some respects, memory here is subsumed under history, because my sense is that memory and history overlap to quite an extent. Traditional formulations of the dynamics of these two often see the latter correcting or clarifying the former. History challenges and trains memory, and memory, for all its personal biases and subjectivity, is also innately historical. It can be "self-correcting" and open to expansion. I personally remember hearing about when Ronald Reagan was shot, but my "memories" of the event now include press footage, journalistic commentary, and the knowledge of subsequent historical developments. Similarly, when caregivers remember, especially when they recollect with others, the memories are open to emendation. When my family tries to remember specific events from our past, we informally do many of the things historians do, gather and compare evidence and evaluate its reliability. Even if such processes are only of our own memories, we acknowledge that one of us may remember an event better, and so we are willing to correct our own "memories" accordingly.

Two aspects of this phenomenon are crucial. First, history does ask the memory to be honest, to acknowledge its limits, biases, and potentially mythic configuring of events. It also asks memory to be ready to admit of correction. Second, history is shared; it is public. (This is one of the reasons why it needs to be honest.) It proclaims a right to exist outside of the persons who experienced the original events. It strives for immortality, for perpetual remembering, and it asks to be significant to later generations. History is part of our public discourse, and by making the claim that caregivers are to be a part of history, I claim that their work should be remembered just as surely as the names and dates of public textbooks are to be memorized. Caregiving is done in private, but it has significant social and historical implications.

Because our thinking about the past has great implications for our conduct in the present, I have preferred a loose construal of history which allows us to consider both history as an objective discipline and as something which we appropriate and actualize (in the sense of *zkr*) in our lives. Any number of paired terms express similar or related phenomena—the etic and emic of anthropology, the external and internal histories of H. R. Niebuhr's *The Meaning of Revelation*, history and memory themselves—and such dualities serve best when they are coordinate, not opposed. Seeing how such cooperation can be the case will be one of the tasks of this chapter, but it should be noted here that one of the reasons why Jews and Christians have been so concerned about history is because of the importance of memory for both.

In his *Lament for a Son*, Nicholas Wolterstorff calls human remembering "one of the profoundest features of the Christian and Jewish way of being-in-the-world and being-in-history."[2] Relative to the ancient Greeks, the Jews, for example, had a much greater respect for historical memories. Although Herodotus and Thucydides are hailed as the fathers of history, their own historical horizons are profoundly limited—their primary subject matter is events which they themselves either participated in or witnessed. By contrast, the history of Israel drew together more generations than the history of Athens, and the genealogy of Jesus with which Matthew begins takes Christian readers back many, many centuries. The transformation of historical thinking from "cyclical" to "linear" history wrought by Jewish and Christian traditions was the result of the importance of remembering God's work. God's unique deeds, especially the covenant and the Incarnation, hammered the loop of time into a purposeful vector.

One can see that the kingship of Solomon or the evolution of the institutional church would belong to history, but it might be objected, too, that caregiving and love are not really a part of what history is all about. As any schoolchild will tell you, history is about names, dates, and facts, and such things are generally about change and progress, the emergence of the new and the publicly significant. I want to challenge such assumptions, and believe that if we begin our thinking with Jesus—whose Incarnation, Crucifixion, and Resurrection are at the center of a Christian understanding of history—and his way of thinking about history, then we can see that we may well need to reconfigure our thinking about what "history" is. As might be gathered from the comparisons with history in public schools, churched history, like multiculturalism, will raise questions about traditional construals of history.

In a forthcoming book which promises to be of great significance, George M. Marsden discusses what he calls *The Outrageous Idea of Christian Scholarship*. He argues that explicit Christian perspectives can and ought to be a vibrant part of the academy. His analysis and recommendations illustrate how specifically Christian concerns (such as God's love) should not be excluded out of hand from professional disciplines such as history. This work certainly will help Christian academics who do wish to reflect on the past in light of their faith, and I believe that it will lend support to the idea of churched history in a university. My own emphasis in this discussion of churched history will be on relating the study of history to the church's mission. It will also suggest how a Christian consideration of history can become related to one's total life. It may be the case that churched history helps us to experience the freedom of a Christian as we participate in the Kingdom of God here on earth.[3]

The Caregiver as Historian

In the broad sense of history used in this chapter, caregivers naturally become historians. They find themselves charged both with remembering another person and with remembering *for* another person. Their daily experience with someone else's diminishing cognitive faculties heightens their sense of trying to remember the patient. However world-historical or simple, the particular experiences shared with a patient become absolutely precious. At the same time, caregivers recognize that they must do the remembering on behalf of this person. This is particularly clear when the caregiver tries to remember *with* a person. One very important method for keeping an early- or middle-stage person connected with the world is to jog his memories by asking him to talk about himself (gerontologists call this "life-review therapy"). Being able to do this requires that the caregiver develop a facility for remembering for a person so that she can ask the questions which will evoke powerful memories from the patient.

Such remembering by caregivers entails what can be called "history" because it requires careful reflection and investigation on behalf of the caregiver. She finds herself asking all the questions of a biographer or a historian. What was it like for him growing up? What did he think of his first job? Did he vote for Kennedy or for Nixon? What was his favorite color? G. Cullom Davis has demonstrated that the historians' experience with taking oral history can be of great aid to caregivers. Working with his own experience as a historian and drawing from the lessons of a project conducted by St. Alban's Parish in Washington, D.C., in which parishioners worked with elderly people to record their life stories, he shows how the field of oral history helps aging patients recover their sense of dignity and purpose. Not only are the elderly encouraged to recover their own past, they also come to take pride in seeing that other people are interested in their lives. Significantly, Davis reveals that as a historian he had never previously understood how history could be therapeutic for its subjects. Churched history hopes precisely for this, to make the study of the past beneficial to our lives in the present, and the St. Alban's project may be a model for caregivers or churches seeking to help the elderly.[4]

A heightened awareness of the fragility of the past also leads the caregiver who stumbles across old letters or mementos to study them with great attentiveness in order to reconstruct their original contexts and significance. At times, for example when the patient seems to regress to childhood experiences, the caregiver is confronted with certain biographical or historical problems. Why is it that she always calls out for her father and not her mother? What incident from her past is she recollecting now? Which house does she think she's in? Even if the caregiver cannot use the knowledge of the patient's background therapeutically, it may be important for the caregiver's own peace of mind to have some awareness of which world the patient seems to be in at the moment. This all requires a sensitivity to historical details and personal memories. Here, the discipline of history is helpful for its experience with constructing biography, discovering details, and establishing social contexts can be of service to caregivers as they exercise their memories.

In particular, the developing field of family history is well-placed to contribute to this labor. Although much of this field is statistical and demographic, much of it concerns the qualities of family life at different periods. Some historians in this field have developed a great sensitivity to recovering familial experience. The "thick description" of human life inside the home has been explored from a great variety of non-traditional sources. Caregivers can benefit from the experience of these historians both directly and indirectly. They can read these works themselves, or their friends or members of their church can read them and train themselves to discuss productively the caregiver's own family memories. Like the experience of beauty, historical reflection and inquiry benefits from the cultivation of sensibilities and training in attentiveness to details. Such preparation comes from a variety of sources—from history, memoirs, movies, novels—and it takes patience, curiosity, and dedication. Perhaps because the stakes now are clearly much higher than they were before the onset of the disease, caregivers and their friends may be better prepared to invest the energy and effort into such work.

It is an additional chore, but it is important for caregivers or their friends to commit their historically-exercised memories to a written record in whichever form they feel most at home. We preserve what we value, and what we value we need to preserve. But here, too, there may be hesitation. I teach a course on family history, and I ask the students to research some aspect of their own families' history. Much to my consternation, I have discovered that many students simply do not feel that their families are worthy of a written history. Their parents were farmers or perhaps local leaders, hardly the national heroes the students studied in other classes. But the New Testament is filled with people hardly worthy of history whom God has chosen for his work. And Jesus' own interest in the poor and the marginalized should remind us all that we are all worthy of historical consideration. Similarly, as historians themselves recognize, modern democratic capitalism has led to a much greater respect for the role of non-elites in history. Many historians are less interested in kings and much more engaged with recovering the lives of ordinary people. Feminist historians are demonstrating that women have been overlooked for too long by traditional history. In a curious way, Jesus' own universal concern for humanity is much more capable of being realized in the modern world precisely because the modern world values people quite differently. Caregivers, I believe, should take advantage of this democratization of history, and realize that the patients they care for, too, deserve to have a historical future. One day, their own grandchildren's grandchildren will want to know about their ancestors.

Still, such historical recollection may be far from easy. A younger person may have fewer memories of the patient than someone of the patient's generation. Or, the memories of happier times may be simply too painful to remember in the present. Perhaps the most difficult of all remembering will be the recollecting done by caregivers who are stricken by anger, bitterness, or guilt. We do not want to remember many things about some patients, and we may be angry that her demented state has prevented any sort of reconciliation. We may be longing for an apology which may never come. We may also not want to remember how we have failed to return the love given to us. Remembering is not an experience unalloyed with grief.

Fortunately, friends are able to help us. I am very grateful for all of our friends who knew my mother long before I was born. I have been given memories of her, and these I cherish. Such gifts also remind us that remembering is both communal and multiple. We can remember together, but we often remember different qualities according to our own interests and experiences. Sharing these multiple perspectives is essential (just as it is essential to have all four Gospels), because no single person can adequately remember another person in her totality. Together, my father, brother, aunts, uncles, and nieces can remember quite a great deal about my mother, but none of us really can do justice to what she meant to the people she worked with in the YWCA in Nebraska many years ago. A full life defies solitary remembering.

Our friends, especially those who do not really know the patient, can ask us to share our remembering. I recall being struck one day when a good friend who knew about our family's situation but who had never met my mother said, "Tell me about your mom." Not only was I given a sympathetic ear—something quite valuable when you feel isolated—but this simple request was also a wonderful invitation as it led me to express my memories formally, something I rarely did. We tend to tell friends about another person in such considered detail on only a few occasions—perhaps after we've met a possible spouse or at a funeral service. Most of the time when we describe people we mention only a few particularly interesting characteristics. Rarely do we share what we know of the whole person. That's why I found this simple invitation so profound. Not only was my memory refreshed, but also I was offered the chance to organize the many feelings, thoughts, and experiences of my mother. For me, this was therapeutic, not in a sense of producing a catharsis (which such a conversation could be for some) but in the sense of discovering deeper appreciations through recovering old memories. Like a careful historian, I found myself quite consciously not wanting to leave out any aspects of her life. Such an offer evoked a concern for artistry and considered details which private recalling does not always do but which history usually evokes. As the Trinity's mysterious nature overflows with the joys of self-communicating love among Three Persons, so, too, can sharing our loved ones with friends engender more joy. Or, to choose another image, the communicating of our knowledge of someone we love is like the lighting of candles during a candlelight service; slowly the flame is spread and the light increases and fills the entire sanctuary.

Recollecting the good times and the better aspects of our relationships with friends can be an important pleasure. But the church is particularly well-prepared to help us remember the more challenging memories, the ones which are not so pleasant. Jesus and the church teach us that forgiveness and love are to be the basis of our relationships. The Lord's Prayer emphasizes the importance of forgiveness in our remembering. If we incorporate a prayer for another person into this prayer, we simultaneously remember this person and confess that we all need forgiveness. Regardless of the wrongs which we feel have been committed by either person, the pray-er accepts that neither life is without fault, and neither life lies beyond the forgiveness of God. When we remember with charity and with full awareness of the need for mutual forgiveness, recalling the angry or guilt-ridden aspects of our relationships becomes easier. It is still painful, to be sure (forgiveness often requires time and much effort), but it is no longer insurmountable. Further, the Lord's Prayer reminds us that in prayer not only do we ask God to act, we also commit ourselves as well. Hence, we confess that we too will forgive, and we acknowledge that we are to follow God's will for the Kingdom.[5]

Ultimately, praying for someone is perhaps the finest way to remember a person (as churches with saints' feast days might tell us). As when we tell a friend about our mother, we recall the many aspects of a person we cherish. In a well-considered prayer, we can enter into a sustained meditation on a person, on her gifts, her quaint foibles,

211

and her particular needs. We become thankful both to the person and to God as we remember the many reasons we pray for this person in the first place. Even in the dark night of caregiving, such a prayer is not a solitary process. As we remember in prayer we enter into a centuries-old relationship between God and humanity, and our concerns become a part of the divine work of restoration. The profound historical life of prayer in which we join Israel and the church superimposes onto our own personal concerns and potentially ambivalent feelings the rich dominant modes of thanksgiving, forgiveness, faithfulness, and love. In the case of Alzheimer's, the "Amen" which concludes our prayers links us through the New Testament church to Israel, and the beauty of this continuity is a communal assertion of faith against a disease which threatens to destroy both continuity and community.

Moreover, as we pray for someone, we pray that God will manifest his love in her life. Such a desire entails a re-imagining of the person in the context of God's providential love. Although we often re-imagine God acting for the person according to our own hopes, we acknowledge that, ultimately, if God chooses some other course, then we must accept that. Praying for someone else, in other words, entails praying for ourselves as well. Fortunately, as Paul reveals in Romans 8:26-7, we know that the Spirit aids us in our prayer, for God knows that those who do not suffer cognitive impairment need help, too. When we pray, we accept that it is God's memory of a person which is most important—this is not always an easy fact to accept, but it is a reality we enter into in prayer. Thus, remembering in prayer is much like history itself, because prayer, like history, forces us to be as honest as possible about our thoughts concerning another person and about our abilities to affect this person's life.

Prayer joins people to the church, and when we remember a person's life as a life within the church, we come to see how a family member who now seems so detached from the world is in fact part of a community which is several millennia old. Linking a person's memories to the church connects a person to Abraham and Sarah. Or, if we think of particular roles in the church or of particular gifts of the Holy Spirit, a person's life becomes related to many others who have preceded him. My mother, for example, is an ordained minister in The United Methodist Church, and so her own history extends all the way back through Wesley and through the apostles even unto the Old Testament priesthood. Similarly, as Director of Children's

Education at Glenn Memorial United Methodist Church in Atlanta, her history extends back through the ages to all of the church's catechists. Our personal memories are enriched and deepened through history. In these terms, her life is important not just to the immediate circle of caregivers, medical specialists, and intimate friends but also to the entire communion of saints, the ultimate circle of friends. When we remember a person as a loyal vice president of a company or as a good Little League coach, we remember a person in terms of valuable but transient institutions. When we remember a person as a member of the Body of Christ, we remember the person in terms of the faithful memory of God and his transhistorical Kingdom.

Jesus as Historian

It is unfortunate that while we consider Jesus historically, we rarely consider Jesus as a historian. As his life is an example to us in holiness, love, and suffering, so too can we see in his life and teachings profound lessons for doing history. Through him we can learn that history, caregiving, and love ought to be inseparable. More specifically, through a consideration of the Gospels, we come to sense that caregiving can, or perhaps, ought to be at the heart of the study of human history. Given our own assumptions about history, especially as a professional discipline, this may sound odd. But it may be the case that what Jesus suggests about how we ought to study the past is no less radical than what he has to say about divine forgiveness and the Kingdom of God. The first church historian, Eusebius, a man who has exerted a great influence on how Christians think about history, was also a biographer of Constantine. Hence, a post-Constantinian Christianity, if that is what we now experience, may be in need of learning from Jesus as a pre-Constantinian historian. I am admittedly employing the phrase "Jesus as historian" here in a heuristic sense; my purpose in so doing is to suggest a different way of thinking about history, one which will help to clarify the crucial relationships between history and caregiving.

Historians make a great number of decisions about subject matter and methodology. They select a period, the particular types of people to study, a set of questions needing to be answered, a body of evidence to explore. And, both implicitly and explicitly, they study the past through their own world view, their own beliefs about the relationship between the past and the present and their expectations about the future. Such assumptions entail beliefs about human nature and the relative importance of different categories of thought. A conservative intellectual historian chooses a different set of concerns and employs a different set of beliefs than a Marxist economic historian. These questions—Who? What? Why? and How?—are central to the historian's task, and if we consider Jesus' approach to them we can begin to see Jesus as a historian.

For Jesus, as for anyone, the work of history is inseparable from the life of the historian. His ministry suggests whom he considers important and how he views them. If we follow our Lord's lead, we see that the historian, too, should be concerned especially with the poor, the outcasts, and those of lowly status. Christians indeed can learn from what is often called social history. We should remember, too, that he is able to empathize with the marginalized masses of history because he himself was despised and rejected. Moreover, whereas we sometimes herd people into terms such as "the poor," Jesus heals and cleanses individual persons, not groups or classes. The person is the locus of his work, and he treats each person as an invaluable member of the Kingdom of God. Christ's temptation (his own rejection of Constantinian glory), his clear sense of his limited time on earth, and his own suffering all point to a profound awareness of the issues of human existence. At stake is nothing less than salvation and eternal life, the joys of the Kingdom of God in both this world and the next. All these are crucial contexts for his ministry, and, by extension, they are central contexts for his thinking historically.

How does he employ the past in his ministry? He has a divine memory, and he is able to encompass all of human history. He chooses to be most concerned with suffering. His clearest expression of this occurs in Matthew 23:34-6, where he links the future persecution of his church with the innocent blood shed in Old Testament narratives. The "righteous blood" which has been shed becomes part of the fundamental dynamic of history. In this sense, history is less about the rise and fall of nations than it is about humanity's struggle for righteousness in a world filled with temptations, afflictions, and sorrows.

As this passage indicates, Jesus often uses the past polemically against the present (see also, for example, Matthew 15:1-9 where he employs a prophecy from Isaiah against the Pharisees). In so doing, he understands the present generation's faithfulness, or lack thereof, in light of the past. History, particularly the Old Testament witness of human sin and divine righteousness, becomes a critique of the present (cf. Matt. 11:23-4). He himself fulfills Israel's prophecies, particularly of the suffering Messiah, and by being obedient to the Law, he also, in some sense, completes the past. The present reality of God transforms the promises and commandments of the Old Testament, establishing a new basis for human existence—and human history. Thus, Christ reconfigures the Law and the prophets by linking love of God and love of neighbor (commandments which appear separately in Deuteronomy and Leviticus) and by revealing that these are to be at the heart of God's work through Israel and the church.

History, for Jesus and the Jews of his era, was inseparable from the Law, but now history becomes inseparable from love. In particular, history becomes inseparable from the preeminent example of love—an example revealing the centrality of caregiving—God's suffering for us on the Cross. As hard as it may be to imagine, the marginalizing work of caregiving, a work of love, may lie at the center of the human pilgrimage through time. As Paul observes in Romans 8:17, our suffering with Christ (and by extension our loving service in his name) is intrinsically related to our future glorification. Paul's words give us a new perspective on how the ministry of caregiving becomes part of the Kingdom of God. It is in light of these new relationships between humans and God and within humanity that we can see how Jesus' ministry is related to his thinking historically.

Hence, useful for a consideration of Jesus as a historian will be a brief consideration of his commands, proclamations, and parables. We often think of history as a matter of public events and public records. But in Matthew 6, Jesus asserts that the opposite is also important. We are not to make our fasts, alms, and prayers a matter of public knowledge. Rather, we are to do these quietly as the Father sees in secret. Here, the caregiver's work, a labor often performed in seeming isolation, becomes the subject of God's intimate concern. Quite clearly, God himself is the historian of caregivers. Should the work of caregiving—however it is manifest in history—not also be our concern when we think historically? It is in this context, at least in Matthew, that Jesus teaches us the Lord's Prayer, a prayer with deep implications for caregivers and for history.[6]

There is much to explore in this prayer, but there is space here to touch upon only two aspects—our need for daily bread and divine and human forgiveness. These are at the heart of the prayer, and so, too, I believe are they central to history. If this is the case, then the caregivers who prepare and serve the daily bread to patients are doing world-historical work indeed. (Jesus himself seems to be much more concerned with providing for the daily needs of individuals than with discussing the current emperor or the economy.) Similarly, Jesus underscores the importance both of forgiving others and of being forgiven. When we offer this prayer, we can enter into a profound understanding of who we all are and what we share. Human relations are interwoven with sinfulness, and our best response is to forgive and ask for forgiveness. Even if Jesus is not speaking as a historian *per se* here, it is not hard to recognize that this prayer sheds light on how Christians are to view their lives and, by implication, human lives in history.

Jesus himself teaches us about the intimate relationship between history and caregiving. In Matthew 26:6-13, Jesus chastises his disciples who criticize a woman for anointing Jesus with a rich oil which could have been sold to give to the poor. "Why do you trouble the woman? For she has done a beautiful thing [*kalon*] to me. For you always have the poor with you, but you will not always have me." Jesus' commandments about Christian giving to sustain the poor yield to the gracious, loving act of caregiving. We might expect that since Jesus is so close to torture and death (the oil is a preparation for his burial), such a use of ointment is a true waste of resources. (Similarly, we might conclude that since an Alzheimer's patient in the latter stages is so close to death, special attention is completely unwarranted.) On the contrary, we learn that it is precisely the willingness to cherish the person without regard to the economic "opportunity costs" which is so beautiful. Faithful human deeds transcend financial concerns, and they are performed often in the full awareness of our mortality. What the woman gets out of this deed is not stated. Could it be that she does not expect any benefit, that she does this simply because it is the right thing to do?

Jesus concludes this pericope, "Truly [*amen*], I say to you, wherever this gospel is preached in the whole world, what she has done will be told in memory of her." (This commandment to remember her beautiful work is especially poignant when we read in the next passage of Judas' plot to sell the "pearl of great price" for thirty pieces of silver.) But who was the woman of Matthew 26:6-14? She, like so many advanced-stage Alzheimer's patients, is all but lost to us. Jesus' prophecy of the global remembering of the unnamed woman contains a note of sadness, for only her deed is remembered, not her full person. Elisabeth Schüssler Fiorenza uses this text as her point of departure for her feminist reconstruction of early Christian history, and she argues that in this woman we can discern "the paradigm for the true disciple."[7] If we wish to know who our Lord is and how to follow him, we must learn about this woman. In this simple event in Simon the Leper's house in Bethany, we are confronted with the necessity of history. Jesus' commandment to remember her (as well as the commandment to love our neighbor whom we do not forget), leads us to try to recover, preserve, and cherish the deeds and persons of the past. In short, the beauty of faithful caregiving—the beauty of loving—evokes history.

Significantly, this event occurs immediately after the apocalyptic passages in Matthew 24–25. Caregiving as history needs to be considered in an eschatological context. As apocalypticism reminds us that we should not understand God's righteousness in terms of a glorious Israel, so too do the eschatological teachings of Jesus remind us that it is a crucified Lord glorified after his death, not a Davidic king, who has established the Kingdom of God. By seeing human history in this light, it becomes possible to see how it may be the case that caregivers are living embodiments of this Kingdom. Their agapic love, loves given as crosses taken up, may be a mysterious foreshadowing of the eschaton, a time when we all may be able to love without concern for our own wants, a time when we are able to give freely to one another.

Moreover, Jesus' unyielding concern with the salvation of souls reminds us that each person's life needs to be understood in the context of her relationship to the Judge of the quick and the dead. Such a belief certainly complicates the study of history as an eschatological context for thinking historically means that history, especially biography, must remain tentative on this side of the eschaton. The knowledge of peoples' fates after death is beyond us, at least in this life, and given the temptation to play God, we would do well to remember that even historians are not the ultimate judges of a person's life. In his *Wolfgang Amadeus Mozart*, Barth makes a whimsical comment about his inquiring first about Mozart's fate when he, Barth, arrives in heaven. In its own way, this is insightful. Barth's own relationship to the composer remains incomplete until he knows of Mozart's ultimate relationship to God. This eschatological context is important, because it reminds us that God's judgment and his forgiveness, not ours, is determinative for human life. Hence, if we can abandon the temptation to judge a person's life, we can allow ourselves to forgive the people whom we might otherwise condemn. This biographical uncertainty creates room for humility, and humility makes forgiveness easier. Humility also makes it easier to be sympathetic, and sympathy is an important quality for the historian. Moreover, humility also makes it easier to be honest and more "objective" as a historian, since humility engenders circumspection and caution.

The final context for considering Jesus as historian is his telling of parables. For our purposes, the central parable for caregivers is in Luke 10:30-37. Responding to the lawyer who was trying to "justify himself" by asking Jesus to set boundaries so that he might know which neighbors he is to love, Jesus offers the story of the Good Samaritan. This story tells us that "neighbor" extends to all people, and it establishes a reference point for evaluating our human actions. Even though we do not play the role of Judge, as historians we do praise, honor, and condemn, and Jesus has given us guides for doing so. This parable is crucial for our thinking about historical behavior as it describes the proper basis for human social relations—it reveals how we should live in history. As we compare this Samaritan's deeds with human history, we see at once how wretched most of us have been, and are led to recognize that all of us need Christ's saving work.

The study of history and the processes of our remembering the past mold our habits in the present. As Jesus suggests that caregiving and love are the most faithful and beautiful deeds, so are we to take these examples to heart. By remembering these achievements—by making them part of our history—we develop our own ability to love and serve as caregivers. Even though professional history is primarily conducted in a university, an institution which seems to care little for the agapic love revealed by Christ, it should not be so strange a notion that the study of history could help us to be better lovers. After all, Frankenstein's creature was inspired by reading an ancient historian: "Plutarch taught me high thoughts; he elevated me above the wretched sphere of my own reflections, to admire and love the heroes of past ages."[8] History, for this poor one, could have been one of the vehicles for his becoming fully human. Moreover, if we view history as we should view much of our lives—as a response to God's work—we should be able to see how history and love are related.

The Freedom of Churched History

Are caregivers overwhelmed by history and circumstances, or are their labors integral to history itself? Is their call to love the sick simply bad luck, or does it reveal to us all the way in which we may become free to participate in the Kingdom of God even amid afflictions? Churched history, this view of history developed in light of the church's teachings and Jesus' ministry, suggests that caregiving is integral to God's redemptive plan for humanity. Consequently, remembering the caregiver's agapic love—a rare and wondrous embodiment of God's love—encourages the entire church to be more Christ-like as it reminds us of what we are capable when we love. A sprinter never knows how fast she can run until she chases someone or is being chased. Similarly, we never know what we can do until we wholeheartedly pursue an ideal or until we find ourselves driven from behind by the *durée* of a challenge from history.

By placing works of care and love at the center of our remembering, we can, I believe, aspire to a sublime, liberating view of history. In the previous chapter, Santayana's description of the sublime, an experience combining sorrow and beauty which can raise us above the world in new-found knowledge of the self amid the vicissitudes of this life, was seen to have Christological potential. Similarly, through a Christian reading of his general description of the sublime (he explicitly allowed for Stoic and Epicurean versions), we can see how placing love and caregiving at the heart of history makes the past, even with all of the human suffering it encompasses, sublime. This view of history is sublime, because it seems so strange, yet so right. It is liberating because it tells us how we become free to live properly.

The "transcendent element of worth" especially amid pain; the triumphant "detachment and liberation" from the categories of the world; the roll-call of millions of righteous suffers, a conception both "immense" and "terrible"; the "moral reaction" to the presence of evil; the "universal standpoint" attained by the sublime contemplator and the "heart choked" which seizes her—all of these become a part of such a vision of history. This view of history is, I believe, "supremely . . . intoxicatingly beautiful" (just as Christ described the deed of the woman with oil). Truly, in this way of seeing the past, "The sense of suffering disappears in the sense of life and the imagination overwhelms the understanding."[9] Here, as we consider

219

history from the perspective of sacrifice and love, we can achieve a sense of calm, repose, and freedom. New possibilities are created, and a fresh awareness of our responsibilities are generated. Whereas Santayana's notion of the sublime entailed a certain profound inactivity, a sublime Christian experience of history as suffering love will yield to a subsequent stirring to praxis. Perhaps for the first time, we can see how human activity unites us to the Kingdom of God and the Lordship of the cosmos.

We can hope to become more free through this view of history because it helps us to realize what Luther described in his treatise, "The Freedom of a Christian." Paul had declared in Romans 8:2 that "the law of the Spirit of life in Christ Jesus has set [him] free from the law of sin and death." Through our faith in Christ, Luther thus argued, we can become free not only from sins, laws, and commandments, but also the dangers of poor health, the vanities of the world, and the temptations of earthly power. These are the true obstacles to Christian freedom, not the challenges of caregiving. The reality of God's forgiveness lifts the burdens imposed upon us by our sinful imperfection, and the new paradigm of Christ's Lordship liberates us from slavery to mammon. (Churched historians may consider how the trappings of worldly academic glory need not be so important to them.) We thus become free to love neighbor and God, because we understand that God's creative desires truly evoke loving service from us. Hence, the paradox Luther offers that Christians are simultaneously lord and servant to all. How can this be?

Luther recognized that for Christians, "power" needs to be understood in light of the Cross. Hence he draws on 2 Corinthians 12:9, "power is made perfect in weakness," as he articulates how Christians are to live in the world. We live with spiritual, not worldly power, and we are often quite "weak" according to the world's standards. Similarly, recognizing the works of love in history entails a redefinition of "power." Currently, "power" and "power relationships" seem to be the buzz words in academic discourse. But such uses of these words assume, I believe, that power resides in human subjects who exercise their wills. An Alzheimer's patient often has little subjectivity left and very little will, but she still has great power. As any caregiver who loves his patient will tell you, the patient, even in end-stage dementia, has real "power" over the caregiver's life. Indeed, as Luther observes, someone who loves is always ready to serve the beloved. To be sure, this power is not absolute, and it does not necessarily prevent anger or violence (love does not destroy sinfulness). Still, it is real, and it suggests to us that the power of loving and being loved is fundamental in human affairs.

Other doctrines and philosophies support this churched emphasis on love in history. That the fundamental events in history, the Cross and Resurrection, are acts of love and that we are made in the image of God who is love both suggest that love (and its crippling or perverting by sin) needs to be central to our view of human affairs. In several speeches in Plato's *Symposium*, it is clear that Eros creates the possibility of thinking thoughts normally forbidden or frowned upon by social conventions. Love, both agapic and erotic, is political dynamite because it refuses to allow mammon or the state to have ultimate authority over its relationships. Love and freedom become inseparable, both for Plato and for Luther. In his *Discourse on the Origins of Inequality*, Rousseau argued that history should be seen, in large part, as the enervation of the original, natural compassion humans were able to feel for one another by the progress of civilization. G. K. Chesterton's *Orthodoxy*, implicitly drawing on a long Augustinian tradition, observes that love describes our primary loyalties and attachments, and it is these primary identities which are the inspiration for our creative energies and the occasion for their realizations. Recently, James Q. Wilson has taken the lead of Adam Smith's understanding of the moral sentiments and has argued for the centrality of sympathy for the formation of moral behavior; such a recovery of a moral sense related to love, altruism, and charity further suggests how the Christian idea of love may be inextricable from history.[10] Through taking love as a historical force seriously, Christians may become better prepared to contribute to the academy. As a non-Marxist may learn from a Marxist the importance of class struggle, so may a non-Christian come to appreciate certain aspects of the churched historian's emphasis on love. Moreover, in light of all these views on the power of love, we can sense that if our primary loves are neighbor and God, then we will be properly oriented in our lives and can experience the freedom of a Christian.

Placing agapic love in the center of history helps us to experience the sublime freedom of churched history. If we presuppose conflict and build it into our historical models (as does an orthodox Marxist approach to the past), then we assume that conflict is inevitable, and we probably become more willing to tolerate it. By contrast, if we believe in the God of love and the real power of love in history, then we are empowered, or made free, to help bring love into the world. Such a view does not ignore the reality of conflict, hatred, and the countless failures of churched people; indeed, it sees these failures as all the more horrible. And such a historical vision does draw on the lessons of many different sub-fields of history as well as the other humanities, social sciences, and natural sciences. Indeed, it recognizes that economic history, literature, sociology, and geology each have something to contribute to the Kingdom of God because they each contribute to our knowledge of God, the creation, and humanity. (I suspect that the unifying power of love is what makes this larger vision possible.) But churched history fundamentally is open to the *durée* of the Cross, of the powerful examples of caregivers, and of the millions who have shed their "righteous blood." It is sublime because it can help us to experience "the peace which passeth understanding" even amid the sufferings of a disease such as Alzheimer's. It is a peace which does defy the world's understanding, and it is a peace brought about by accepting that the awful sacrifice on the Cross is constitutive for human history. As Paul understands, such a quickening, life-transforming peace is also related to the Spirit; to reject the life of the flesh and to "set the mind on the Spirit is life and peace" (Rom. 8:6).

In light of this chapter's brief observations, I believe it is now possible to approach the mystery of divine providence and God's work in history. If we approach providence through a juxtaposition of the image of the omnipotent throne-sitting God with the horrors often experienced in this world we will forever be confounded. A Constantinian understanding of providence will not sit comfortably with pain. By contrast, if we explore this subject from the incarnated reality of Christ's crucified Lordship, then we may be able to make some sense of the suffering we share as well as ground our prayer life in the reality of God's work through history. Both "crucified" and "Lordship" need to be remembered. The first tells us that God's most fundamental act in time is of suffering love. In this sense, if nothing else, Bonhoeffer's deep awareness of the primacy of the Cross for understanding God's work in history was accurate.

Lordship is an accurate term for thinking about history from a Christian perspective because this word recognizes the importance of the Lord's stewards. That is, any lord depends on his followers for the exercise of his rule and the administration of his kingdom. Human agency, as manifest in error, fidelity, or ignorance, is crucial to lordship in history. Similarly, God works, in part, through his people, and when they are faithful to his will, then the Kingdom becomes a greater reality. And when we recognize both the peculiar nature of crucified Lordship and the terrible responsibilities it devolves to us, we can sense how the history of the Kingdom of God is sublime, something simultaneously awe-inspiring, disturbing, ecstatic, and peaceful. To return to Santayana's expression, "The more of the accidental vesture of life we strip ourselves of, the more naked and simple is the surviving spirit; the more complete its superiority and unity, and consequently, the more unqualified its joy."

But is the Lord powerless in this world as some "death of God" theologians might maintain? Is his rule exercised only through human agents? When we ask such questions we are scrutinizing the mysteries of God's providence, and as Dante underscores in canto VII of the *Paradiso*, we need to be matured in God's love if we are to be able to fathom how he works in human affairs. I am far from matured in such power, but I suspect that each of us when confronted with such mysteries can only confess. On the one hand, God's nature and ways so transcend the linguistic and intellectual capacities of humanity that it sometimes seems proper to recognize the inability of the human mind to contemplate God. On the other hand, God has become a man, and he has suffered so that we might live. Such intimate love draws forth attempts to express the inexpressible.

For my part, as I have tried to show in this book, there are some things which seem clear to me. The Spirit does work through the soul and through the *durée* of doctrine and history. When our discernment is accurate, we can sense guidance and illumination through our prayer life and through the sacraments. The resurrected Lord whose life was given up on the Cross because God so loved the world *is* with us. Prayers are answered, grace is recognized in the soul, and the peace which passes understanding is bestowed. Our sins are forgiven, and we recognize that we, too, are to forgive. The workings of God are mysterious, serendipitous, and multiple, and I, for one, can only give thanks and seek to follow his Lordship. These confessions are not an argument, but I hope that this book as a whole has provided a convincing description of the reality of things unseen.

Because I believe that the Lord is indeed omnipotent, I still face the question: Does God, then, in some sense "intend" Alzheimer's? Does he tolerate its ugliness for a reason? Is it true, as Paul says in Romans 8:28 that "in everything God works for good with those who love him, who are called to his purpose"? Stephen Sapp suggests that Alzheimer's disease and Paul's understanding of the ways of the crucified Lord in 1 Corinthians 1:26-31 can be mutually intelligible.[11] Paul observes God's seemingly odd choice of the poor, the lowly, and the foolish and argues that God must be up to something here. God must be out to "shame the strong . . . so that no human being might boast in the presence of God." Alzheimer's certainly does chasten the human ego. By placing this experience of dementia and disempowerment at the heart of human affairs, we accept that we are fundamentally dependent creatures. We need the care both of other people and of God, and love helps make this possible. Moreover, as Sapp observes, it may be that Alzheimer's providentially reminds us of God's love for all, even the "weak . . . low and despised." Are we not to follow God's example, as difficult as it may be? Marginalization, whether through being a patient or a caregiver, while it does inhibit achievement according to worldly standards, does not distance the person from God. As Paul declares (Rom. 8:39), nothing, not even principalities and powers, can "separate us from the love of God in Christ Jesus our Lord." God is not only the caregiver's historian but also his Redeemer. And, as Handel's magnificent aria proclaims, "I Know That My Redeemer Liveth."

Afterword

An Alzheimer's Hermeneutic
and the Love of God

In the last chapter, I drew repeatedly from Romans 8. This remarkable passage reminds us of God's providential directing of all things for the good, of the freedom of Christian life and peace, of the aid the Spirit provides in our prayers, and of the centrality of Christ's resurrection. Romans 8 also should serve well for some brief concluding reflections for this book, because it incorporates many of the themes discussed. Paul's repeated emphasis on the fact that nothing "will be able to separate us from the love of God" becomes, as we saw in chapters 4 and 5, a central way we can understand God's sustaining the soul between death and the resurrection. Paul's recognition of the impatience Christians often experience leads him to remind us to live "with patience"; we know that God's great work of reconciliation has already been wrought. The apostle shows that despite our sinfulness we have been "set . . . free from the law of sin and death." His reflections on the "groaning" of the creation for the eschaton resonate with one of the descriptions of the beautiful—that experiencing beauty provides us with a foretaste of the glories to come. Finally, concluding with Paul seems appropriate because it is clear, at least to me, that my father's sustained reading of the apostle helped to prepare him for his sustained caregiving.

Paul's statements about suffering in Romans 8 do not "explain away" Alzheimer's, but they do help us fathom what is really going on and what is at stake. The apostle observes that through Christ, we become children of God, "and if children, then heirs, heirs of God and fellow heirs with Christ, provided we suffer with him in order that we may also be glorified with him." Paul takes suffering seriously because he recognizes that God has chosen his own pain on the Cross as the vehicle for our redemption: God "did not spare his own Son but gave him up for us all." If we think about Alzheimer's with the help of Paul, then we see that the painful experiences of caregivers and patients are not alien or anomalous or even to be feared, for we come to see that such experiences are consistent with what is central to God's own work.

Thinking along these lines may seem unusual today, as an unfortunate comment in *The Oxford Annotated Bible* suggests. The text of Romans 8:35 reads "What shall separate us from the love of Christ? Shall tribulation, or distress, or persecution, or famine, or nakedness, or peril, or sword?" The comment says that "To be a Christian in the first century was both difficult and dangerous." Somehow we seem to assume that tribulation, distress, and other sufferings were limited to the early church and the days of persecution. Although Paul does have the experience of his contemporaries in mind, he widens his statement: "For I am sure that neither death, nor life, nor angels, nor principalities, nor things present, nor things to come, nor powers, nor height, nor depth, nor anything else in all creation will be able to separate us from the love of God in Christ Jesus our Lord" (8:38-9). That is, he recognizes that the life in this world is filled with all kinds of perils and threats, and these things are not limited to any particular social order. By over-historicizing Paul's own context, we may have missed how his words apply to believers at all times.

Fortunately, Paul helps us to understand his particular vision of suffering, and he does so by interpolating into his epistle verse 22 from Psalm 44. As I tried to show in chapter 2 of this study, the New Testament re-remembers the Old in light of Christ. Paul here appropriates a psalm of lament and reinterprets it triumphantly in terms of the Cross. When experiencing Alzheimer's disease, we may be very much like the Israelites of the psalm who had recently experienced a great military defeat and humiliation. This disease, as we have seen previously, invites an intimacy with Old Testament suffering, and hence we too sense that we are being overcome by an oppressive force that mocks and destroys us. We too feel "cast . . . off and abased." We may or may not declare that we have faithfully remembered God and his Law, but we certainly echo the sense of blamelessness which the Israelites exhibit. They cry out for God to do something: "Deliver us for the sake of thy steadfast love!" Paul's re-remembering Psalm 44 transforms the suffering of God's people entirely. Paul does not echo the Israelites' cry for help, rather he responds that God has already sent the Messiah on our behalf, affirming that "Christ Jesus, who died, yes, who was raised from the dead, who is at the right hand of God, who indeed intercedes for us." Because the Cross is a revelation of how God's providence unfolds, afflictions do not challenge God's lordship, rather they become an integral part of it.

This passage illustrates the implicit procedure of much of this book, a procedure for understanding the Gospel message which might be called an "Alzheimer's hermeneutic." Paul does not ignore the reality of famine, persecution, and death. He does not overlook our ultimate helplessness before sin and death. But above all of these, he places his confidence in the resurrected Lord. He suggests to us that when we acknowledge our limits, our suffering, and our total dependence on God's work, then we can begin to allow the Cross and Resurrection to change our lives. Thus, we interpret our lives differently because we interpolate our dependence and misery into the story of the Cross, into the revelation of God's prior acceptance of our human suffering and mortality.

Similarly, with Alzheimer's disease, the patient is thrown into a cognitive chaos which entails total dependence on the love of care-givers and God. The caregiver is confronted with human dissolution and death, and becomes aware of her own inadequacies and needs. At these moments, Alzheimer families are so humbled that they may allow Christ's presence in the text and his resurrected Lordship to transform their own worlds. As the daughter of a patient strengthens her efforts through remembering that the woman she tends once diapered her, so too does the daughter grow stronger through re-membering that God gave us all the loving service of the Cross. That is, the fundamental perspective for one's reflection and action is seen as a response to what has already been done, a response to something determinative for the caregiver's existence. In different ways, both the patient and God have made it possible for the caregiver to have life, and the caregiver begins with this reality. This study has empha-sized the importance of memory precisely because beginning our reflections with remembering God—remembering whose we are—means that we are already in quite a different world.

Such experiences of subordinating one's self-understanding to God's revelation may be called a hermeneutic, as they resemble Barth's and Ricoeur's understanding of how readers make them-selves open to the message of the Bible. The hermeneutics of both stress that the self needs to be set aside so that it may be enlarged by Scripture. One commentator summarizes: "The displacement of the self in the experience of listening for the word of God is a hallmark of both Barth's and Ricoeur's hermeneutics—and a position that separates their standpoints from other philosophical and theological positions that use the experience of the sovereign self as the basis for a theological interpretation theory."[1] Particularly for Barth, the idea that we approach the Bible as people capable of interpreting (or judging) as neutral arbiters of truth and meaning overlooks the fact that it is precisely God's Word which interprets (and judges) our lives. Ricoeur's term for what is needed of faithful readers, *dépouillement* ("self-divestment"), also describes what many Alzheimer's caregivers may do, for these people learn from seeing the patient being divested of his self.

An Alzheimer's hermeneutic learns through the humiliation of disease, dissolution, and death that we approach the Bible's narratives as creatures in need, creatures whose own selfhood is dependent on the support of the family, the church, and God. It is a disposition which acknowledges that, above all, we must interpolate our narratives into the narrative of Christ's suffering, death, and resurrection. In several places, this study has cited David H. Smith's observation that "loss of control and suffering belongs at the *beginning* of religious thought"; now we can see indeed that Christ's loss of control and suffering belong at the beginning of our theological reflection.

For Alzheimer families, this hermeneutic means that they may come to understand their conditions in light of the Bible's witness to God's love. Christ's agony on the Cross, the suffering of the Father, Mary, and even the disciples—these now come to have priority over our own suffering. These agonies do not eliminate the sufferings of Alzheimer's but they relativize them. And as we learn how Christ shares our afflictions, we learn more deeply how we imitate his ministry as caregivers. This hermeneutic, an interpreting vision of the Bible and the world, is not a method for eliminating pain, service, and sacrifice but for appreciating its significance. Caregivers may participate in the Kingdom of God even (especially!) as they confront the worst experiences of full-time care for the demented.

This book has followed this approach of allowing God's work to be prevenient. The soul has been considered not as a statement of the powers of the human subject but as the locus of God's work. We have seen that the ecclesial body of Christ precedes our existence and hence is able to share our grief and sustain us. Christ's forgiveness has anticipated and answered our sins before we have even committed or acknowledged them. The Cross has relativized our apocalyptic intimations. Following Barth's recognition that the cosmos is beautiful even though we fail to recognize it fully, we have let the objective beauty of God's creation qualify the ugliness of Alzheimer's. We have come to understand caregiving in the language of 1 John 4:19, "We love, because he first loved us." Returning to Bergsonian language, this approach has helped the Cross exercise its *durée* by reminding us that God has already acted in history on our behalf. We now acknowledge that our experiences are chronologically, ontologically, and soteriologically secondary to his. Such an approach softens the hardened, angry heart so that the "peace which passeth understanding" may at times be present even amid great suffering.

Significantly, the endurance through time which *durée* suggests is a central category for understanding the love of God. 1 John is suffused with the vision of God's enduring love and its transformation of the Christian. "God is love, and he who abides in love abides in God, and God abides in him" (1 John 4:16). Paul's hymn to love in 1 Corinthians 13 also observes that "love . . . endures all things. Love never ends" (vv. 7-8). The Greek word *menein* used in many of these passages suggests remaining, abiding, being steadfast, enduring. It suggests a powerful permeation of the cosmos; it describes a love which in Dante's language "moves the sun and the other stars"; it is a love which stirs and inspires our souls through the Holy Spirit. God's love has *durée*. It impinges on our lives, if we let it. "Let what you have heard from the beginning abide in you" (1 John 2:24). We can be confident in the resurrection because God's love desires our eternal existence. God's love has priority over all things visible and invisible, over powers and principalities, over diseases and brain cells.

To help make this a part of our lives, we need the church's help. As 1 John suggests, the loving, caregiving community of the church helps manifest God's love in the world. I have underscored the church's role in this book because Alzheimer's families do need the assistance of prayer, preaching, and communal support. Prayers do make a difference. Preaching is an ever-needed reminder. Sharing the joy of the Good News with sorrowful caregivers is crucial. The communion of saints provides us with centuries of traditions as well as a vision of ultimate concelebratory worship and love. Indeed, they are as stunning as a large, beautifully-robed choir rising as one to sing a hymn of praise.

229

This study began with the question, Is there a balm in Gilead? We now know that we can sing the spiritual, "There Is a Balm in Gilead." We now know that we have been given a balm "to make the wounded whole, a balm to heal the sin-sick soul."

Let us sing!

Notes

Notes to Introduction

1. Glenn Weaver, "Senile Dementia and a Resurrection Theology," in *Theology Today* 42 (1986): 444–56; Cecil Murphy, *Day to Day: Spiritual Help When Someone You Love Has Alzheimer's* (Louisville: Westminster/John Knox Press, 1987).

2. Nancy L. Mace and Peter V. Rabin, *The 36-Hour Day* (Baltimore: Johns Hopkins University Press, 1981).

3. See, for example, Stephen Sapp, *Light on a Gray Area: American Public Policy on Aging* (Nashville: Abingdon Press, 1992), and Robert H. Binstock, Stephen G. Post, and Peter J. Whitehouse, eds., *Dementia and Aging: Ethics, Values, and Policy Choices* (Baltimore: Johns Hopkins University Press, 1992).

4. Stephen G. Post, *The Moral Challenges of Alzheimer's Disease* (Baltimore: Johns Hopkins University Press, 1995); James Lindemann Nelson and Hilde Lindemann Nelson, *Alzheimer's: Hard Questions for Families* (New York: Doubleday, forthcoming).

5. See, for example, Irving Rosow, *Socialization to Old Age* (Berkeley: University of California Press, 1974). See also Jack Levin and William C. Levin, *Ageism: Prejudice and Discrimination Against the Elderly* (Belmont, CA: Wadsworth, 1980), for a review of recent gerontological research on these issues.

6. See, for example, William M. Clements, ed., *Ministry with the Aging* (San Francisco: Harper and Row, 1981) and Barbara Payne and Earl D. C. Brewer, eds., *Gerontology in Theological Education* (New York: The Haworth Press, 1989).

7. Simone de Beauvoir, *The Coming of Age*, trans. Patrick O'Brian (New York: G. P. Putnam's Sons, 1972).

Notes to Chapter 1

1. Existing texts which discuss these issues are listed in the notes to the Introduction and in the Bibliography. I have relied on them for my discussion of the medical aspects of the disease.

2. Some denominations will be particularly affected by this disease. The

May 1995 report of the United Methodist General Council of Ministries, for example, indicates that this church is graying faster than others; 61.4% of laypeople are over the age of fifty (the national average is 25.5%).

3. Mary Shelley, *Frankenstein* (New York: Bantam Books, 1991), 115.

4. William Shakespeare, *Julius Caesar*, §IV.iii.191–92.

5. Ronald Dworkin, *Life's Dominion* (New York: Vintage Books, 1994), chapter 8, "Life Past Reason."

6. For each of these observations, see their respective articles in Binstock, Post, and Whitehouse, eds., *Dementia and Aging*, 37, 49.

7. Jenijoy La Belle, "No Memory Means No Self: The Pain of a Fading Mind," *International Herald Tribune* (Feb. 2, 1995), 7.

8. Diana Friel McGowin, *Living in the Labyrinth: A Personal Journey through the Maze of Alzheimer's* (New York: Delacorte Press, 1993), and J. Bernlef, *Out of Mind*, trans. Adrienne Dixon (Boston: David R. Godine, 1988).

9. Glenn Weaver, "Senile Dementia and a Resurrection Theology," in *Theology Today* 42 (1986): 447.

10. Stephen Sapp, "The Dilemma of Alzheimer's: Valuing Autonomy and Acknowledging Dependence," *Second Opinion* 9 (1988): 99–101.

11. Susan Sontag, *Illness as Metaphor* (New York: Doubleday, 1989), 20.

12. Sapp, "The Dilemma of Alzheimer's," 94. The unnamed minister was one of many people with experience with this disease whom Sapp has interviewed.

13. Sherwin B. Nuland, *How We Die: Reflections on Life's Final Chapter* (New York: Alfred A. Knopf, 1994).

14. This study was published in the November 1995 issue of the *Journal of the American Medical Association*.

15. Allan Bloom, *Love and Friendship* (New York: Simon and Schuster, 1993), 107.

16. The phrase derives from Philip Rieff and I quote it from E. Brooks Holifield, *A History of Pastoral Care in America: From Salvation to Self-Realization* (Nashville: Abingdon Press, 1983), 12.

17. James W. Ellor, John Stettner, and Helen Spath, "Ministry with the Confused Elderly," *Journal of Religion and Aging* 4 (1987): 27. In addition to this article, see the useful essay by Marty Richards and Sam Seicol, "The Challenge of Maintaining Spiritual Connectedness for Persons Institutionalized with Dementia," *Journal of Religious Gerontology* 7 (1991): 27–40.

Notes to Chapter 2

1. Brevard Childs, *Memory and Tradition in Israel* (London: SCM Press, 1962). I will make frequent reference to this important study.

2. On the figurative parabolic sense of Scripture, see Aquinas, *Summa Theologiae*, §1.1.10.

3. Childs, *Memory and Tradition*, 77–79.

4. See, for example, Exod. 32:13, Lev. 26:45, Jer. 14:21, and Ezek. 16:60.

5. See Childs, *Memory and Tradition*, 31–33.

6. For a good discussion of the church's communion described through the shared liturgical memory of Christ, see David S. Yeago, "Memory and Communion: Ecumenical Theology and the Search for a Generous Orthodoxy" in Ephraim Radner and George R. Sumner, eds., *Reclaiming Faith: Essays on Orthodoxy in the Episcopal Church and the Baltimore Declaration* (Grand Rapids: Eerdmans, 1993), 247–71.

7. This is one of the central theses of Childs, *Memory and Tradition*.

8. Ibid., 85–89.

9. Ibid., 25–27.

10. The link between memory and our personal narratives is important in John Kotre, *White Gloves: How We Create Ourselves Through Memory* (New York: The Free Press, 1995), and Theodore Plantinga, *How Memory Shapes Narratives: A Philosophical Essay on Redeeming the Past* (Lewiston, NY: The Edwin Mellen Press, 1992). As their subtitles might suggest, Alzheimer's disease renders their notions of memory's creative and redemptive powers ultimately suspect.

11. See Leander E. Keck, *The Church Confident* (Nashville: Abingdon Press, 1993), chapter 1.

12. Article on *"zakhar"* by H. Eising in G. Johannes Botterweck and Helmer Ringgren, eds., *Theological Dictionary of the Old Testament*, 7 vols. (Grand Rapids: Eerdmans, 1973–1974), 4:74. The list provided here includes Exod. 20:24; Isa. 26:13; 48:1; and Ps. 45:18 (17). See also Childs, *Memory and Tradition*, 14.

13. See Childs, *Memory and Tradition*, 59–60.

14. A. C. Cawley, ed., *Everyman and Medieval Miracle Plays* (New York: Dutton, 1958), 223.

15. Nicholas Wolterstorff, *Lament for a Son* (Grand Rapids: Eerdmans, 1987), 65.

16. Hesiod, *Theogony*, trans. Norman O. Brown (New York: The Liberal Arts Press, 1953), section 1, 54–56.

17. See, for example, J. D. Zizioulas, *Being as Communion: Studies in Personhood and the Church* (Crestwood, NY: St. Vladimir's Seminary Press, 1985), chapter 1.

18. Wolterstorff, *Lament for a Son*, 102.

19. Augustine, *On the Trinity*, §14.12.15.

20. Polybius, *The Rise of the Roman Empire*, trans. Ian Scott-Kilvert (New York: Penguin Books, 1982), Introduction, 41.

21. Ibid.

22. See Childs, *Memory and Tradition*, 50–52.

23. Thomas à Kempis, *The Imitation of Christ*, §3.4. Quoted from the translation by Leo Sherly-Price (New York: Penguin Books, 1984).

24. The information in this paragraph comes from the good introduction to the problem of forgetting to be found in Alan Baddeley's "The Psychology of Remembering and Forgetting" in Thomas Butler, ed., *Memory: History, Culture, and the Mind* (Oxford: Basil Blackwell, 1989).

25. Augustine, *Confessions*, §8.7.

26. Thomas à Kempis, *The Imitation of Christ*, §1.22.

27. See Robert H. Stein, *The Method and Message of Jesus' Teaching* (Philadelphia: Westminster Press, 1978), 32.

28. Thomas à Kempis, *The Imitation of Christ*, §3.10.

29. On this point, see Johann Baptist Metz, "A Short Apology of Narrative," in Stanley Hauerwas and L. Gregory Jones, eds., *Why Narrative? Readings in Narrative Theology* (Grand Rapids: Eerdmans, 1989), 251–62.

30. Jacques Le Goff, *History and Memory*, trans. Steven Rendall and Elizabeth Claman (New York: Columbia University Press, 1992), 51. This text contains a useful review of how problems of memory have become important for modern historians.

31. Specific references to the *loci classici* on memory and a good introduction to the problem can be found in the article on "Memory" in *The New Catholic Encyclopedia* (New York: McGraw-Hill, 1967).

32. A good introduction to modern ways of thinking about memory can be found in Baddeley's "The Psychology of Remembering and Forgetting," in Butler, ed., *Memory*. On instrumental memory and for another discussion of memory see Kotre's *White Gloves*.

33. This remark by a British philosopher, Samuel Alexander, in 1890, is quoted in Stephen Kern, *The Culture of Time and Space, 1880–1918* (Cambridge: Harvard University Press, 1983), 33.

34. Peter Burke, "History as Social Memory," in Butler, ed., *Memory*, 107. This essay is a very good introduction to modern discussions of the social aspect of memory.

35. For a scathing, if idiosyncratic, evaluation and critique of Bergson's thought, see Bertrand Russell, *A History of Western Philosophy* (New York: Simon and Schuster, 1972), 791–810. Bergson is discussed extensively and compared with other modern thinkers in the first four chapters of Kern, *Culture of Time and Space*.

36. Some passages from Niebuhr's *The Meaning of Revelation* read as if they were straight from Bergson. For a discussion of the particular influence of Bergson's understanding of faith and religious institutions on Niebuhr, see Jaroslav Pelikan, "Bergson Among the Theologians," in Thomas Hanna, ed., *The Bergsonian Heritage* (New York: Columbia University Press, 1962), 54–73. For Bergson's influence on Maritain, see Maritain's *Bergsonian Philosophy and Thomism*, trans. Mabelle L. Andison and J. Gordon Andison (New York: The Philosophical Library, 1955).

37. For a review of this problem, see Brevard Childs, *Biblical Theology of the Old and New Testaments: Theological Reflection on the Christian Bible* (Minneapolis: Fortress Press, 1992), 413–21.

38. See, for example, Plantinga, *How Memory Shapes Narrative*, 45–47.

39. Stephen Crites, as quoted by Julian Hartt in Hauerwas and Jones, eds., *Why Narrative*, 281. For a dicussion of different views of the imagination as they pertain particularly to the problem of narrative, see the essays by both Crites and Hartt in this volume.

40. Harold Bloom's discussion of how the imaginative and creative powers of great writers emerge from a struggle with the impinging literary memory of the canon illustrates both how how memory is canonical (here,

in a literary sense) and how imagination and memory may interact. See his *The Western Canon: The Books and Schools of the Ages* (New York: Harcourt Brace, and Company, 1994).

41. David Hume, *An Inquiry Concerning Human Understanding*, §5.2.

Notes to Chapter 3

1. Flannery O'Connor, "The Church and the Fiction Writer," in *Collected Works* (New York: The Library of America, 1988), 811.

2. Sally McFague, *Models of God: Theology for an Ecological, Nuclear Age* (Philadelphia: Fortress Press, 1987), 37.

3. See, for example, Bernard E. Meland, *Fallible Forms and Symbols: Discourses on Method in a Theology of Culture* (Philadelphia: Fortress Press, 1976), 129.

4. H. Richard Niebuhr, *The Meaning of Revelation* (New York: Macmillan, 1941), 139. This is one of the many pages in this text which reads as if it were from Bergson. I should note that for Gregory of Palamas, doctrines would not be called energies, a term he applied to God's creative activities. (Still, for doctrine to be true, it must be God's.) Despite my misuse, the term suggests the dynamism of doctrine, a conceptual dynamism of the reality of God's cosmos.

5. See David S. Yeago, "Memory and Communion: Ecumenical Theology and the Search for a Generous Orthodoxy," in Ephraim Radner and George R. Sumner, eds., *Reclaiming Faith: Essays on Orthodoxy in the Episcopal Church and the Baltimore Declaration* (Grand Rapids: Eerdmans, 1993), 247–71.

6. Walker Percy, *The Last Gentleman* (New York: Ivy Books, 1966), 237.

7. As quoted in *The Christian Century* (Oct. 18, 1995): 949.

8. David Tracy's "Theological Method," chapter 1 of Peter C. Hodgson and Robert H. King, eds., *Christian Theology: An Introduction to its Traditions and Tasks* (Philadelphia: Fortress Press, 1985), is particularly dependent on this "we." For the quotations above, see 36–38.

9. Paul L. Holmer, "Wittgenstein and Theology," in Dallas M. High, ed., *New Essays on Religious Language* (New York: Oxford University Press, 1969), 28.

10. David Damrosch, *We Scholars: Changing the Culture of the University* (Cambridge, MA: Harvard University Press, 1995), 9.

11. Ibid., especially chapter 3, "The Scholar as Exile."

12. McFague, *Models of God*, 33.

13. Post, *The Moral Challenges of Alzheimer's Disease*.

14. As can be detected from this text, I personally have been most strongly influenced by what is called post-critical or post-liberal theology. Hence, I am primarily interested in developing a theological description of what is sometimes called the grammar of faith in light of the phenomena of Alzheimer's disease. This is certainly not the only way of proceeding, but I suspect that it may be the most helpful way of engaging pastoral concerns.

15. Keck, *The Church Confident*, 64–65.

16. James W. Ellor, John Stettner, and Helen Spath, "Ministry with the Confused Elderly," *Journal of Religion and Aging* 4, no. 2 (1987): 29.

Notes to Chapter 4

1. Charles Taliaferro, *Consciousness and the Mind of God* (Cambridge: Cambridge University Press, 1994).

2. Karl Rahner, *Theological Investigations*, Volume 6: *Concerning Vatican Council II*, trans. Karl-H. and Boniface Kruger (Baltimore: Helicon Press, 1969), 157.

3. See, for example, J. N. D. Kelly, *Early Christian Doctrines* (San Francisco: Harper and Row, 1978), 345–46.

4. See Ernst Käsemann, *Essays on New Testament Themes*, Studies in Biblical Theology 41 (London: SCM Press, 1964), chapter 4, "The Canon of the New Testament and the Unity of the Church"; and Karl Barth, *Church Dogmatics*, ed. G. W. Bromily and T. F. Torrance, 4 vols. in 14 (Edinburgh: T and T Clark, 1985), 2.2:326.

5. In general, the New Testament approaches the human being through Christ, but different authors exhibit different Christological tendencies, and since the great controversies concerning the nature and work of Christ were still several centuries away, it seems hard to establish a clear picture of New Testament anthropology based on the image of Christ.

6. See, for example, "The Formula of Concord," Solid Declaration, Article 1, in *The Book of Concord* (Philadelphia, Fortress Press, 1983), 508. For Calvin, see his introductory comment to *Institutes of the Christian Religion*, §1.15.2.

7. On Clement, see Kelly, *Early Christian Doctrines*, 344. For Luther, see "The Sacrament of the Body and Blood of Christ—Against the Fanatics," in *Luther's Works: American Edition*, gen. eds. Jaroslav Pelikan and Helmut T. Lehmann, 54 vols. (St. Louis: Concordia, and Philadelphia: Fortress Press, 1955–1976), 36:338–39; hereafter cited as *LW*.

8. *Decrees of the Ecumenical Councils*, ed. Norman P. Tanner, S.J., 2 vols. (Washington, DC: Georgetown University Press, 1990), 1:361.

9. See chapter 12.

10. See, for example, Augustine, *On the Trinity*, §9.12.18 and §14.4.6; Calvin, *Institutes*, §1.15. A good overview of early views of the *imago Dei* can be found in *Christian Spirituality: Origins to the Twelfth Century*, ed. Bernard McGinn and John Meyendorff (New York: Crossroad, 1985), chapter 12.

11. Calvin, *Institutes*, §1.15.4–5.

12. Because the soul is present with such regularity in these texts, I have omitted detailed citations save for direct quotations. On the particular point of God's providing food for the soul, see also Luther's "Large Catechism" in *The Book of Concord*, 449.

13. "Decree on the Apostolate of the Laity," chapter 6, section 30, in *Decrees*, ed. Tanner, 2:1000.

14. Martin Luther, "Two Kinds of Righteousness," in John Dillenberger,

ed., *Martin Luther: Selections from His Writings* (New York: Anchor Books, 1961), 86–90. Calvin, *Institutes*, §2.2.19 and §4.16.25.

15. Thomas à Kempis, *The Imitation of Christ*, §3.23 (p. 126 and 125). Many of the examples cited here are to be found in the third chapter, significantly titled "On Inward Consolation." For Weaver's use of Genesis 1, see chapter 1 above.

16. Thomas à Kempis, *The Imitation of Christ*, §3.31 (p. 136); emphasis added.

17. Allan Bloom, *Love and Friendship* (New York: Simon and Schuster, 1993), 543–45.

18. For a more thorough, though idiosyncratic, discussion of the different contributions to the decline in soul-speak, psych-ology, see William Barrett's *Death of the Soul: From Descartes to the Computer* (Garden City, NY: Doubleday, 1986).

19. For an example of a critique of Descartes, see Fergus Kerr, *Theology after Wittgenstein* (Oxford: Basil Blackwell, 1986).

20. For Schleiermacher's consideration of the soul, see *The Christian Faith*, ed. H. R. Mackintosh and J. S. Stewart (New York: Harper and Row, 1963), 709–22.

21. David Kelsey, "Human Being," in Hodgson and King, eds., *Christian Theology*, 167–93.

22. A good review of the status of the "soul" today in contemporary theology can be found in the Introduction to Taliaferro's *Consciousness and the Mind of God*.

23. Charles V. Gerkin, *The Living Human Document* (Nashville: Abingdon Press, 1984), chapter 5, "The Hermeneutics of the Self and the Life of the Soul." The quotations are from pp. 97 and 104.

24. For an example of how the use of phenomenology in a discussion of the soul or spiritual dimension of humanity leads to what may be an over-emphasis on consciousness and epistemology, see Wolfhart Pannenberg, *Anthropology in Theological Perspective*, trans. Matthew J. O'Connell (Philadelphia: Westminster Press, 1985), 515–32. For the defence of the soul in the context of the philosophy of mind, see Taliaferro's *Consciousness*. For Barth, see *Church Dogmatics*, 3.2:325–436, "Man as Soul and Body."

25. John Bunyan, *The Pilgrim's Progress* (New York: Penguin Books, 1985), 42, 39. It is worth noting that in the earlier part of Bunyan's century, William Harvey had published his medical discoveries, and Francis Bacon had written his works on the inductive and scientific methods.

26. For a discussion of different approaches to matter in the modern world, see Ernan McMullin, ed., *The Concept of Matter in Modern Philosophy* (Notre Dame: University of Notre Dame Press, 1978). For a review of the problematic of matter in the modern world, see 271–98.

27. The full title is *Matter and Consciousness: A Contemporary Introduction to the Philosophy of Mind* (Cambridge, MA: MIT Press, 1990). Another good introductory book, one which is much more overtly materialist in its aims, is Peter Carruthers' *Introducing Persons: Theories and Arguments in the Philosophy of Mind* (New York: Routledge, 1992). A good shorter introduction can

be found in John Searle's "The Mystery of Consciousness" in the November and December, 1995, issues of *The New York Review of Books*.

28. Churchland, *Matter and Consciousness*, 1, 18.

29. Charles Dickens, *Hard Times* (New York: New American Library, 1980), 15–16.

30. Richard Rorty, "Mind-Body Identity, Privacy, and Categories" *Review of Metaphysics* 19, no., 1 (1965): 30. It is possible that Rorty has changed his views in thirty years, but this text seems to have assumed the status of something of a prophetic text for materialists.

31. For his summary of the strengths of dualism, see *Matter and Consciousness*, 13–18.

32. Richard Swinburne, *The Evolution of the Soul* (Oxford: Clarendon Press, 1987).

33. Charles Arthur Campbell, *On Selfhood and Godhead* (New York: Macmillan, 1957).

34. Roger Penrose, *Shadows of the Mind: A Search for the Missing Science of Consciousness* (Oxford: Oxford University Press, 1994), 416–17; see also 35–37.

35. It is curious to observe how some modern theologians accept the noumenal/phenomenal distinction as a way of limiting theology rather than as a vehicle for delineating the possible subjects of peculiarly theological discourse. See, for example, David Kelsey, "Human Being," in Hodgson and King, eds., *Christian Theology*, 178–81. It appears that for many, the subject as a knower interferes with the subject as a believer.

36. It is possible for materialists to appeal to quantum theory and the indeterminacy of matter, but this view would suggest that we neither have free will nor are determined but are rather creatures of randomness. Eliminative materialism and its willingness to abandon any traditional category would be able to say farewell to freedom rather consistently. Most materialists, however, do follow the Hobbesian or Humean formulation of the problem of free will; all that remains, it would appear, would be some sort of freedom of action not of the will. Regardless of the formulation, materialists have serious difficulties with the moral problem of responsibility. For a good review of the problems with references to ancient and modern authors, see the article on "Determinism" by Richard Taylor in *The Encyclopedia of Philosophy*, ed. Paul Edwards, 8 vols. in 4 (New York: Macmillan & The Free Press, 1967), 2:359–73. For Calvin, see *Institutes* §3.19.

37. Hobbes, *Leviathan*, §1.6.

38. Richard Klein, "The Power of Pets," in *The New Republic* (July 10, 1995): 23.

39. For Vatican II, see "Church and World," chapter 2, section 29, in *Decrees*, ed. Tanner, 2:1086. For Luther, see his *Secular Authority: To What Extent it Should be Obeyed*, part 2, in Dillenberger, ed., *Martin Luther*, 382–92. For Barth, see *Church Dogmatics*, 3.4:324–97.

40. Alexis de Tocqueville, *Democracy in America*, ed. Philipps Bradley, 2 vols. (New York: Random House, 1945), §2.15–16 (2:154, 157).

41. Kelsey, "Human Being," in Hodgson and King, eds., *Christian Theology*, 181.

42. Kerr, *Theology after Wittgenstein*, 3–27. While I agree with Kerr's critique, my response to the problem is different. Indeed, I suspect he would disagree quite strongly with me.

43. Kelsey, "Human Being," 191.

44. Reinhold Niehbur, *The Nature and Destiny of Man* (New York: Charles Scribner's Sons, 1964). For Niebuhr's statement on self-transcendence, see the Preface.

45. Kelsey, "Human Being," 190. For Churchland's discussion, see *Matter and Consciousness*, 85–87.

46. David H. Smith, "Alzheimer's, Theology, and Religious Studies" (unpublished paper presented at the Experimental Session on "The Theological Dimensions of Alzheimer's" held at the 1993 meeting of the American Academy of Religion), 4–5 (emphasis his).

47. Rahner, *Theological Investigations*, 6:156–57.

48. Jonathan Shear, "On Mystical Experiences as Support for the Perennial Philosophy," *Journal of the American Academy of Religion* 62 (1994): 320.

49. Bruno Bettelheim, *Freud and Man's Soul* (New York: Alfred A. Knopf, 1983), esp. chapter 10.

50. For a sustained discussion of these points, see Michael Frede, "On Aristotle's Conception of the Soul," in R. W. Sharples, ed., *Modern Thinkers and Ancient Thinkers: The Stanley Victor Keeling Memorial Lectures, 1981–91* (Boulder, CO: Westview Press, 1993), 138–56.

51. Harvey Cox, "Healers and Ecologists: Pentecostalism in Africa" in *The Christian Century* (Nov. 9, 1994): 1045. Taliaferro, *Consciousness*, 16. Rahner, *Theological Investigations*, 6:177.

Notes to Chapter 5

1. Suetonius, *The Twelve Caesars*, trans. Robert Graves (New York: Penguin Books, 1979), §82 (p. 50). On Caesar's wish for a swift death, see §87 (p. 53).

2. Henri J. M. Nouwen, *Our Greatest Gift: A Meditation on Dying and Caring* (San Francisco: Harper and Row, 1984), 106. On this same page, he is even more explicit, declaring the resurrection to be the "foundation of [his] faith."

3. Wolterstorff, *Lament for a Son*, 31, 38–39, 65, and 77–78.

4. Ibid., 56, 34, and 7.

5. The sustained use of Julius Caesar as a backdrop for this Introduction was suggested by the Victorian James Anthony Froude's *Caesar: A Sketch*, which he concluded with a suggestive comparison of the founders of the empire and the church.

6. Reinhold Niebuhr, *Beyond Tragedy* (New York: Scribner's, 1937), 289.

7. Carl E. Braaten, "The Kingdom of God and Life Everlasting," in Hodgson and King, eds., *Christian Theology*, 330.

8. John Patton, *Pastoral Care in Context: An Introduction to Pastoral Care* (Louisville: Westminster/John Knox, 1993), 116–18.

9. Carter Heyward, "The Power of God-Within-Us," in James M. Wall

and David Heim, eds., *How My Mind Has Changed* (Grand Rapids: Eerdmans, 1991), 16.

10. Glenn D. Weaver, "Senile Dementia and a Resurrection Theology" in *Theology Today* 42 (1986): 444–56.

11. Paul Hessert, *Christ and the End of Meaning: The Theology of Passion* (Rockport, MA: Element, 1993), chapter 7, "Life as Resurrection."

12. See, for example, Gerald O'Collins, S.J., *What Are They Saying About the Resurrection?* (New York: Paulist Press, 1978), and Peter Carnley, *The Structure of Resurrection Belief* (Oxford: Clarendon Press, 1987), 1–21.

13. See his *Church Dogmatics*, 3.2:441ff.

14. Carnley, *The Structure of Resurrection Belief*, esp. 25–28.

15. O'Collins, *Resurrection?*, 41 (emphasis his).

16. See, for example, Hans Küng, *Eternal Life?*, trans. Edward Quinn (New York: Doubleday, 1984), 116.

17. Carolyn Walker Bynum, *Fragmentation and Redemption: Essays on Gender and the Human Body in Medieval Religion* (New York: Zone Books, 1993), 19.

18. John D. Zizioulas, *Being as Communion: Studies in Personhood and the Church* (Crestwood, NY: St. Valdimir's Seminary Press, 1985), 59.

19. Reinhold Niebuhr, *Nature and Destiny*, 289–99.

20. For his views on the resurrection, see Schleiermacher, *The Christian Faith*, 696–722.

21. On the importance of this point, see Küng, *Eternal Life*, 160–61.

22. Küng, *Eternal Life*, 164.

23. Stanley Hauerwas, *Suffering Presence: Theological Reflections on Medicine, the Mentally Handicapped, and the Church* (Notre Dame: University of Notre Dame Press, 1986), 96.

24. See Luther's sermon, "Two Kinds of Righteousness," in John Dillenberger, ed., *Martin Luther: Selections from His Writings* (New York: Doubleday, 1961), 86–87.

25. Flannery O'Connor, "The Church and the Fiction Writer" in *Collected Works* (New York: The Library of America, 1988), 809.

26. Hauerwas, *Suffering Presence*, 88. Certain exceptional cases (such as comas and brain trauma) and the medical and ethical responsibilities for care which they entail may well be cases when the church does need to provide guidance for families.

27. Ibid.

28. The phrase is Schleiermacher's (from his discussion of the Resurrection and the Last Judgment in *The Christian Faith*, 722), but it could also have come from any of the great theologians who recognized the importance of the affective role of theology.

29. See, for example, Nouwen, *Our Greatest Gift*, 108 and Nicholas Peter Harvey, *Death's Gift: Chapters on Resurrection and Bereavement* (London: Epworth Press, 1985), 6–7.

30. Arthur C. McGill, *Suffering: A Test of Theological Method* (Philadelphia: Westminster Press, 1982), chapter 4, "Self-giving as the Inner Life of God."

31. Wolterstorff, *Lament for a Son*, 81 and 102.

32. Harvey, *Death's Gift*, 7.

33. Braaten, "Kingdom of God," 348. Hauerwas also has stressed the importance of communal presence in suffering and grief; cf. *Suffering Presence*, 6 and 178, and *Naming the Silences: God, Medicine, and the Problem of Suffering* (Grand Rapids: Eerdmans, 1990), xi.

34. James discusses the sick soul in chapters 6 and 7 of *The Varieties of Religious Experience* (New York: Macmillan, 1961). In chapters 4 and 5 he examines the religion of healthy-mindedness.

35. James, *Varieties*, 118–19.

36. Harvey, *Death's Gift*, 9.

37. James, *Varieties*, 139.

38. Smith, "Alzheimer's, Theology, and Religious Studies," 4–5 (emphasis his).

39. For a treatment of Edward's views of the afterlife, see John H. Gerstner, *Jonathan Edwards on Heaven and Hell* (Grand Rapids: Baker Book House, 1980).

40. See, for example, Dante, *Paradiso*, §XIV.61–66. See Bynum, *Fragmentation*, 256.

41. Most Christian commentators enthusiastically have seen Dante as a man of the church. But for a critique of such unbridled enthusiasm in light of Dante's rare hubris, see Harold Bloom's *The Western Canon: The Books and School of the Ages* (New York: Harcourt Brace and Co., 1994), chapter 3. All quotations from the *Divine Comedy* are from John D. Sinclair's translation (New York: Oxford University Press, 1982).

Notes to Chapter 6

1. Individual experiences of caregivers and patients vary enormously, but I believe that the phenomena I describe here are not uncommon. The poignant collection of prayers for Alzheimer's families in Cecil Murphy's *Day to Day*, for example, directly addresses many of the tribulations and anxieties discussed here.

2. James, *Varieties*, 114. For his discussion of the religion of healthy-mindedness, see chapters 4–7.

3. I take this list from Childs, *Biblical Theology*, 571.

4. Leander E. Keck, "Death and Afterlife in the New Testament," in Hiroshi Obayashi, ed., *Death and Afterlife: Perspectives of the World Religions* (New York: Greenwood Press, 1992), 88.

5. Augustine, *Confessions*, §2.3.

6. Bernard of Clairvaux, *On Consideration*, §5.12.25.

7. For a recent example of how remembering the link between sin and death can be crucial for a Christian ethic of dying, see Vigen Guroian, *Ethics After Christendom: Toward an Ecclesial Christian Ethic* (Grand Rapids: Eerdmans, 1994), chapter 8.

8. See, for example, Stephen G. Post, "The Inadequacy of Selflessness: God's Suffering and the Theory of Love," *Journal of the American Aacademy of Religion* 56 (1988): 213–28, esp. 223.

9. For a discussion of the problematic character of the term, see Leander E. Keck, "Paul and Apocalyptic Theology," *Interpretation* 38 (1984): 229–41. I have found this article and the pages cited in note #11 to be useful overviews of the problems.

10. Ibid., 235.

11. For a brief review of scholarly literature on Apocalyptic and the problematic character of this kind of text, see Childs, *Biblical Theology*, 181–86 and 317–22.

12. Eiesland misreads the Lukan passage by seeing forgiveness and healing as "equivalent." See Nancy L. Eiesland, *The Disabled God: Toward a Liberatory Theology of Disability* (Nashville: Abingdon Press, 1994), 71.

13. Childs, *Biblical Theology*, 576.

14. Luther, "The Sacrament of Penance," *LW* 35:17 and 10.

15. Ibid., *LW* 35:21.

16. Keck, "Death and Afterlife," 92.

17. Ignatius, *Epistle to the Romans*, §7.

18. Wolterstorff, *Lament for a Son*, 81.

19. Thomas à Kempis, *The Imitation of Christ*, §4.14.

20. As quoted in Eiesland, *Disabled God*, 85. She discusses the ALC text, which was written in 1980, in chapter 4.

Notes to Chapter 7

1. See, for example, James, *Varieties*, 120 and 126.

2. George Santayana, *The Sense of Beauty, Being the Outline of Aesthetic Theory* (New York: Dover Publications, 1955 [orig. 1896]), 5.

3. Jacques Maritain, *Art and Scholasticism*, trans. Joseph W. Evans (Notre Dame: University of Notre Dame Press, 1974), 24.

4. Perry Miller, *Errand into the Wilderness* (Cambridge: Harvard University Press, 1956), 169. The following quotations are from Ralph Waldo Emerson, "Beauty," in *The Conduct of Life*, as printed in Perry Miller, ed., *The American Transcendentalists* (Baltimore: Johns Hopkins University Press, 1981), 171–86.

5. Santayana, *The Sense of Beauty*, 163–64.

6. Each of these descriptive terms is discussed by Burke in part 2 of *A Philosophical Enquiry into the Origin of our Ideas of the Beautiful and the Sublime* (New York: Oxford University Press, 1990 [orig. 1757]).

7. Santayana, *The Sense of Beauty*, 145–46. This Christological reading is suggested by Santayana's own text.

8. Memory is particularly important for discerning and evaluating art. See, for example, Carlo Ginzburg, *Clues, Myths, and the Historical Method*, trans. John and Anne C. Tedeschi (Baltimore: Johns Hopkins University Press, 1984), 53.

9. Barth, *Church Dogmatics*, 2.1:655, 651, and 650.

10. William M. Thompson, "The Saints, Justification, and Sanctification: An Ecumenical Thought Experiment," *Pro Ecclesia* 4, no. 1 (1995): 16–36, esp. 32–34.

11. An excellent, fair review of the opus may be found in Robert E.

Wood's "Philosophy, Aesthetics, and Theology: A Review of Hans Urs von Balthasar's *The Glory of the Lord,*" *American Catholic Philosophical Quarterly* 67 (1993): 355–82.

12. Patrick Sherry, *Spirit and Beauty: An Introduction to Theological Aesthetics* (Oxford: Clarendon Press, 1992).

13. John Paul II, Apostolic Constitution, "Fidei Depositum," Prologue, in *The Catechism of the Catholic Church* (Manilla: ECCCE and Word and Life Publications, 1994), 3.

14. Barth, *Church Dogmatics,* 2.1:662.

15. Barth, *Church Dogmatics,* 2.1:665.

16. Santayana, *The Sense of Beauty,* 144.

17. Barth, *Church Dogmatics,* 2.1:661.

18. Barth, *Church Dogmatics,* 2.1:668.

19. Frank Burch Brown, *Religious Aesthetics: A Theological Study of Making and Meaning* (Princeton: Princeton University Press, 1989), 136.

20. Hans Urs von Balthasar, *The Glory of the Lord: A Theological Aesthetics,* trans. Erasmo Leiva-Merikakis, ed. Joseph Fessio and John Riches, 7 vols. (San Francisco: Ignatius Press, and New York: Crossroad, 1983–1991), 7:19.

21. Barth, *Church Dogmatics,* 2.1:677.

22. Protopriest Anatoli Volgin, "What is an Icon?" *Tvorchestvo,* 1:9–10 (Moscow, 1991), trans. Jean Laves Hellie (a text that was electronically transmitted via the Internet to the Orthodox Christianity discussion group by Lev. A. Pokrovsky and forwarded to me in the Philippines by Russ Martin).

23. Josef Pieper, *Leisure, The Basis of Culture,* trans. Alexander Dru (New York: Pantheon Books, 1964), 59.

24. For a discussion of Nebel's *Das Ereignis des Schoenen* (Klett, 1953), see von Balthasar, *The Glory of the Lord,* 1:58–70.

25. Pieper, *Leisure,* 63.

26. Paul Holmer, *Making Christian Sense* (Philadelphia: Westminster Press, 1984), 9. Note that Richard Mouw, citing Patrick Ryan, S.J., defends kitsch, glow-in-the-dark statues in the context of his exploration of how popular religion can teach us all a great deal. In particular, we are reminded that Jesus was not born into "high-brow" status or tastes. See Mouw's excerpt from his recent *Consulting the Faithful: What Christian Intellectuals Can Learn from Popular Religion* (Grand Rapids: Eerdmans, 1994) in *The Christian Century* (Aug. 10–17, 1994): 740–41.

27. For Barth, see for example, *Church Dogmatics,* 2.1:650–62, and for von Balthasar, see *The Glory of the Lord,* 1:121–23.

28. Kerr, *Theology After Wittgenstein,* 23–25.

29. Ibid., 166–67.

30. For example, see Ellor, Stettner, and Spath, "Ministry with the Confused Elderly," 28–29.

31. Von Balthasar, *The Glory of the Lord,* 1:65.

32. See Pelikan's chapter on "The Beauty of Holiness" in his *Fools for Christ: Essays on the True, the Good, and the Beautiful* (Philadelphia: Fortress Press, 1955).

33. See Gari Lesnoff-Caravaglia, "The Aesthetic Attitude and Common Experience," in his edited volume *Values, Ethics, and Aging* (New York: Human Sciences Press, 1985), 13–25.

Notes to Chapter 8

1. That the discipline is somewhat confused can be seen from the enormous number of books in recent years on "history." Different theories, pronouncements, and manifestos abound, and in many ways this is quite healthy as it is related to the opening up of new areas of research and discussion. Still, there seems to be very little agreement among professionals as to what "history" is. Despite a focus on European thought, a good introduction to recent discussions, as well as to considerations of the relationship between history and memory, can be found in Jacques Le Goff, *History and Memory*, trans. Steven Rendall and Elizabeth Claman (New York: Columbia University Press, 1992).

2. Wolterstorff, *Lament for a Son*, 28.

3. Unfortunately, the space here is all too limited for an extended consideration of this way of doing history. I hope only to make some suggestions at this time, and to develop this way of thinking about the past in a subsequent work on the idea of churched history. I am grateful to George M. Marsden for allowing me to read *The Outrageous Idea of Christian Scholarship* (New York: Oxford University Press, forthcoming) while still in manuscript form.

4. Information about the St. Alban's Parish project is available in Sara Jenkins, *Past Present: Recording Life Stories of Older People* (Washington, DC: St. Alban's Parish, 1978). See also G. Cullom Davis, "Oral History: Accounts of Lives and Times," in Gari Lesnof-Caravaglia, ed., *Values, Ethics, and Aging* (New York: Human Sciences Press, 1985).

5. While we do not usually make the association, forgiveness is not completely alien to the discipline of history. Donald W. Shriver, Jr.'s *An Ethic for Enemies: Forgiveness in Politics* (New York: Oxford University Press, 1995) demonstrates through his study of remembering World War II how history can foster the process of forgiveness between nations. Churched historians may be able to develop this link and make it one of its particular contributions to the professional study of history.

6. The shorter Lord's Prayer in Luke is preceded by the story of Mary and Martha (Luke 10:38–42). Here, Jesus' rebuke of Martha suggests that service, like caregiving, needs to be performed in the context of His teachings, for it is God's Word which links human caregiving with His love and His own sacrifice.

7. Elisabeth Schüssler Fiorenza, *In Memory of Her: A Feminist Theological Reconstruction of Christian Origins* (New York: Crossroad, 1983), xiv.

8. Shelley, *Frankenstein*, 113.

9. Santayana, *The Sense of Beauty*, 143–50.

10. For Chesteron, see his *Orthodoxy: The Romance of Faith* (New York:

Doubleday, 1990), 68. For Wilson, see *The Moral Sense* (New York: The Free Press, 1993), esp. 29–54.

11. Sapp, "The Dilemma of Alzheimer's," 99.

Note to Afterword

1. Mark I. Wallace, *The Second Naiveté: Barth, Ricoeur, and the New Yale Theology* (Macon, GA: Mercer University Press, 1995), 102.

Bibliography

Balthasar, Hans Urs von. *The Glory of the Lord.* Translated by Erasmo Leiva-Merikakis. Edited by Joseph Fessio and John Riches. 7 vols. San Francisco: Ignatius Press, and New York: Crossroad, 1983-91.

Barrett, William. *The Death of the Soul: From Descartes to the Computer.* Garden City, NY: Doubleday, 1986.

Barth, Karl. *Church Dogmatics.* Edited by G. W. Bromily and T. F. Torrance. 4 vols. in 14. Edinburgh: T and T Clark, 1985.

Beauvoir, Simone de. *The Coming of Age.* Translated by Patrick O'Brian. New York: G. P. Putnam's Sons, 1972.

Bernlef, J. *Out of Mind.* Translated by Adrienne Dixon. Boston: David R. Godine, 1988.

Bettelheim, Bruno. *Freud and Man's Soul.* New York: Alfred A. Knopf, 1983.

Binstock, Robert H.; Post, Stephen G.; and Whitehouse, Peter J., eds. *Dementia and Aging: Ethics, Values, and Policy Choices.* Baltimore: Johns Hopkins University Press, 1992.

Bloom, Allan. *Love and Friendship.* New York: Simon and Schuster, 1993.

Bloom, Harold. *The Western Canon: The Books and Schools of the Ages.* New York: Harcourt Brace, and Company, 1994.

Brown, Frank Burch. *Religious Aesthetics: A Theological Study of Making and Meaning.* Princeton: Princeton University Press, 1989.

Burke, Edmund. *A Philosophical Enquiry into the Origin of Our Ideas of the Beautiful and the Sublime.* New York: Oxford University Press, 1990.

Butler, Thomas, ed. *Memory: History, Culture, and the Mind.* Oxford: Basil Blackwell, 1989.

Bynum, Carolyn Walker. *Fragmentation and Redemption: Essays on Gender and the Human Body in Medieval Religion.* New York: Zone Books, 1993.

Carnley, Peter. *The Structure of Resurrection Belief.* Oxford: Clarendon Press, 1987.

Carruthers, Peter. *Introducing Persons: Theories and Arguments in the Philosophy of Mind.* New York: Routledge, 1992.

Cawley, A. C., ed. *Everyman and Medieval Miracle Plays.* New York: Dutton, 1958.

Chesterton, G. K. *Orthodoxy: The Romance of Faith.* New York: Doubleday, 1990.

Childs, Brevard. *Biblical Theology of the Old and New Testaments: Theological Reflection on the Christian Bible.* Minneapolis: Fortress Press, 1992.

———. *Memory and Tradition in Israel.* London: SCM Press, 1962.

Churchland, Paul. *Matter and Conciousness: A Contemporary Introduction to the Philosophy of Mind*. Cambridge: MIT Press, 1990.

Clements, William M. *Ministry with the Aging*. San Francisco: Harper & Row, 1981.

Damrosch, David. *We Scholars: Changing the Culture of the University*. Cambridge: Harvard University Press, 1995.

Dante. *The Divine Comedy*. Translated by John D. Sinclair. New York: Oxford University Press, 1982.

Dillenberger, John, ed. *Martin Luther: Selections from His Writings*. New York: Anchor Books, 1961.

Dworkin, Ronald. *Life's Dominion*. New York: Vintage Books, 1994.

Eiesland, Nancy L. *The Disabled God: Toward a Liberatory Theology of Disability*. Nashville: Abingdon Press, 1994.

Ellor, James W.; Stettner, John; and Spath, Helen. "Ministry with the Confused Elderly." *Journal of Religion and Aging* 4 (1987): 21-33.

Frei, Hans. *The Eclipse of Biblical Narrative: A Study in Eighteenth and Nineteenth Century Biblical Narrative*. New Haven: Yale University Press, 1974.

Fukuyama, Francis. *The End of History and the Last Man*. New York: The Free Press, 1992.

Gerkin, Charles V. *The Living Human Document*. Nashville: Abingdon Press, 1984.

Ginzburg, Carlo. *Clues, Myths, and the Historical Method*. Translated by John and Anne C. Tedeschi. Baltimore: Johns Hopkins University Press, 1984.

Le Goff, Jacques. *History and Memory*. Translated by Steven Rendall and Elizabeth Claman. New York: Columbia University Press, 1992.

Guroian, Vigen. *Ethics After Christendom: Toward an Ecclesial Christian Ethic*. Grand Rapids: Eerdmans, 1994.

Hanna, Thomas, ed. *The Bergsonian Heritage*. New York: Columbia University Press, 1962.

Harvey, Nicholas Peter. *Death's Gift: Chapters on Resurrection and Bereavement*. London: Epworth Press, 1985.

Hauerwas, Stanley. *Naming the Silences: God, Medicine, and the Problem of Suffering*. Grand Rapids: Eerdmans, 1990.

———. *Suffering Presence: Theological Reflections on Medicine, the Mentally Handicapped, and the Church*. Notre Dame: University of Notre Dame Press, 1986.

———, and Jones, L. Gregory, eds. *Why Narrative? Readings in Narrative Theology*. Grand Rapids: Eerdmans, 1989.

Hesiod. *Theogony*. Translated by Norman O. Brown. New York: The Liberal Arts Press, 1953.

Hessert, Paul. *Christ and the End of Meaning: The Theology of Passion*. Rockport, MA: Element, 1993.

High, Dallas, M., ed. *New Essays on Religious Language*. New York: Oxford University Press, 1969.

Hodgson, Peter C., and King, Robert H., eds. *Christian Theology: An Introduction to Its Traditions and Tasks*. Philadelphia: Fortress Press, 1985.

Holifield, E. Brooks. *A History of Pastoral Care in America: From Salvation to Self-Realization*. Nashville: Abingdon Press, 1983.

Holmer, Paul. *Making Christian Sense*. Philadelphia: Westminster Press, 1984.
James, William. *The Varieties of Religious Experience*. New York: The Macmillan Publishing Comp., 1961.
Jenkins, Sara. *Past Present: Recording Life Stories of Older People*. Washington, DC: St. Alban's Parish, 1978.
Käsemann, Ernst. *Essays on New Testament Themes*. Studies in Biblical Theology 41. London: SCM Press, 1964.
Keck, Leander E. *The Church Confident*. Nashville: Abingdon Press, 1993.
———. "Death and Afterlife in the New Testament." In *Death and Afterlife: Perspectives of the World Religions*, ed. Hiroshi Obayashi, 83–96. New York: Greenwood Press, 1992.
———. "Paul and Apocalyptic Theology." *Interpretation* 38 (1984): 229-41.
Kern, Stephen. *The Culture of Time and Space, 1880-1918*. Cambridge: Harvard University Press, 1983.
Kerr, Fergus. *Theology after Wittgenstein*. Oxford: Basil Blackwell, 1986.
Kotre, John. *White Gloves: How We Create Ourselves Through Memory*. New York: The Free Press, 1995.
Küng, Hans. *Eternal Life? Life After Death as a Medical, Philosophical, and Theological Problem*. Translated by Edward Quinn. New York: Crossroad, 1995.
Lesnoff-Caravaglia, Gari, ed. *Values, Ethics, and Aging*. New York: Human Sciences Press, 1985.
Levin, Jack, and Levin, William C. *Ageism: Prejudice and Discrimination Against the Elderly*. Belmont, CA: Wadsworth, 1980.
Lewis, R. W. B. *The American Adam: Innocence, Tragedy, and Tradition in the Nineteenth Century*. Chicago: University of Chicago Press, 1955.
Lindbeck, George. *The Nature of Doctrine: Religion and Theology in a Post-Liberal Age*. Philadelphia: Westminster Press, 1984.
Luther, Martin. *Luther's Works*. ed. by Helmut T. Lehmann and Jaroslav Pelikan. Philadelphia: Fortress Press, 1955-76.
Mace, Nancy L. and Rabin, Peter V. *The 36-Hour Day*. Baltimore: Johns Hopkins University Press, 1981.
McFague, Sally. *Models of God: Theology for an Ecological, Nuclear Age*. Philadelphia: Fortress Press, 1987.
McGill, Arthur C. *Suffering: A Test of Theological Method*. Philadelphia: Westminster Press, 1982.
McGowin, Diana Friel. *Living in the Labyrinth: A Personal Journey through the Maze of Alzheimer's*. New York: Delacorte Press, 1993.
Maritain, Jacques. *Art and Scholasticism*. Translated by Joseph W. Evans. Notre Dame: University of Notre Dame Press, 1074.
———. *Bergsonian Philosophy and Thomism*. Translated by Mabelle L. Andison and J. Gordon Andison. New York: The Philosophical Library, 1955.
Marsden, George M. *The Outrageous Idea of Christian Scholarship*. New York: Oxford University Press, forthcoming.
Meland, Bernard E. *Fallible Forms and Symbols: Discourses on Method in a Theology of Culture*. Philadelphia: Fortress Press, 1976.
Miller, Perry, ed. *The American Transcendentalists*. Baltimore: Johns Hopkins University Press, 1981.

———. *Errand into the Wilderness*. Cambridge: Harvard University Press, 1956.

Mouw, Richard. *Consulting the Faithful: What Christian Intellectuals Can Learn from Popular Religion*. Grand Rapids: Eerdmans, 1994.

Murphy, Cecil. *Day to Day: Spiritual Help When Someone You Love Has Alzheimer's*. Louisville: Westminster/John Knox Press, 1987.

Nelson, James Lindemann, and Nelson, Hilde Lindemann. *Alzheimer's: Hard Questions for Families*. New York: Doubleday, forthcoming.

Niebuhr, H. Richard. *The Meaning of Revelation*. New York: Macmillan Publishing Company, 1941.

Nouwen, Henri J. M. *Our Greatest Gift: A Meditation on Dying and Caring*. San Francisco: HarperSanFrancisco, 1984.

Nuland, Sherwin B. *How We Die: Reflections on Life's Final Chapter*. New York: Alfred A. Knopf, 1994.

O'Collins, Gerald, S.J. *What Are They Saying about the Resurrection?* New York: Paulist Press, 1978.

Patton, John. *Pastoral Care in Context: An Introduction to Pastoral Care*. Lousville: Westminster/John Knox Press, 1993.

Payne, Barbara and Brewer, Earl D. C., eds. *Gerontology in Theological Education*. New York: Haworth Press, 1989.

Pelikan, Jaroslav. *Fools for Christ: Essays on the True, the Good, and the Beautiful*. Philadelphia: Fortress Press, 1955.

Penrose, Roger. *Shadows of the Mind: A Search for the Missing Science of Consciousness*. Oxford: Oxford University Press, 1994.

Pieper, Josef. *Liesure, The Basis of Culture*. Translated by Alexander Dru. New York: Pantheon Books, 1964.

Plantinga, Theodore. *How Memory Shapes Narratives: A Philosophical Essay on Redeeming the Past*. Lewiston, NY: Edwin Mellen Press, 1992.

Post, Stephen, G. "The Inadequacy of Selflessness: God's Suffering and the Theory of Love." *Journal of the American Academy of Religion* 56 (1988): 213-228.

———. *The Moral Challenges of Alzheimer's Disease*. Baltimore: Johns Hopkins University Press, 1995.

Radner, Ephraim, and Sumner, George R. *Reclaiming Faith: Essays on Orthodoxy in the Episcopal Church and the Baltimore Declaration*. Grand Rapids: Eerdmans, 1993.

Rahner, Karl. *Theological Investigations*, Vol. 6: *Concerning Vatican Council II*. Translated by Karl-H. and Boniface Kruger. Baltimore: Helicon Press, 1969.

Richards, Marty, and Seicol, Sam. "The Challenge of Maintaining Spiritual Connectedness for Persons Institutionalized with Dementia." *Journal of Religious Gerontology* 7, no. 3 (1991): 27-40.

Rorty, Richard. "Mind-Body Identity, Privacy, and Categories." *Review of Metaphysics* 19, no. 1 (1965): 24-54.

Rosow, Irving. *Socialization to Old Age*. Berkeley: University of California Press, 1974.

Santayana, George. *The Sense of Beauty, Being the Outline of Aesthetic Theory*. New York: Dover Publications, 1955.

Sapp, Stephen. "The Dilemma of Alzheimer's: Valuing Autonomy and Acknowledging Dependence." *Second Opinion* 9 (1988): 90-107.
———. *Light on a Gray Area: American Public Policy on Aging.* Nashville: Abingdon Press, 1992.
Schleiermacher, Friedrich. *The Christian Faith.* Edited by H. R. Mackintosh and J. S. Stewart. New York: Harper and Row, 1963.
Schüssler Fiorenza, Elisabeth. *In Memory of Her: A Feminist Theological Reconstruction of Christian Origins.* New York: Crossroad, 1983.
Sharples, R. W., ed. *Modern Thinkers and Ancient Thinkers: The Stanley Victor Keeling Memorial Lectures, 1981-1991.* Boulder: Westview Press, 1993.
Shear, Jonathan. "On Mystical Experiences as Support for the Perrenial Philosophy." *Journal of the American Academy of Religion* 62 (1994): 319-42.
Shelley, Mary. *Frankenstein.* New York: Bantam Books, 1991.
Sherry, Patrick. *Spirit and Beauty: An Introduction to Theological Aesthetics.* Oxford Clarendon Press, 1992.
Shriver, Donald W., Jr. *An Ethic for Enemies: Forgiveness in Politics.* New York: Oxford University Press, 1995.
Smith, David H. "Alzheimer's, Theology and Religious Studies." Unpublished paper presented at the Experimental Session on "The Theological Dimensions of Alzheimer's" held at the 1993 meeting of the American Academy of Religion.
Sontag, Susan. *Illness as Metaphor.* New York: Doubleday, 1989.
Stein, Robert H. *The Method and Message of Jesus' Teaching.* Philadelphia: Westminster Press, 1978.
Swinburne, Richard. *The Evolution of the Soul.* Oxford: Clarendon Press, 1987.
Taliaferro, Charles. *Consciousness and the Mind of God.* Cambridge: Cambridge University Press, 1994.
Taylor, Richard. "Determinism." In *The Encyclopedia of Philosophy,* edited by Paul Edwards, 2:359-73. New York: Macmillan and the Free Press, 1967.
Thomas à Kempis. *The Imitation of Christ.* Translated by Leo Sherley-Price. New York: Penguin Books, 1984.
Thompson, William M. "The Saints, Justification, and Sanctification: An Ecumenical Thought Experiment." *Pro Ecclesia* 4, no. 1 (1995): 16-36.
Voltaire, [François Marie Arouet de]. *Philosophical Dictionary.* 2 vols. Translated by Peter Gay. New York: Basic Books, 1962.
Wallace, Mark I. *The Second Naiveté: Barth, Ricoeur, and the New Yale Theology.* Macon, GA: Mercer University Press, 1995.
Weaver, Glenn. "Senile Dementia and a Resurrection Theology." *Theology Today* 42 (1986): 444-56.
Wilson, James Q. *The Moral Sense.* New York: The Free Press, 1993.
Wolterstorff, Nicholas. *Lament for a Son.* Grand Rapids: Eerdmans, 1987.
Wood, Robert E. "Philosophy, Aesthetics, and Theology: A Review of Hans Urs von Balthasar's *The Glory of the Lord.*" *American Catholic Philosophical Quarterly* 67 (1993): 355-82.
Zizioulas, J. D. *Being as Communion: Studies in Personhood and the Church.* Crestwood, NY: St. Vladimir's Seminary Press, 1985.

Index

Many subjects, such as Alzheimer's disease, caregiving, Christ, and the church, appear throughout the text, and readers will be better served by approaching such subjects through the Table of Contents.

31836276R00144

Made in the USA
Middletown, DE
13 May 2016